IRON TIMES WITH THE GUARDS

IRON TIMES
WITH THE GUARDS

BY AN "O. E."

The Naval & Military Press Ltd

Published by

The Naval & Military Press Ltd
Unit 5 Riverside, Brambleside
Bellbrook Industrial Estate
Uckfield, East Sussex
TN22 1QQ England

Tel: +44 (0)1825 749494

www.naval-military-press.com
www.nmarchive.com

TO

THE ALLIED DEAD

Cast down at last by Time's irreverent hand,
Proud marble crumbles, beauty turns to clay;
By his respite such for an era stand,
Then, as the laurel wreath, they fade away—
Thus do frail human arts live but a day.
For you who bore your Motherland's suspense
Can fitful dross provide fit recompense ?

Ordained through mortal ages to survive,
A monument of mem'ry let us raise,
That with each generation shall revive
The legacy of your immortal days :
Let Gratitude rebuild what Time decays.
On you who paid the price of our defence
May our remembrance shed true recompense !

PREFACE

ENGLISHMEN of to-day may be divided into two groups : one that derives its knowledge of the war from direct observation, another which is dependent on hearsay and on the newspapers. It is solely to the latter, the people at home, that this book is offered. It claims to be neither authoritative nor historical, being only a chronicle of such episodes as have come within the writer's experience. Yet contemporary narratives of memorable events, however fragmentary and whatever their merit, must surely deserve to be placed upon record. This belief must be the author's justification for adding to the ever-growing number of books dealing with the present war.

Apart from the interest these works may have eventually for historians, such a literature undoubtedly does possess in these days a practical value ; it serves a purpose ; it broadens and deepens the public's source of information. In measure as hostilities progress, it is coming to be realised that final success will lie with that side which retains longest its moral resources ; for the might of modern armies is proportionate to the steadfastness of public resolution behind them. A superfluity of such strength is hardly possible, and for that reason, any effort aimed to foster its growth may surely be excused.

With regard to scope, the period here dealt with opens in the second month of the war, and closes in the spring of 1917. It will be found that the narrative is by no means chronologically complete. Intervals represent terms of illness that necessitated convalescence in this country; yet such interruptions served but to intensify the writer's impressions at each subsequent return to France.

This want of continuity not only governed the general arrangement of the book, but its character also. While a cumulative effect has been attempted, endeavour has been made to give to each part its own peculiar aspect. Thus, in turn, the reader may see something of our national unpreparedness for war, together with our consequent lack of great achievement at the front. Accordingly it is not surprising that for a time British efforts in Flanders should appear dwarfed by those of France. Next come the gradual results of our exertions. Two formidable armies arise: one carves its way forward on the Somme, the other transforms our factories into arsenals. Lastly comes the incident of Hindenburg's retreat, which, as it would seem to fix the close of the war's first phase, forms the ending of this series of impressions.

With respect to this final scene, a word of explanation appears desirable. Events subsequent to the date when it was written may be thought to falsify its sanguine tone; but as most people do not question the ultimate triumph of our cause, the author has left it as originally sketched. Possibly our hopes at that time have proved themselves delusions; but who doubts they were shadows cast by coming events?

August 1918.

CONTENTS

PART I

NIGHT

PART II

DAWN

CONTENTS

PART III

DAY

PART III

DAY

PART I

NIGHT

"There were giants in the earth in those days."

CHAPTER I

THE CALL TO ARMS

" . . . And will observe and obey all orders of His Majesty, his Heirs and Successors, and of the Generals and Officers set over me. So help me God."

THE officer's voice ceased, and with it our repetition, leaving our group awaiting the next formality. For an instant his glance swept our ranks, then : " Kiss the Book."

One by one we did so, as it came to each in turn. Thus we became recruits in the Territorials.

So quickly had one event followed another through the last half-hour that I could hardly realise the momentous change that had come into my life. The medical examination, the filling in and signing of attestation papers, and, lastly, this ceremony of being sworn in, impressed a civilian mind by their unfamiliarity and gravity.

" Party—'Shun ! "

A sergeant, instructed by another officer who had preserved hitherto an air of detachment, called our squad of raw recruits to attention ; thereby banishing individual thoughts.

" Parade 9 o'clock, Russell Square, to-morrow morning ; wear anything you like. On the command ' Dismiss,' turn smartly to your right and dismiss."

" How does one do that ? " I wondered.

" Party—Dis-miss ! "

We turned as ordered, horribly uncertain whether

3

to salute or not. For a moment we stood there wavering, then, our civilian habits overcoming our doubts, we fell out.

"Hi! *You* there!" Our steps toward the exit of the drill hall were arrested by the sergeant's voice, and each one turned in expectation of finding himself the object of the remark. The discovery that the words were addressed to someone else came as a relief. "Who told you to salute? I never said anything about saluting. Don't ever do that unless you're in uniform, and then only when you're properly dressed." His victim mumbled something and followed us sheepishly. Apparently my own performance had been correct, although quite by accident. A moment later we found ourselves in the road outside the regimental headquarters, full-blown privates of the Artists' Rifles, and committed for good or evil to a new life. Thus the war claimed yet other pawns.

Proceeding homewards, one could not help feeling that henceforth everything was changed. So great did the change in my own lot seem, that I fancied something of it must be visible to every passer-by. For oneself, during the last month, the world had turned upside down, and the incident just finished seemed to complete the final overthrow. As I made my way toward the "Tube," it seemed incredible that the surrounding world could continue in just the same leisurely fashion as before. Surely so great a crisis should leave some token of its presence, some fresh landmarks on the scene?

But along the streets, little or nothing in the outward appearance of things served to indicate the great catastrophe which had visited us. True, the crowds had a sprinkling of khaki, but nothing more that suggested the new epoch. Buses, taxicabs, and pedestrians wore just the same aspect of unconcerned preoccupation as ever.

However, Trafalgar Square revealed signs of the

war's presence in our midst, for, above a crowd of
bowler hats and caps, the red coat of a Chelsea pen-
sioner was visible. He, at least, had grown restless at
the tramp of marching feet. The Past, no less than the
Present, had called to him " Fall in ! ", and so he had
taken the field once more. The sight of him beneath
the shadow of the Nelson Column still haunts my
memory : gloriously decrepit, he was still strong enough
to preach the new crusade.

Down in Whitehall the recruiting offices were busy.
Though the war was now nearly six weeks old, long
queues of volunteers still waited patiently outside.
Old names have at times the defects of their associations. The volunteer, as we were now to know him,
is better described by the name he came to be known
by in France, *le Volontaire*—the voluntary regular.
In this sense do I like to think of those patient, often
dripping figures, who awaited daily hour after hour the
privilege of donning the King's uniform.

But though in the middle of September '14 these
men were stepping forth in their thousands, yet the
bulk of their fellow countrymen seemed slow to understand. The voice of Custom still smothered the whisperings of Duty, and many who desired to shoulder
their share of the burden were tied by circumstances.
Nevertheless, through these weeks of September, Londoners beheld an ever-growing number of uniforms in
their midst ; but though their eyes were for the ama-
teurs in their streets, their hearts were with the meagre
Expeditionary Force across the water. There it had
just shared in the glorious victory of the Marne.

For several weeks life became one monotonous round
of squad drill in Russell Square, varied somewhat by
route marches to Hampstead and other localities. A
large proportion of my comrades were aspirants for a
commission, engaged " for the duration," volunteers

for foreign service. I do not recollect many of us who
had not been through a well-known school or university.
Our uniforms were mostly procured from private tailors,
but our equipment followed sooner than we had dared
hope for. The 2nd Battalion, to which we belonged,
presented at the beginning of October quite a military
appearance. Its physique was noticeable, for my company itself, out of eight that comprised the battalion,
could boast of nine " Blues."

The organisation of camps had not yet produced any
remarkable effect in the London District. Housing
already existed, so the need was not so pressing as in
the country. We lived at our homes and proceeded
daily, except Sunday, to the various points announced
beforehand in " orders."

Many of the parade grounds of different units were
to be found in the strangest localities. Russell Square,
Hyde Park, Regent's Park, even Holland Park, were
soon trampled bare by the mobs of London recruits.
Organisation certainly did exist, discipline flourished
most astonishingly, but the appearance of these battalions beggars description.

Except in the case of three or four non-commissioned
officers lent them by reserve depots, uniforms and
equipment were entirely lacking. An old leather belt
or a forage cap, dating from volunteer days, gave an
air of conspicuous distinction to its proud wearer.
Caps, bowlers, straw hats, almost every variety of
head-gear, undulated in serpentine fashion as one's
gaze travelled down these long columns of men. Every
tailor, storeman, or pawnbroker must have contributed
to the clothing of these battalions when on parade.
These hordes of lusty men, whistling on the march the
newly discovered air of the " Marseillaise," or the
popular " Tipperary," swinging along with measured
step, would have been laughable, had they not been
sublime. Average Londoners are not prone to demonstration, but the passage of a battalion of "Kitchener's"

men, as they were popularly called, was in those days greeted with uncovered heads. Recognition of their spirit was general everywhere, and familiarity with it had not yet dulled the first instincts of spectators. I never saw more than three officers in one of these battalions until October. Their discipline, taught by those few they could boast of, was maintained by the men themselves. A number had grown up under the codes of our public schools, and the vast majority asked no more than to be made trained soldiers as soon as possible.

Rifles of the old " long pattern " were available for the use of about half of our battalion. Thus, company programmes of training required careful interadjustment. In Russell Square squad drill became evidently an object of great interest to the public, and the spectators on the farther side of the railings usually included in their number a large proportion of French and Belgian refugees. The northern *départements* of France being now in enemy occupation, and Belgium similarly subjected, a large influx of fugitives from *Kultur* had reached London. Everywhere one could hear French spoken, and the Strand, Kingsway, Bloomsbury, and Soho ceased for a while to be really British. On those occasions when the battalion did a route march, or was returning to the St. Pancras Headquarters, scenes of great enthusiasm often occurred. Bus-loads of refugees would give us a miniature ovation, rising from their seats on top, or gesticulating wildly from the inside.

" Vivent les anglais ! " would attract our attention ; this being promptly answered by " Vivent les alliés ! " This was safe, for they might be either French or Belgian.

" Vive l'entente ! " Thus their nationality was obvious.

" Vive la France ! Vive Joffre ! " came our response.

" Vive l'Angleterre ! "

" À bas le Kaiser ! "

Then were the flood-gates opened.

Less frenzy, but possibly more amusement, was to be witnessed at other chance encounters. A soldier and a seaman would discover at the farther end of a crowded omnibus a Belgian uniform, a gleam lighting up the eye of the British casualty from France as his gaze encountered that of his ally.

" I'm just going to have a chat with that bloke, Jack."

Jack was visibly impressed.

" Mons ! "

The ejaculation, together with the gesture toward the speaker's waist belt, successfully engaged the attention of all present. The Belgian started, then smiled.

" Ah ! Mons, monsieur ? "

" Wee, Mons." Then after a pause, " Kompeen."

" Compigne ? "—the other's perplexity was only momentary—" Tiens ! Compiègne ? "

" Wee, Kompyaine."

Again silence ensued, soon ended by another gesture intended to be French.

" Marne ! "

" Bon ! " The bus echoed the word. " On les flanquait un joli coup là-bas. Sales cochons ! "

Atkins nodded a non-committal agreement with this observation.

" Soyssons."

This came in an inimitable accent. Complete stupefaction veiled the other's expression; but not for long, for seeing an opening to cover his own confusion, the foreigner exclaimed with an angelic smile :

" Ah—saucissons ! "

Here a titter arose, quelled for a moment by the intrusion of Jack, who, with a heavy dig into his companion's ribs, gave utterance to a growing scorn :

" Go along with yer ! Yore a-gassin' the bloke's head
off. I reckon you learnt ter parleyvoo in the backwoods
o' Frarnce ! "

By November, the 1st Battalion having departed
overseas, various drafts began to be called for from our
battalion. From the mysteries of forming fours when
turned about, we were now initiated into the higher
arts of war. Field work and musketry on the miniature
range came as a relief after the tortures of " frog marching " and other sundry inflictions beloved of the in-
structor in physical training. So, in company with
various other units, we repaired to Hampstead Heath,
which soon became in the eyes of London a diminutive
Salisbury Plain. Then, after a lapse of several weeks,
our course of instruction was amplified and rendered
more comprehensible by lectures. These were delivered by the Commanding Officer in the lecture theatre
of the London University in Gower Street.

The company on an early morning parade now began
to present a new interest. Gaps appeared, and the
absence of familiar faces began to be noted from day
to day. These indicated the arrival of commissions
for the more fortunate of us. One, we would learn,
had gone to join a brother in his Regular battalion ;
another had had access to the colonel of a Territorial
unit in process of formation. Every day changes
were to be found among our ranks, and the programme
of work grew more varied. One day it would be battalion drill in Regent's Park, where our uniforms dis-
tinguished our parade from the motley formations in
our vicinity ; on another, with ardour we soiled those
same uniforms among the sand and bracken of Hampstead. By now we were adepts with shining-kit and
button-stick ; puttees caked with mud had ceased to
trouble us, or ignorance of the care of service boots to
torment. Looking back on those days, I suppose we
were a fairly creditable body of recruits. At the time

we imagined ourselves soldiers. But into whatever self-complacency we may have been tempted, I confess that it was not the sight of ourselves, but of those hybrid bodies of men on all sides that called for most enthusiasm.

Labouring under every conceivable disadvantage— lack of officers, N.C.Os, instruction, and military spirit —they laboured on, doggedly indifferent to what others thought of them. Their appearance as soldiers was ludicrous, for they neither seemed military nor aped militarism. No well-known marches rose from their ranks, for they brought with them to the Army the full spirit of their civilian life. The music halls provided their regimental marches, the haberdasher their uniforms ; but beneath their shabby clothes their hearts were pure metal. Old gentlemen upon the pavement, whose experience of the world no doubt endowed them with a more prophetic eye, expressed the sentiments of many of us as they gravely saluted these passing columns. No doubt to the cynic they appeared as so much cannon fodder, but to the more human mind these fellows represented an ideal.

"Aux armes, citoyens !   Formez vos bataillons !"

The immortal refrain arose on every side. Whistling battalions of volunteers, street-organs, restaurant orchestras, all swelled into one great harmony, which expressed better than anything in our language the spirit of the country. So, all through the remaining days of autumn, the tide of recruits flowed in, and the approach of winter saw little abatement. To those who remember these autumn weeks, the recollection must remain ever vivid. Recruits in their thousands, marching to and from the public parks, held up the traffic in all parts of the metropolis.

With the passing weeks it was remarked that the Territorials far surpassed their rivals, the " regular " volunteers, in matters of kit and equipment, though, even in the case of the former, supplies were still hopelessly inadequate. "Getting into khaki" became with them less a figure of speech and more a matter of accomplishment. Occasionally a Territorial battalion would pass in the street one of the "Kitchener" units. Their respective manners were amusing, for criticism of the unsoldierly appearance on one side was met with good-humoured toleration of the "irregular" branch of the Service on the other.

The spirit of enterprise and readiness to face any class of work now displayed by the Territorials contributed largely to their re-establishment in that place in public esteem from which, for one reason or another, they had fallen during their few years' existence before the war.

November brought with it its wintry conditions, but even these, apparently, did not hamper the sequence of military events in France. Our ideas in England upon the subject of a winter campaign were very vague. The memory of the last of which the country had had any knowledge had long faded into oblivion. Two generations had never known it. Between Sebastopol and Ypres lies a great interval of time ; but a few there were who noted with surprise the revival of long-disused methods of warfare. Trenches were familiar to many, but the growing talk of sandbags and hand grenades seemed like the echo of a past age.

It is no exaggeration to say that during the year 1914 England, as a people, had hardly begun its education in war. A few startling pages had been read, but beyond a certain feeling of great unpleasantness, the public had no real conception of the book before them. The country was at war, fighting for a somewhat vague object—was it Belgium ? The forces arrayed against us were recognised to be immense, yet there was no understanding of the need of conscription. That, we were informed, was precisely what we were fighting against. The German Army, according to popular fancy, was, above all continental armies, the outcome of this pernicious measure. Conscription and Militarism were unquestionably a pair of Potsdamese twins, both highly objectionable. Except for those who cared to give up all in order that the Empire might remain a free and independent Power, " Business as usual " became the favourite watchword. Whose business ?—England's ? Charity demands that we should assume so.

How firmly Habit, that legacy of pre-war times, was still rooted in our midst is well shown by a matter which about this time began to give rise to a certain amount of controversy. The sentiment of the so-called " Kitchener Posters " was pronounced to be undignified and unworthy of the country. Who does not remember their appeals to " best girls," their admonitions of " I want *you*," and their queries whether a gigantically and badly drawn service cap fitted its beholder ? But, though the tenor of this form of publicity by a Government Department admittedly shocked other than University Dons and the inmates of certain learned London Clubs, the success of the new venture was beyond question. Judged by their results, these posters were justified, and should we have got the men without them ?

CHAPTER II

THE last week of November had now arrived, and with it came my commission in a battalion of the London Regiment. Though one was now invested with certain responsibilities, life underwent no great change. The unit was still in process of being recruited, there being not more than 400 men on its strength. Companies were organised on the new double-company basis, which became at this time universally adopted in the Territorial Army; but as my training hitherto had conformed to the old system, I could not help feeling in consequence somewhat at a loss for the first week or so.

The headquarters of my new regiment were situated in the neighbourhood of Oxford Street; so Hyde Park came to be our usual training ground. I shall never visit the vicinity of the Marble Arch without recalling those days; indeed, so strange has their memory become, that they seem now barely credible.

Physical drill, with which companies generally commenced the day's work, was followed by company training, and the whole battalion assembled later for battalion drill under the second-in-command. Occasionally, as our training progressed, we carried out simple attacks, our objective being usually the Magazine near the Serpentine. The variety of formations and tactics adopted escapes my memory, but we must have assaulted that devoted position in every way known to man.

The approach of winter compelled us in great measure to revert to indoor instruction, and in this we fared very well, for our spacious premises allowed practically half of the small battalion to carry out its programme of training simultaneously. A large basement, besides an excellent miniature range, afforded ample means for musketry instruction. At the same time the main hall above could be used for physical drill, squad drill, or lectures. We were crowded, it is true, but were heartily thankful for the advantages we enjoyed over the great majority of other units. In this respect, as I have already indicated, Territorial Battalions in London were far better provided for than the " Kitchener " units, which were compelled for the most part to go into most uncomfortable quarters in the country, or to find temporary premises in London itself.

Accustomed to the physique of my late battalion, I was not greatly impressed by the appearance of the majority of our recruits, though I confess that, in many cases, surprising results began to appear after several weeks of hard drilling and physical training.

About the commencement of the New Year, a marked falling-off in the rate of recruitment began to appear, not among ourselves alone, but throughout many London battalions. It was perhaps inevitable under the prevailing conditions that this should have been so, since a large proportion of the unmarried men had already joined the colours, and the remainder, having more at stake, either found it embarrassing to leave their employment, or were waiting for their fellows to join up. The uprising of the country's manhood, fanned into flame by the battle of the Marne, had not maintained itself. This unsatisfactory state of affairs was largely the outcome of our insular situation. With the Navy holding the enemy at bay, there came a sense of isolation and security that made it hard for the masses to realise we were engaged in a struggle for our Imperial existence. The country was still largely un-

affected by the war ; even educated persons failing at
that time to realise its gravity.

The question of how to promote recruiting in the
battalion became for its officers a most pressing one.
Frequent route marches through the City and West
End were resorted to, and these proved moderately
successful. The sight of several hundred men in khaki
with mounted headquarters and company officers,
coupled with the strains of "Tipperary" and "Your
King and Country Need You," seemed to inspire those
clerks and shop assistants from whose circles the regiment had been always largely recruited. Smoking
concerts held in the Y.M.C.A. hut in Grosvenor Square
also proved lucrative in results. To these the men were
encouraged to ask their civilian friends and lady acquaintances ; thus the "best girl" proved for us a
most valuable ally. The object we had in view was
a battalion at full strength.

We never accomplished that, however, during my
period of service with this regiment, owing to the constant drain on us from our service battalion, which
was now taking its share of the fighting that fell to the
lot of Territorial units overseas. These had been hurried into the line as a result of the furious struggle
around Ypres. Though every bit as significant as the
Marne, and no less critical, that great episode was
not fully appreciated at this time. Unlike the battle
of Mons and the Marne, it produced no great effect at
home in England.

In this manner therefore did we continue our training through January and the commencement of February. Though progressing in one's own elementary
knowledge of soldiering, one could not escape from a
sense of monotony and uncertainty. Several causes
accounted for this. I had discovered that most of my
fellow officers were commissioned for Home Service
only. Moreover, the time was fast approaching when
I should have to join the 2nd Battalion in the country,

and the prospect of having to join a fresh unit where one would be a complete stranger, coupled with the existence of most uncomfortable surroundings, was not calculated to atone for the loss of my friends with whom I had joined. Though anxious with the desire of a novice to see something of the war, I wished to do so under conditions as congenial as possible. None of us had joined the Army for our own enjoyment, and I fully realised that in such matters it was generally impossible to pick and choose ; but though that maxim is often laid down, it would seem at times rather the outcome of necessity than for any other reason. Moreover, in February I had ascertained through friends that an alternative course lay before me.

A prospect of soon proceeding overseas began to unfold itself in a most alluring fashion, and though it necessitated a transfer to the Special Reserve of the Regular Army, there was every likelihood of its being obtainable. In the regiment to which I aspired, I should have not only every opportunity to become efficient, but the certainty of serving in the vanguard of the British forces. So, after undergoing the necessary preliminaries, and obtaining the consent of my Commanding Officer, I sent in my application for transfer.

CHAPTER III

THE depot of the Reserve Battalion of the Coldstream Guards was at Windsor, so it was at that place that I joined it in the last week of March. In it I found a number of former friends dating from school and Cambridge days. As the considerable number of officers on our strength exhausted the accommodation in barracks, most of the newly joined Ensigns put up at "The White Hart." There, it was not long before a couple of entire stories was converted into the semblance of officers' quarters; for what with the number of one's comrades and our servants, the place soon resembled a kind of bee-hive.

After several months of instruction in the somewhat unsuitable surroundings of London, it would be a pleasure to gain a little experience of field training in a locality suggestive of such work. The days of Kensington Gardens and the Serpentine Magazine were over.

I was very quickly made to realise, however, that work with one of the training companies was not immediately contemplated for me. Though urgently in need of junior officers, the Service Battalions demanded, as in the past, a supply that should approximate as nearly as war conditions would allow to their customary standard of former days.

A great deal is said concerning the training of the Foot-guards; especially by those who have but little acquaintance with it. Through several centuries their

3   17

discipline has grown to be proverbial. It has been generally conceded by those officers with whom one has discussed the matter at various times, that the Guards are looked upon in this respect as a model. In general, the majority of officers of experience outside the Brigade have expressed this opinion, though some, regarding the matter as if it were a claim to exclusive efficiency, have expressed a contrary view. But were it possible for the thoroughness of the Guards' instruction to be imparted to every infantry unit in the Army, one supposes that most people would regard it as an end most desirable of attainment. That state of affairs is, however, for a variety of reasons quite impossible ; at any rate under the present conditions. The Foot-guards excel in this respect, not by reason of any superior intelligence or method, but rather owing to a marked superiority in the *application* of a standard method to the ordinary raw material. It is a common mistake to suppose that all recruits are picked men. In reality, save for the height standard of five feet seven, they are drawn from exactly the same sources as the rest of the Army. Still, larger resources in personnel, especially in the non-commissioned ranks, are at their disposal, and not only do they find the necessary complement of experienced instructors for their own requirements, but, in addition, a considerable number for the needs of Army Schools of Instruction all over the country.

It is sometimes suggested that, as their duties in normal times comprise far more " Ceremonial " than other infantry, their distinctive qualities of drill and discipline become their sole end in view, and accordingly characteristics unfitted for the adoption of an Army that regards itself as essentially an Expeditionary Force capable of adaptation to warfare over-seas. But in spite of this view, the fact does remain that these distinctive qualities have been long regarded as merits. This would not have come about unless it had been felt that these same characteristics were responsible for a general soldierly efficiency. Moreover, the records of the Brigade of Guards do not suggest any loss of adaptability or fighting capacity, but rather an enhanced power to carry out orders in the gravest circumstances. No troops can wish for a higher reputation than that of constant reliability. These remarks are put forward solely in relation to the non-commissioned ranks and men, for it is on them that the reputation of the Brigade mainly rests, though, in common with every self-respecting regiment, its officers may lay claim to a highly trained efficiency.

A sense of rivalry between the various regiments of our forces has been in no small measure the cause for the Army's high reputation, and this spirit of emulation is therefore deliberately fostered within its ranks. Perhaps the spirit of the above remarks will suffice to show how thoroughly one's own education in this respect was carried out. I cannot conceive, either in the present or the future, any newly joined Ensign thinking otherwise than that he had been admitted to the finest brigade on earth. Of all the British regiments, the Coldstream Guards alone can trace a direct descent from the famous Ironsides. No more need be said of a child whose sponsors were Cromwell and Monk.

Though a considerable modification in the training of junior officers had taken place since the outbreak of war, no change was made in the procedure at the outset of their work. All newly joined Ensigns had to go through a course of setting-up drill and ceremonial on " The Square." Such is the designation by which their drill parade grounds are known to regiments throughout the Army. The " young " officer—the term applied to the newly joined officer whatever his age—is assumed to know nothing. Any previous acquirements are ignored, and, for the purpose of the system, wisely so. Throughout the Brigade there is one way of doing a thing and one only—the Brigade way.

As a result, squad drill " by numbers " became our daily experience. Before we might proceed to the work of an officer, a thorough knowledge of the work of a private soldier was demanded of us. Then, according to their individual aptitude, beginners were called out of their place in the squad to begin their training in how to drill others. The capacity for drilling others is far from being identical with a knowledge of how to perform drill movements oneself, though this would appear to be insufficiently realised in certain units, especially those " new " ones that were then being formed.

Having passed from squad drill " by numbers," the young officer proceeds next to drilling " judging the time." Concurrently with this work on parade, he has also to learn how to inspect men, kit, and so forth, and attends lectures from some senior officer of his battalion.

Daily attendance at his company commander's " orders " is rigorously expected of him later on. Off parade or duty, he is a member of a club with regard to all mess-mates. The wild frenzy of saluting frequently expected of young officers in other units is not encouraged, it is discouraged even. By contrast with the punctilious conduct of a parade, life at other times seems strangely free and easy.

On " the square " our progress took the form of a series of progressive " acting " ranks. From his place as a private, an Ensign under instruction rises to be a section commander, then platoon sergeant, company quartermaster-sergeant, and company sergeant-major. Not until he has familiarised himself with their duties is he allowed to act in his proper rôle of platoon officer. The training of the new Ensign does not end, however, with education in all the duties of his own rank. He has to be instructed as much as time will allow in those of his Captain, so that, in the event of being called upon, he may " carry on " with some chance of success. After a while, he may be tempted to believe he has a real knowledge of his Captain's work. This conceit will end abruptly on the day of his promotion to that rank.

In the early months of '15, so urgent were the requirements of the battalions abroad, that the course of our instruction was necessarily somewhat curtailed. The duration varied from about a month to three months according to the previous experience of the individual, but with the men the period of training was usually nearer a year.

Recruits to the Brigade commence their recruit's course at the Brigade Depot at Caterham, passing there a term varying from twelve to sixteen weeks, after which the normal man is passed out to his Reserve Battalion wherever that may be. There he continues his training for a similar period; in many cases for longer. This method was only made possible by the number of reservists at the disposal of the various regiments by reason of their short-service system. The old guardsman of pre-war days was in most things unique, but his place was to be filled by no discreditable successor.

Apparently even my previous experience was of some service to me, for, slender as it was, at the end of a fortnight it caused my removal from off "the square" to a training company. But this reason was a subsidiary one in reality; the true cause was the call for officers. The constant wearing down of effectives at the Front was resulting in over-much work devolving on the survivors, and, though it was coming to be realised that trench warfare did not call for the full complement of officers to a battalion, there was a certain irreducible minimum below which it would be dangerous to fall.

A call for an officer draft would be likely to arrive at any moment; so our training was accelerated as much as possible. The party passed off " the square " was now split up among the four training companies, so the new nature of my instruction commenced with fresh fellow officers.

From conversations concerning training programmes I began to suspect the existence of another tactical *bête noire*, this time not a powder magazine, but the Copper Horse in Windsor Great Park. Happily, my week of field work proved to be a horseless one. As the prospect of our gaining any experience of " open " warfare in France was small, we were rushed through a variety of tactical schemes. At that time means were lacking for imparting any real instruction in trench warfare, and I can only suppose it was felt that we should gain experience in that branch at a fairly early date.

However that may be, my week of make-believe consisted of much manœuvring by day and night, together with a very real route march following on a twenty-four hours' outing. I have vivid recollections of that march home, and its timely relief in the form of " The Drums." These had come out several miles to meet us on our homeward way, and their effect was plainly discernible to all as the battalion descended the Long Walk in column of route.

On arriving in barracks, I was informed that I should be proceeding to France with the next draft, which was due to leave in a week; I could go on draft leave until further orders. In a few hours I was in London for what might be the last time.

CHAPTER IV

THE pleasure of draft leave is always apt to be marred by sundry troubles, among which those caused by purchases of kit are not the least. The young Ensign setting out on active service for the first time is looked upon by many tradesmen in the light of legitimate prey. Warnings of their wiles had been given me, so I was to some extent prepared. In the earlier months of the war experience was not so generally obtainable as now, and pitfalls were many.

All too soon the time arrived for dismal calls on friends and relatives, dismal on account of their unnatural hilarity and cordiality. These also may be classed among those things which we generally term "horrors of war." One gloomy night toward the end of April, I left for Windsor, whence the draft was proceeding on the following day. Many strange and memorable things were to occur before I set foot again in London.

The following morning witnessed an unusual stir at "The White Hart." Busy servants swarmed to and fro in all directions; officers made anxious inquiries after belated items of kit; and on all sides one could hear lively discussions as to what might be wisely left behind. An unusual desire to please was noticeable on the part of the hotel staff. Their assiduity was almost touching.

At last the time came for us to cross to the barracks

for lunch, but even there the atmosphere was no less marked by activity. Mess waiters would announce from time to time the existence of "most important documents" in the orderly room requiring one's urgent signature ; it seemed even doubtful whether one would be able to accompany the draft unless they were attended to.

"Oh, yes! Most important, sir! The orderly room sergeant says——" ; but here the human mind fails to remember more : it is doubtful whether it ever understood.

Outside, across the large expanse of grass that spread in front of the Officers' Block, groups of men were beginning to appear from the neighbouring barrack rooms. Somehow, the excitement of our departure drove away our usual appetites. Disquieting thoughts kept recurring ; perhaps, even now, your servant might be late with your equipment ? Hastily finishing our last meal, some of us repaired outside to make a final inspection of our belongings. Behind me I heard the familiar movement of the guardsman's salute. "Your kit, sir! All correct."

Indeed it was, like everything else the excellent fellow had done for me that day.

A movement toward "the square" by the bunches of men around the side blocks now began. Among the khaki throng, the scarlet tunics of the Bandsmen from London showed up conspicuously; it was time to be getting on our equipment. Already my man was impassively waiting.

Webbing equipment, complete with full pack, constitutes another necessary evil of war. However, after a few moments to adjust a buckle or two, we were ready to move on to parade, feeling for all the world like an out-of-season group of Father Christmases. The draft, very smart in their new outfit, had already fallen in. They were between three and four hundred strong, under the command of a senior Captain, Bruce. Ac-

companying him was another newly joined Captain
and seven or eight Ensigns.

From our positions on " the square " we could see
at the farther end of the barrack enclosure groups of
fellow officers at the windows and steps of the Officers'
Mess. Nearer, bounding either side of the roadway
that ran towards the barrack gates, was a dense throng
of non-commissioned officers and men who had come
out to take their last farewell of comrades on parade.
All this we took in at a glance, for time was short.
Already the Regimental Colonel was giving to Bruce
permission to march off.

" Parade—'Shun ! Slope hah ! "

The serried ranks sprang to life, giving forth the
three movements of " the slope." The order to march
was barely out before its echoes were drowned in a
crash from the Band stationed on our flank. Short
men though some of them were, their bearskins rose
above the wall of khaki that lined the road. Now, I
reflected, one was really off to the war.

" Good luck t'yer, Ted. Love t'Fritz."

" Not 'arf ! Same ter you," would come the somewhat inconsequent reply. On every side arose a babble
of greetings, some in what one felt to be real earnest,
others jocularly ribald.

" Goodbye, sargint-major ! Sorry I can't stop."
The note of chaff drew forth instant applause from
those who were able to appreciate its full significance. A twinkle came to the eye of the sergeant-
major.

" Take care of your mascot, lads," came the reply,
aimed not so much at the individual as at those in his
vicinity.

And now, wheeling to the right, we passed the barrack guard, salute answering salute. A moment later,
wheeling once more, we had left them behind us. Ahead
of me, the long column, moving rhythmically in step,
and displaying a vista of caps and beautifully arranged

packs, spread forward down the road. From my
position in rear, I could note with appreciation the
magnificent body of men. Five feet eleven inches was
our actual height in those days, and they looked every
inch of it. Powerfully built miners from Tyneside,
strapping fellows from Birmingham and Devon, they
were indeed good to look upon.

Presently we were descending the steep slope of the
Castle Hill, and from the houses on one hand and the
walls of the Castle opposite resounded the notes of
" The girl I left behind me." Never until that moment
had I understood the full beauty of that old English
tune. Cheer answered cheer and hand replied to
waving handkerchief, as we glanced up to window and
balcony. There, you could not help noting every
variety of human emotion. Assuredly, it was to no
ordinary war we were bound. Often I had read of such
scenes as this, but it was hard to realise that the present
moment was actual fact. It all seemed so unreal.
My world had not acquainted me with such things
beyond the artificial thrills of a patriotic drama.
Behind the footlights one had heard the roll of
drums and even the music now ringing in one's ears,
but it had all been unreal ; moreover, the knowledge
that presently one would be motoring homeward to
supper had not enhanced its appeal. But this *was*
real : it was fact. Tears and smiles and sparks from
the cobbled streets—yes, this was different. I suppose
the cobbles revealed it most ; they are wanting on a
stage, however much supers may exert themselves in
doing " pathetic business."

Along the footpath on either hand rolled waves of
civilian friends, or were they merely sightseers ? At
any rate, they would not readily forget the scene before
them. " Cheero, boys. Good luck to you ! " The
voice of a hale old cabman died amidst a yell of " Roll
on the Coalies ! ", which proceeded from a neighbouring
public-house. And so, amidst a scene very moving

and very fine, we passed onwards to the station where
our train was in waiting.

With a ring of heavy feet upon the platform, the
platoons came to an abrupt halt. Under the glass roof,
rifle-butts rang smartly as the men " ordered arms."

" In fours, left—turn." Now they were ready to
entrain.

Presently, the men being all accommodated after
an orderly tumult, I was accosted by my servant, from
whom I learnt that a seat was being kept for me in an
officer's compartment at the end of the train. It was
not long before we moved off. A whistle from the
engine was the sergeant-drummer's signal for his last
contribution to our departure. A moment later the
station was resounding to a tempestuous rendering of
" Auld Lang Syne," while from the carriage windows
poured forth a roar of cheers.

" Good-bye, good-bye ! "

Voices were drowned in the noise. It was impossible
to make oneself heard above the crash of drums, to
whose rolling echoes we set out to the war.

CHAPTER V

At dawn the following morning we were steaming slowly up the harbour of ——, our port of disembarkation. At this early hour, the windows of the old-fashioned houses along the quay were still shuttered, and the town to all appearances was still asleep. Owing to a rather rough sea, many of the men had lain all night on deck in the throes of sea-sickness; but as they now commenced to assemble in readiness to go ashore, very few seemed the worse for their journey.

After the usual preliminaries, the draft filed over on to the quay-side and began to fall in. A certain number of civilians had already arrived, and among them, the inevitable gang of small boys.

Little time was lost in getting started for our destination, which we now knew to be the Infantry Base Camp. A few minutes were allowed us in which to swallow some hot coffee and a few biscuits, after which we were ready to move off.

Taking my place with the rearmost platoon, I found myself close to some of the bystanders, who speedily commenced a fervid discussion of my identity.

" Regardez donc ce grand ! Il porte des boutons differents."

" C'est peut-être un sergent."

" Pas possible ! Les sergents ont les manches galonnées. Il me semble plutôt un officier."

" Mais, voyons ! il ne porte pas une épée ! "

By this time I was beginning to wonder what status

I should be awarded by the expert of the party. However, I was soon gratified to know that I was the " Porte-drapeau," though some doubts were raised at this on account of the absence of any colour. The matter was still under discussion when the order came to move off.

We arrived in camp about 10 o'clock after a very tiring march. The cobbled streets of the town were bad enough for feet unaccustomed to them, but when we cleared the outskirts our discomfort was, if anything, increased by a dense cloud of dust from the road. This soon began to slope upwards as it approached our destination. Some of the draft, which had to do this march in full kit amid great heat, were glad to arrive ; especially as many had been upset somewhat in the night.

The Infantry Base Camp in April 1915 was in its infancy, a very different place from the well-ordered and comfortable spot it has subsequently become. The heat of the first day there was quite unusual and led many of the men to fancy that they had been transported overnight to a strange tropical country. Rain fell abundantly on the following day and quickly converted the lines into a mass of mud.

Our stay proved very brief, for on the third day a party including myself received orders to proceed up the line. Attached to us were drafts of Munster Fusiliers and of the Welsh Regiment. The second Captain of our party from Windsor was to accompany me to the same battalion.

There is no need to dwell upon the journey. In those days it possessed all the discomforts of travel by troop train. Chocques, at that time our railhead, was reached after thirty hours.

There, one discovered that nobody except a guide had been sent down to meet the Irish and Welsh ; so I was compelled to set out with them in search of their billets, having first arranged to meet my travelling companion at Chocques in the evening. We reached

the battalion of the Welsh Regiment about the middle
of the afternoon, and I began to imagine that my
labours would soon end for the day. But, as our march
progressed, I was soon undeceived ; no sign of the
Munsters became visible. I was getting very tired,
for not only were the roads in an abominable state
from the recent rain, but the long railway journey had
proved more fatiguing than I had thought. It was
getting on toward evening when, after losing the way,
my " guide " announced that his battalion was near
at hand. Having handed over the men and their
sundry papers, I was entertained to tea and kindly
offered an orderly and horse for my return. Having,
in my ignorance, set off earlier in the day in my
webbing equipment, I was very glad of the offer.

On reaching railhead once more, I discovered that
my companion had given me up on account of the late-
ness of the hour. A note from him informed me that
he had obtained a lift in a car and was proceeding to
our battalion.

Night had fallen before I discovered my servant
installed in an *estaminet*. Though compelled to sleep
in the town that night, I was far from certain of finding
a billet, for the *Chef de gare* informed me that the
whole place was overflowing with British troops. Fortunately, after some abortive visits, I discovered he
was mistaken. My temporary quarters were in an
attic, fairly comfortable, but, what was more important,
perfectly clean. Dinner that night, the first I was
destined to take at the Front, was among the worst
I have ever had. Troubles had dogged me all day,
even up to the last moment, so it was with genuine
relief that I presently turned in, wondering whether
this was a sample of what lay before me.

At an early hour next day I was ready to start out
in quest of my battalion, which was in billets at a
small village named Le Préol. On my way, I should
have to pass through Béthune, and being at railhead,

I did not anticipate any difficulty in getting a motor lorry to take me there. This proved to be the case, and an hour later I was put down at the Headquarters of the 2nd Division, where I procured all information necessary for the completion of my wanderings. The battalion mess-cart, which visited the town daily, would take me and my kit on its return journey.

Le Préol, which we reached about midday, proved to be a rambling and unattractive village lying beside a tributary of the Béthune–La Bassée Canal. The weather was still unsettled and much rain had fallen lately. This no doubt accounted for my finding most of the battalion in their billets. That afternoon, I obtained my first glimpse of the war. I was on the point of going round from my company mess to my own billet, when someone announced that an aeroplane was being shelled outside. To one freshly arrived this seemed something not to be missed, but my companions evidently considered the news of no importance whatever. Stepping into the road, I was shown a sight which, though interesting at the time, I likewise came to regard as drearily commonplace. Away to the southward the sky was mottled by an irregular line of small clouds gleaming brightly against the blue background. Even as one watched, others were spinning themselves out westward. Glistening like a speck of silver dust as the sun's rays caught its planes, a machine was visible travelling smoothly ahead of this string of shells. The scene was an utterly silent one owing to its remoteness, and seemed strangely unlike warfare.

.   .   .   .   ﹡

The following day was abominable, for it rained steadily hour after hour, so it was with some dismay that we learnt the battalion was to go up to the trenches that night. The wet roads outside seemed bad enough, but what the state of the trenches might be I did not try to imagine. This was to be a great experience, equally memorable, I suppose, to all those thousands who have met with it. A first visit to the lines, in addition to being the modern equivalent to the old baptism of fire, is an experience unique and surpassing most others in life; thus it was with a sense of great expectancy and curiosity that one made the arrangements necessary for a stay of four days in the line. Beyond the vague knowledge that our position would be opposite La Bassée, I had no idea of it all.

The evening of a " relief " is for the in-going battalion always a time of great activity. Servants, especially, have good cause to dislike such occasions, as their masters' trench kits have to be prepared, and this necessitates on their part an irksome amount of thinking. If the period " in " be of any duration, much foresight is required. Kits left out, valises are then packed, and are either called for by the kit waggon or dumped at a given point in readiness for the battalion transport. Usually these preparations are left until the last moment, with the ever-recurrent result that wild haste ensues.

A fine drizzle set in shortly after the departure of the battalion, so that we were dripping before long from every part of our clothing and equipment. The road at first skirted the La Bassée Canal, which lay dark and turbid below us in the gloom. Gradually the mud became worse, because we were compelled at last to leave the road and take to a track that ran onwards to a ruined village ahead. Amid the night and the windings of the trail, one's sense of direction became lost, but away in the darkness an occasional gleam of a Verey light denoted the direction of the line.

The men's greatcoats were now becoming sodden with rain, which had not ceased descending in a steady downpour. Under foot, the ground sucked tenaciously at our feet. We were marching at intervals between platoons, since we were now within the shelled area, and as we struggled on, the only sounds that broke the monotonous hiss of the rain were the tapping of our equipment and the squelching of the mud. Following the glare of a Verey light came the rapid " toc-toc-toc " of a machine-gun, whose reports sounded curiously clear upon the night air.

A couple of hours of such marching had elapsed before we entered a deep communication trench. There we discovered the platoon ahead of us, for now, as the risk of losing touch became greater, companies were closing up. Onward through the slough of mud we staggered, the men's mess-tins clattering against the wall of the trench as the procession lurched from side to side. The form of our guide, whom we had picked up in the village behind, loomed in the darkness ahead. As we advanced, the sound of occasional shots cracked viciously, and the hiss of a Verey light became audible where it soared upwards in the darkness. Now the voice of a machine-gun took on a sharper note, while away on the flank a shell burst abruptly, drowning for an instant the mysterious sounds around us.

Then at last the voice of our company commander spoke from out the darkness. Yes, we were Number 14 Platoon ; yes, we knew our frontage. The guide was here. Another 200 yards ? All right. By and by his voice called from behind that he would be round presently. If I wanted to know anything, D——would be just along the trench on my left.

Another five minutes elapsed. A rifle banged loudly from somewhere just ahead ; then came a bend in the trench, followed by what appeared to be a cross trench.

" Round to the right, sir. Straight along to the road embankment." My guide beckoned us forward. We had reached our journey's end. This dark, shadowy path, hedged in with its damp walls of earth, was the front line.

4

CHAPTER VI

SOMETHING was happening to my foot, what exactly, it took me a few moments to realise. Then I woke and sat up.

"It's 4 o'clock, sir. Mr. Hotham said as how I was to call you now."

I rubbed a sleepy eye and surveyed a black mass at the entrance of my dugout.

"Quite right, corporal. Is Mr. D—— still in the front line ? "

"Yes, sir. I believe he'll carry on till morning, as Mr. Hotham has gone back. Anything you want, sir ? "

"No thanks, that's all right."

"Thank you, sir." The squelching footfalls of the corporal died away in the trench outside.

Four in the morning, a chilly damp one too—this was a pretty dismal start for a day in May. Where was I this time last year ? In a comfortable bed, wherever it was. Something tickled my neck, and with a quick motion I carried my hand to the spot. I hated insects, always had; this I disliked above all others as I was unable to see it. How dark it was, and chilly ! That grey patch beyond my feet was the wall of the trench. My dugout was not long enough to take a man, and to avoid having one's feet knocked by those passing by it was necessary to draw up one's knees. The sound of rain had ceased. How it had rained a few hours before as I had groped my way along the communication trench to this hole!—a comparatively dry hole at all events.

I passed a hand over my trench coat and found it was still sodden. The empty sandbags on which I lay had also been reduced to a state of clammy dampness by my clothes. I peered down, endeavouring to see the sky under the lintel of the doorway. Yes, there were some stars ; evidently the weather was clearing. Putting on my cap, I next groped for and discovered my electric lamp, but not until I had overturned the bottle that served as candlestick. Did I require anything else, I wondered ? There lay my revolver holster where I had placed it a little while ago. I slipped it on to the belt of my trench coat—no use going unarmed round the front line, I thought.

Then followed a short scramble through the dugout entrance. How infernally low these places were ! I rubbed my head and set off down the trench, slowly picking my way through the puddles gleaming under the ray of my lamp. This I kept as low as possible, using it only in short flicks in order to have some idea of what lay ahead, for my fellow officers had warned me against showing any unnecessary amount of light. The only sound audible as I approached the front line was the sucking of mud around my boots.

Bang—His-s-s-s—a Verey light streamed upwards a few yards ahead. All remained silent; evidently no target had been surprised this time. Coming out into the front-line trench, I saw several dark figures seated on the fire-step. At the noise of my approach their voices died away.

" Who is that ? " inquired D——'s voice. Then, recognising me, " There is no need for you to turn out, I have only been up two hours. Got another two to go."

" I wanted to see what the place was like at night," I explained.

" You'll soon be satisfied. That won't last long,"
he retorted with a laugh, " but as you are here, you
can go down the company front and let me know
if they have heard anything of No. 2 Company's
patrol."

At this hour of the morning life in the trenches is at
its quietest. Working-parties have usually " knocked
off," and the opposing lines retire to snatch a brief rest
before dawn gives the signal to " stand to arms." No
shell arrives with disconcerting shriek, no shot is fired
from the parapet. Stealing along quietly from one
fire-bay to another, one notes at intervals a silent
figure upon the fire-step. There stands the sentry
keeping his vigil until the next relief, his head
showing black against the stars, his bayonet gleaming
in the moonlight by his side. At the sound of your
approach he turns his head, and you feel, rather than
see, that he is scrutinising you.

" 'Oo are yer ? " In his tone lurks an irrepressible
desire to know. This is no empty formality. Though
not to be found in *Infantry Training*, this formula
represents the only form of challenge for which his
mind has any use when in the vicinity of the enemy.

Such was my first experience of life in the trenches.

Hastily I considered whether to tell him my name or
not. Most probably he would not know it, as I had
so recently arrived in the company.

" 'Alt ! 'Oo *are* yer ? " The low but insistent tones
were repeated. His bayonet vanished from the light,
and his hand fell to his rifle.

" Officer ! No. 4 Company."

Bending, he examined me closer, then, satisfied, he
turned his face to the parapet, where he resumed his
watch. Here was a fellow of few words, probably an
old soldier before the war. I mounted the fire-step
and looked across in the direction of the enemy.
Though now accustomed to the darkness, my eyes
could make out nothing beyond twenty paces. The

night was dark, and the moon was even then being obscured by passing clouds.

A mass of black shapes indicated where the wooden stakes supporting our entanglements loomed out of the ground, and among them I could make out a confused jungle of shadow, which I took to be barbed wire. Beyond, a chaotic surface spread to where the darkness grew impenetrable. Here the ground had been turned up by a shell, and the crater thus formed was already in process of being filled again by mud washed in by rain.

" How far are we from the enemy lines ? " I inquired, turning in the direction of the sentry. He did not move, but I caught his reply clearly, though it was uttered in a tone lower than my own.

" About a matter of two 'undred an' fifty yards, sir."

Once more I turned my face to the mysterious expanse ahead. So here lay No Man's Land, that sinister strip of the Unknown of which I had so often heard. What secrets did the darkness veil by night and the rank grasses by day ? I pictured to myself somewhere ahead another row of tumbled coils writhing around a line of posts. Behind that would be the gentle rise of a parapet merging into the darkness on either flank. There, immobile, and therefore hardly discernible against the background, might be the shape of a *pickelhaube* ! At that moment I realised why my companion had not turned his head.

Certainly, out there in the night, lynx eyes were on the watch even as ours, and ears were strained, as those of the sentry beside me, for the least suspicious sound of the night. Did that dark blotch really move ? Was that only the whisper of the breeze in the long grass, or was it caused by something else ?

His-s-s-s ! Down the flank toward the direction of the Brick Stacks there shot upward a graceful curve of light, scattering at the summit of its flight into a splash of fire. Beneath its brilliancy, the surface of

No Man's Land gleamed strangely white, like a snow-field. Backwards and forwards across the flaring region of desert land the eye travelled with unwonted speed, probing the heavy shadows that moved un-cannily with the motion of the flare. Abruptly, swell-ing instantaneously to its full-throated tune, a sound of rapid hammering burst forth somewhere on our left. This was no casual gust of fire ; evidently the machine-gunners had sighted a target. Nearer to where we stood, a desultory splutter of reports arose from the direction of the British line. The scene was now fast fading into obscurity, when from the enemy's direction flared an answering light. I could not fail to remark the steadiness and brilliancy of this compared with ours. Under its white glare the landscape stood out harshly. Now the splutter of a machine-gun came from beyond No Man's Land ; for a moment the two machine-guns continued their staccato duet, then gradually the opposing parapets sparkled with spurts of rifle fire. The regular reports of the machine-guns were notice-ably different, the British brisker than its opponent. Other Verey lights rose hovering over the rival posi-tions, and the rhythm of the Vickers gun was soon drowned by an outburst of firing. Stabbing flashes rippled slowly along toward our company front, flash answering flash from out of the misty landscape oppo-site. A bullet flitted past with a screech that ripped the air, and from the neighbouring fire-bay a sharp crack came in reply. Then by degrees the lights waned ; the machine-guns had already ceased their chorus. For another few minutes a few scattered shots con-tinued to be exchanged, but these also died away in their turn, until silence reigned once more. In my ears there still sang the ringing impact of a report near at hand.

"Nothing, sir, worse luck," replied the sentry in answer to my query as to what he had seen. No, he had not fired. It was no doubt, he suggested, the bullet which had struck our parapet that I had heard.

" Only a little wind, sir," was his final comment before resuming his scrutiny of the night.

Doubtless he was right, but to the novice the episode proved how imaginary was the tranquillity brooding over the enshrouding darkness.

. . .

It was not until daylight revealed features in detail that any general picture of the trenches was obtainable. The dawn held out prospects of a fine day, and it was with a fervent hope for its realisation that I retired once more to my dugout at the termination of " stand to."

Breakfast was reported ready some hours later, but as the accommodation of the company mess did not permit of all four officers breakfasting together, I first obtained a very make-shift wash and shave. Breakfast over, I set forth on a tour of inspection.

The right flank of the company rested against the La Bassée road, which ran at this point along an embankment at right angles to our frontage. Lining its borders stood a long line of truncated tree-trunks, scarred and splintered by shell fire, and it was curious to observe how these gaunt poles receded behind the German lines in lessening degrees of demolition. Far away to the rear they were already in leaf.

From a machine-gun embrasure, one could catch sight of an irregular line of earth and sandbags about three hundred yards distant from our parapet. This was evidently the enemy's front line, for, straggling across it some score of yards nearer, there ran a darker smudge of barbed-wire entanglements jagged with stakes and *chevaux de frise*. Hanging limply among these like scarecrows, a number of bodies were to be seen, apparently Germans, as their weather-beaten and sodden uniforms seemed somewhat darker than our own.

Leaving the machine-gunners, I gradually made my way along the windings of our front line. Here, from the bottom of the trench, nothing but the muddy walls remained visible. Overhead the sky blazed brilliantly, giving every promise of a warm day. Everywhere along the trench groups of men were seated, or reclined upon the narrow fire-step by the parapet, engaged in sundry tasks of cleaning rifles or equipment, and from time to time the crackle of a fire would reach one's ears.

"Here, you there! Watch that show of yours!" A sergeant's eye had detected smoke that was curling upward from beneath a mess-tin of unsavoury-looking tea. "You'll be getting something worse than smoke if Fritz sees that."

My education in trench lore was merely commencing. The sergeant's words speedily had the desired effect.

The result of "Fritz's" attention became apparent an hour or so later, when news of disaster reached us from the machine-gun emplacement on the right. A Whizz Bang had suddenly crashed into it, scattering the sandbags in ruins, and wounding a gunner on sentry outside the crew's dugout.

Contrary to the custom at night, watch was now kept by only a few sentries scattered along the line, who observed what was going on over the parapet by means of small mirrors. These, fixed to a bayonet or a cleft stick, were placed in the front face of the parados at such an angle that the watcher sitting on the fire-step below could see into No Man's Land behind him. In a corner a couple of men was engaged in improving the fire-step, which had become worn away by rain. One held the mouth of a sandbag open while the other filled it with his shovel. Every twenty yards the view along the line was interrupted by a traverse. These were sometimes revetted to render their sides more durable; their corners, in some cases, being worn quite smooth by the passage of men. There were few dugouts ; the majority of shelters were merely proof against the weather, and these were often of a most inadequate kind. A ground-sheet, propped on a few pieces of stick, was often the only contrivance possible, and the occupant was regarded as a fortunate fellow to be able to enjoy even that. Scattered in wild profusion upon the earth thrown on top of the parados were dozens of empty jam and bully-beef tins, among which lay a liberal sprinkling of pieces of bread and bacon parings. As a result of the warm sun, the ground was beginning to dry, and an odour of damp earth, combined with tobacco smoke and fried bacon, pervaded the air ; the resulting scent defies description by reason of its subtlety.

Branching from the trench at various intervals, passages led into communication trenches, which, in their turn, wound in irregular fashion toward the second and third lines. In them an occasional dugout was to be found, but the majority of these were used for the company stretcher-bearers and as tool stores. Having no fire-step, these passages were only half the width of the fire-trenches, and were in consequence far muddier, because the sun could not reach them so easily. So narrow were they, that in places recesses had been cut to permit men to pass one another. In a corner, seated on an ammunition box, a platoon orator was brandishing a copy of *John Bull*, enforcing his remarks with various lurid expletives. Thereupon, a hitherto appreciative corporal, noting my approach, ordered the speaker to "modderfy his langwidge."

Full of appreciation of the non-commissioned officer's sensitiveness, I rapidly passed on, directing my steps toward my dugout. My trench coat had dried on me during my tour, and the sun, combined with the buzz of stray flies and my tiring night, began to produce a sense of drowsiness.

My dugout, in comparison to the thickening mud outside it, seemed invitingly dry. During my absence my man had put out my towel, and had erected, goodness knows how, a wooden shelf in the interior upon which was laid out various odds and ends. Assuredly this was home, I thought. A sudden shriek overhead followed by a distant spurt of smoke announced the commencement of the day's work. I entered the dugout.

CHAPTER VII

ALARUMS AND EXCURSIONS

EVERY moment the tree-trunks along the La Bassée road were becoming more visible. The early morning mist appeared to be thinning.

"It won't be long now, sir, before the sun will be showing up." The sergeant with whom I had been doing a round during the "Stand to arms" evidently had hopes of another nap before breakfast. But on such mornings as these, when No Man's Land remained obscured by mists issuing from the ground, the patience of all ranks was apt to be sorely tried. The previous day, in spite of the heavy rain overnight, we had been able to see the enemy's line a full hour sooner. With the presence of fog, however, our period of watchfulness was inevitably prolonged, for no man either in the front or support line would stand easy until word came from the company commander.

The air around struck damp and chilly, beads of dew glistening on the wire entanglements in front. Slowly but surely, the pale opalescent light filtered through the obscurity. Someone in the next fire-bay loaded up a clip. No sound save the sudden snap of his breach-bolt was audible in the silence of the new day.

"How far should you reckon we would have to see, to stop an attack, sergeant?" The veiled quest for information was put abruptly in the tones of a cross-examiner.

My companion on the fire-step sucked his teeth before replying.

"Depends, sir, on the tactical situation." Then, realising the glaring insufficiency of the reply, he added : "I should expect these chaps to bring 'em up in the time they took to cover two hundred out there."

"What about the machine-guns ? "

"They'd get those that we might overlook."

I smiled my appreciation of his faith in our "ten rounds rapid."

"Fact, sir ! You can't miss your man all over at point-blank. Why, I knew a fellow once, a colour sergeant he was, back at——"

Here the inevitable anecdote, which was to carry conviction to my mind, was interrupted. A rifle leaning against the parapet slipped down with a clatter into the bottom of the trench. The sergeant swallowed his first instinctive remark, and, fixing its owner with a basilisk eye, watched the offender scramble after his weapon.

"Why weren't you holding your rifle ? " I inquired.

"D'you hear what the officer says ? " The sergeant pounced on his prey before he had time to reply. The matter, I saw, could be left to his masterly powers, so I moved away.

"See that your fingers are warm next time you stand to." With this I left them.

The voice of the sergeant, freed from my embarrassing presence, floated over the intervening wall of the traverse. "I'll warm you, m'lad. Blowing on your fingers you were. I saw you, you clumsy cabman." The remainder of his remarks became inaudible.

"Stand easy, stand easy." The cry was coming down the line, N.C.Os following in its wake to make sure that their sentries were properly posted. Soon all was quiet once more. The trenches had emptied somewhat : the dugouts were filling up.

Away in the sky, somewhere behind our position, arose the faint hum of a motor engine. The Royal Flying Corps was early awake.

Gradually the sound approached, rising upwards in volume to a humming drone, but nothing was visible owing to the stray wisps of ground mist still hanging about the lines. The aeroplane seemed to be coming very near. Now the roar of its propeller filled our ears—then, gazing aloft, we all saw an amazing sight.

Gliding over our heads at a great pace into No Man's Land, the outline of one of our machines loomed into view. The forms of the pilot and observer were silhouetted clearly against the yellow planes, for it was apparently not more than 150 feet up. Heads were upturned now all down the trench, amazement on every feature. Though climbing rapidly, the machine would be in deadly peril if it held on its present course.

With the thought came the report of a rifle fired from the enemy's direction. Others followed in a spluttering gust, until the whole line opposite seemed crackling with shots. Into this medley of sounds burst the throbbing beat of a machine-gun. All eyes were fixed on the plane, which was now driving over the enemy's lines. It seemed to many in our trench that we could hear the splatter of bullets as they struck it. Then, after a moment of breathless suspense, it appeared to falter. It was swerving now to the right and turning down the German line. Another instant passed. It was *not* turning, for the engine had stopped, and—horrors !—the machine was gliding downwards !

A pandemonium of firing now reached our ears. Evidently hit, it was wheeling round as if wishing to land within our lines. Would they do it ? The next moment, it was obvious that it was gliding downwards too fast. Then, with a swoop, the aeroplane vanished below the parapet some three hundred yards on our right. No use wondering whether they had reached safety, for the air was now filled with cheers that floated in a joyful tumult towards us. One's blood boiled at the sound. If only we could have done something! But the Germans, firing upward from below the level of their parapet, had given us not so much as a sporting target.

The whole incident was over almost before we could realise it had begun : the swoop over No Man's Land ; the vain effort to make a full turn ; then the final glide to death. What on earth had possessed those two ? Before our eyes they had gone in reckless fashion to fruitless and sudden annihilation. It seemed as senseless and pathetic as a moth's attraction for a flame, but a hundred times more horrible. Then I remembered the ground mist and swore.

This episode, the first which I had really witnessed, filled me with disgust. It was unquestionably the most futile sacrifice of human life of which I had knowledge. The exultant glee manifested at the destruction of these two brave men, though not altogether surprising, suggested something very repulsive. But I was to live and learn many things beyond the scope of a civilian's philosophy.

Nothing is so contagious as the sound of rifle fire. The line was now on the alert, ready to pour in a hail of bullets at anything which might be suspect. For a while, a machine-gun situated in a commanding position in the second line kept up a series of bursts, but by degrees everything became quiet once more.

It was about three hours later, while the company commander was making a tour of inspection, that I received orders from him to visit this machine-gun's emplacement with a view to warning them of the risk they ran. For several minutes a steady series of short bursts of fire had been rapping out from its direction. The gun, I was told, was located in a ruin

near my dugout, a spot of evil reputation, as its name
" Whizz Bang Villa " implied.

" Be careful when crossing the ruin. The gunners
are just on the other side." I acknowledged the
warning as I turned into the communication trench
that led to my objective.

There was no difficulty in finding my way, since it
lay along a route by which I had already travelled
several times. Approaching the villa, I was careful
to keep my head down ; the sandbag parapet screening its entrance was none too high. Peering inside,
one could only see a concrete floor, over which lay a
wild profusion of broken scattered bricks. Many
hits had been obtained on the walls, and these, jagged
and perforated by shell fire, rose only some five feet
above floor level. Across the ruins stood what I
took to be the entrance to the emplacement, but to
reach this, one had to cross a gap in the wall which
was visible to the enemy. This I had no difficulty in
passing at a run, crouching as best I could.

In reply to my questions, the N.C.O. in charge informed me that he thought he had located a sniper's
post across on our left front.

" The Captain wants you to remember that you are
likely to incur retaliation, if you keep it up too long."

" Very good, sir."

His manner was irreproachable, but I caught a
suspicion as if he thought our solicitude was not
entirely for himself and his gun's crew ; retaliation
has a reprehensible tendency to fall, not on those
who provoke it, but upon the hapless occupants of the
adjoining trenches.

A few moments later it seemed as if an earthquake
and I had entered the passage to the communication
trench together. Barely had my ears caught the
slightest warning of its approach before a loud crash
and concussion enveloped me. The next moment,
having ducked into the bottom of the trench, I was

hit on the back by some missile, while a shower of
damp earth came pattering down around me. After
a moment I straightened myself and carried my hand
to my back. Withdrawing it, I saw it was smeared
with mud ; a flying clod had chosen me for a target.

"That must have been a Whizz Bang," I thought.
As if in reply, a loud shriek, followed instantly by
another crash, sounded somewhat farther off behind
the villa. Looking up, I beheld a blotch of black
smoke hanging lazily in the air several yards beyond
the edge of the trench ; then another shell landed
perilously near, sending up a splash of mud and fragments of brick. This spot seemed no health resort.

.   .   .   .   .

Although our front line was heavily defended by
wire entanglements, it was announced by our company
commander later in the day that further strengthen-
ing of the position had been decided upon. Tasks
were allotted so that the four platoons worked near
their own bit of trench, so in our capacity as a supporting one, our portion of the work was on the support line. The position of the La Bassée road on our
right flank has already been described. Cutting through
the opposing positions at right angles, it was naturally
for us an object for close observation. At night, the
machine-gun in Whizz Bang Villa was trained on it
in such a way as to sweep the road for a considerable
distance. At the point where the front line abutted
against it, the road was wired across, but no such
defensive measures existed in the support line. Our
orders were to lash a number of *chevaux de frise* across
it sufficient to block it effectively at a short distance
in advance of our trench.

At dusk, therefore, I surveyed this ground in company with the platoon sergeant, and decided on the
arrangements for carrying out the work. Visibility
was now quite low, yet sufficient to render objects
recognisable at twenty paces.

Several hours later we filed along a disused trench that ended about thirty yards short of the road. On our right, somewhere in the darkness and at no great distance, lay the support position ; from behind came the stumbling footfalls of the fatigue party carrying our material. This had come from the battalion dump.

Climbing out at the end of the trench where it had fallen in, I set out, followed by a single man, to take a final view of the road and to discover if possible the easiest track for the carriers. Everywhere around, the ground was cut up by shell craters and obstructed by tufts of wild grass and obstacles. On reaching the road, I placed my man in a suitable spot whence he could observe the direction of the enemy line, and ordered him to warn the party at the first sign of a pistol light. Dim and ghostly in the darkness, the track of the roadway receded toward our front line. Upon its surface, dark patches denoted splinters fallen from the flanking rows of trees, and one noted with surprise that already a scattered carpet of thin grass had made its appearance in many places. This had sprung up in so short a period as seven months. The lonely melancholy of the shattered trunks and the abandoned road seemed strangely emphasised by the dim light.

Pacing the width of the road and its ditches, I estimated that the number of *chevaux de frise* would suffice with something to spare. Five minutes later, we were engaged in lashing the first into position with the supply of wire we had obtained.

We were halfway across before a sharp warning from the observer caused us to fall flat on our faces. Around us, the brightly lit road and ditches were dancing with gliding shadows, among which the forms of our party lay frozen into immobility. It was, perhaps, some twenty seconds before we were again enveloped in darkness. The gloom, as the light from the German rocket subsided, seemed to leap upon us. Then in the dusk recumbent figures came to life once more, and another section of the barricade was lashed into position. For several minutes our work proceeded in stealthy fashion ; in a very short while our task would be completed. The whispers of those around me were interrupted suddenly by a splutter of rifle shots from the direction of our front line. Then, once again the night became still.

"Only two more will be wanted now, sir." The guarded tones of the corporal in charge of the working party came from a dark mass crouching near at hand. "Down ! "

The whispered exclamation flew from the observer. Once more we became petrified, as it were, in those very attitudes which the flare had surprised. Presently the returning darkness was greeted by another outburst of scattered shots from the obscurity ahead. Quickly the next *chevaux de frise* was carried into its place, to be pounced upon by the wirers who awaited it. Away overhead, a bullet moaned through the night air, followed by a quickly repeated drone as others followed on its course.

"Next one," whispered the corporal. In response, a sound of deadened footfalls came from the shadows by the roadside.

Rat-tat-tat-tat ! Like ghosts in the night, a chorus of shrill wails careered forlornly overhead, the moans swelling in volume as the bullets were traversed towards us. Now we were on our faces once more, snuggling closely into the very hollows of the ground. Swish, swish, crack ! Their tearing notes sounded like whip-thongs in our ears. Something hit the wooden frame of the barricade with a resounding impact, and at the same instant there arose the shriek of a ricochet where it faded away behind us like the dying voice of a banshee. Close to where we grovelled something flicked on to the road, but, after investigation, nothing was to be seen: a flying splinter most likely.

Away on our right, in the direction of the French line, the waning sound of the swinging traverse reached our ears.

" 'Spects them blurry Allemans 'as seen us." The voice, issuing from the refuge of the ditch, addressed apparently the world at large.

The firing having died away, a wait of a minute or two seemed prudent, then, all being quiet once more, the last section was carried to its place. The wirer seemed to be curiously clumsy in fastening this final portion of our work, but at last it was done. To collect the party and dispatch them toward the old trench occupied only a few moments, for no one wished to spend unnecessary time out here. After a final examination and a few pulls at the barricade, I too had finished, and followed in the direction taken by the working-party. Steering toward the direction of a low hail from the darkness, I presently saw the gaping shadow of the trench below me. The next moment I was in it, and discovered the form of the corporal.

" We have made a pretty good job of that, I think."

" Yessir."

Certainly I fancied we had. I had also felt, for the second time that day, the sensation known in the trenches as " wind."

CHAPTER VIII

THE secret had been well kept, for it was only on the evening of May 7th that news of great events began to circulate in our company messes.

Once again the battalion was in the line, occupying its former position. Amidst much speculation the eve of the day of battle passed away. Our hopes were high, because it was now known that a heavy blow was to be delivered by the allied forces along this sector of the front. To the south of us, extending for several miles past the high-standing ridge of Notre Dame de Lorette, the French 10th Army under the personal command of Foch, was understood to be about to open a great attack. Portions of our troops operating to the northward would pass simultaneously to the offensive. As at Neuve Chapelle, another effort was to be made by the British Army to obtain possession of the Aubers Ridge, and in the event of both attacks proving successful, the town of La Bassée facing us would become gripped between two salients.

By the evening of the 8th, it was common knowledge in the trenches that the hour of commencement had been fixed for 10 o'clock on the following morning. This time we were to repeat the tactics of Neuve Chapelle on a wider frontage.

Even the most anxious hours have their ending. After a night of waiting, the dawn at last appeared, bringing with it a day charged full of destiny to many thousands. Over the misty landscape a profound silence reigned, disturbed only by an occasional far-off shot or the twitter of birds. The day seemed just as any ordinary day, and yet, to us waiting between the two sectors of attack, it seemed almost strange that the very heavens themselves could appear so unconcerned.

By the time breakfast was announced, the sullen mutter of guns was wafted to our position from the southward. Had they started ? The question was uppermost in the minds of all.

Our rôle was one of active immobility : the enemy was to be kept uncertain of our intentions by means of gusts of fire.

Emerging from the mess dugout after breakfast, one's ears were assailed by a steady roll of thunder from the direction of the French front, for the hour of their artillery preparation had been fixed somewhat in advance of our own. Throbbing above the disturbance, the rapid concussions of their 75's were easily distinguishable. So far, the noise of the battle came only from the south. As their opening attack was not yet to extend sufficiently to the north for us to see it, nothing was visible to us from our points of vantage. From the direction of La Targette and Carency a steady crescendo of gunfire was audible. Never had I imagined such a volume of artillery. Later, it transpired that nothing approaching it had been heard up to then on the Western Front.

Before long, our watches announced that the hour of the British Army was at hand. The last minutes crawled by in seeming eternity. Suddenly, behind us, as we faced toward the French, a roar of gunfire ascended from the north : yonder, nearer and more awe-inspiring, pealed the voice of England. Attacking on the sector Festubert-Bois Grenier, part of the 1st Corps and the Indian Corps were moving against the southern end of the Bois du Biez, while the 8th Division, carrying out the main operation, advanced from Rouges Bancs toward the northern point of the Aubers Ridge. Very little of the action was visible to us. Away in the direction of Festubert a thick line of shrapnel bursts mottled the enemy's position, its dun colour darkened from time to time by the black of high explosive. In each ear, as we gazed toward the chimney stacks of La Bassée, there rolled the din of a different battle. Gradually the noise decreased as the hours passed by, and our patience was rewarded at last by news of successes along our front. Several lines of trenches had been taken, in spite of certain checks due to uncut wire.

By nightfall, the British sector had quietened down to a very great extent; but though our guns slackened their fire, the German retaliation showed no signs of a corresponding diminution. Although unknown to us until a few days later, the results of the day seemed, even at the time, lacking in real importance. Before long, rumours of heavy casualties began to circulate.

As yet, no news had come through from the southward. There, far into the night, the thunder of artillery rolled on, causing the ground to quiver about our position and the air to pulsate in our ears. From my dugout door, I saw over in the direction of the French attack a sight grandiose beyond words. Gleaming brilliantly above the black-edged outline of the horizon, rising and falling in ceaseless fluctuation, and filling the sky with its glare, was displayed a sheet of flame. Now waning to a dull yellow, now flaring with renewed intensity, the blazing firmament alternately veiled and disclosed the stark outline of the ridge of Notre Dame de Lorette. Above all rolled and drummed the clamour of battle. Never had I seen so grand or so terrible a sight.

Inside my dugout the earth tremors seemed still

heavier. In the doorway, a ghostly gleam reflected the glare of the sky, playing upon the surface of the smooth earth in weird flickers, while from the roof, a few feet above my head, the dust pattered upon my coat and ground-sheet as it was dislodged by the concussions outside. The sound suggested slow drops of rain. I found myself counting them; and as I counted, I fell asleep.

CHAPTER IX

TAMBOURS BATTANTS

" Je veux enfant de la Patrie
Quand le clairon résonnera,
Quand le canon dans sa furie
Sur l'ennemi rétentira ;
Et l'Empereur au sein de la mitraille,
L'Empereur viendra de nouveau,
L'Empereur viendra de nouveau !
Et toutes les ombres de la Grande Armée
Sortiront de la tombeau ! "

By a great stroke of fortune my platoon was adjoining the French, so one had not far to go in search of news.

Proceeding through the tunnel beneath the La Bassée road on the following afternoon, I found myself among the light-blue uniforms of their *fantassins*, who, lounging about in nonchalant fashion, were gossiping among themselves until my appearance afforded a welcome relief from their routine. From time to time I stopped to exchange a few remarks. The offer of a freshly rolled cigarette indicated that I was supposed to be a private soldier, since to these fellows all English uniforms were strange. How should they know ? My inquiry for an officer brought enlightenment.

" Monsieur est officier ! "

" Mais oui, mon brave."

" Pardon, mon lieutenant, je ne le savais pas. Monsieur ne porte pas des galons d'officier ? "

"Par ici." I indicated my shoulder straps, smiling
at his mistake. "C'est l'habitude de la Garde."

"Vous êtes de la Garde, monsieur?"

"Si! Tout près, à côté de vous." Then, with a
smile, "Comme autrefois à l'Alma et Inkerman."

Nothing more was required to establish the most
cordial relations, for my allusion, imperfectly understood by some, was genially applauded by most.
The trench was filling rapidly with men, come to see
one of "les angliches" from the other side of the
road, thus it was amid quite an escort that I was guided
along their second line to where their company headquarters lay. There I explained my errand to be
quite unofficial, though prompted by a desire to know
the news of the battle on their right.

A young lieutenant, sitting alone in the gloom of a
deep dugout, bade me welcome, and invited me inside
with that hospitable air so common to his countrymen.

"You heard our bombardment?" he asked with
a grin. I assured him that some echo of it had penetrated to the north side of the road.

"Well, La Targette is ours; also part of Neuville
St. Vaast, they say. The White Works, in the centre,
were carried at the bayonet point. There also things
have gone well."

This was good news. I congratulated him on his
countrymen's success.

"And Carency?" I inquired. This lay nearer
than the other places named.

"We are still fighting there. The Boches are
tenacious. To-day we attack on the ridge, and if
Monsieur can prolong his stay, he will see, perhaps,
something of the attack over on this side."

Here was news indeed: an invitation to witness a
battle! Most assuredly, Monsieur would be delighted.

"We must go very soon, then, for the artillery has

been active for some time. From a place I know of, we shall see what there will be to be seen."

Learning that I was no stranger to his country, my companion soon became most talkative. Before long, we had arrived at our position, which proved to be a slightly elevated observation post in their second line.

Gazing in the direction pointed out to me, I saw that the ground, forming a slight valley, curved toward the right. Yonder arose the twin towers of Loos; beyond these again, to the right of them, lay Lens. Nearer to us by some distance in front ran the line of the enemy's trenches near the Loos–Béthune road. A chequered smear along the top of the slope indicated the sandbags of their positions, but these, unlike our own, were made of a variety of materials that presented a motley effect.

The gunfire, which had recommenced earlier in the day, now attained a great intensity. Within a whirl of smoke and spouting earth, the German position could be easily seen. It looked a strong one, as before it, sweeping down toward the bottom of the dip, the farther slope extended without interruption like a giant glacis. From our position the bottom of the valley was invisible; for our vision was obstructed by the edge of the nearer ridge occupied by the French. Lining this like a row of sentinels at regular intervals stood a ragged line of small trees, and it was between these that the view in the direction of Loos was obtainable.

Suddenly, a glimmer of flashes appeared away on our right along this row of trees. Our eyes were immediately arrested by these moving details. Through glasses, figures were clearly visible pouring over the edge of the brow, and before one realised it, a thick line of leaping infantry had vanished down the near slope. The salvos of the 75's firing heavily in our rear shrieked and howled across the valley. The din became tremendous.

Then, descending abruptly like a fringe of clouds along the line of trunks, appeared the smoke of the German barrage. Through this veil of bursting shells the landscape grew patchy and unreal. A bank of haze soon formed along the line of stems, and as we watched, a second wave of men surged into it and vanished down the hill.

Both armies were now pouring forth their full volume of fire, and amidst the thrashing tumult of the attack one's pulse stirred to life and excitement slowly grew. The storm of shell fire drowned all other sounds, but, at irregular intervals, fleeting glimpses of the enemy's trench revealed a faint bluish mist hanging over its line of sandbags: their infantry was in action. Still, at the lowest visible point of the farther slope, nothing was to be seen for several minutes. Anxiously we watched in spellbound silence for the first sign of the leading wave. Still the enemy's barrage crashed along the French position, but by watching this, we should miss the opening of the drama on the hill-side yonder.

Would they never appear ? Had they been caught by a curtain of fire, invisible to us in the hollow ? The thought was a torture.

Glinting in scattered clusters, something called for attention down in the valley. There they were— Frenchmen storming into battle as in the days of the *Grande Armée* !

As the line of black figures stumbled into view, it presented a magnificent spectacle. There the sun flashed upon a bayonet, there—there—everywhere ! Slowly, as it seemed to me, but with rapid movements, they were moving forward in a tattered line, leaving in their wake a trail of dark dots that grew thicker every moment. In the face of that fire they could never reach their goal ; but though men were falling fast, the remnants still advanced.

Scattered in their track, curved streaks of bodies

showed where a traversing machine-gun had caught the wave, the first man to be hit lying slightly in rear of the last. The German fire was murderous.

Then came another surge of men, the second wave, fine and strong in comparison with the straggling mob ahead of it. Intently our eyes followed their progress. Why did they not charge ; their *pas de charge* was famous ? Little could we, idle spectators, imagine at that moment the gasping lungs of those devoted troops as they stumbled resolutely up the farther slope. From the reeling forms within their ranks we realised the hail of bullets that must be tearing past, but its shrieking tumult was not for our ears. There, each pack must weigh a hundredweight, every stride seem challenge to death. Farther and farther they advanced, never faltering, never flinching.

" Allons, enfants de la patrie " !

A few moments later they had become the first line, since of the leading one scarcely anything remained.

Now the view was becoming clearer, for the German barrage had shortened into the valley, whence it rose as a dim haze visible between the trees.

Despite the intensity of the French gunfire, several machine-guns had been able to open from the enemy's position. These were playing across the slope up which the irregular groups of men were moving. Far along the hill-side a dark fringed line was slowly creeping. Now, in the teeth of the gale, they had reached the farthermost bodies of their comrades ; now, they were surging upward in the face of a terrible sleet. Feverishly one wondered whether they would reach the German entanglements.

Moving forward in similar formation, yet another line of supports appeared, and, cantering in a zigzag course up and down their frontage, a mounted officer was visible at their head. Every now and then a streak flashed above him, caused by his sword circling in the sunlight. Our gaze followed that solitary hero in fascination. Already a few men were dropping in the ranks behind him, but he himself bore a charmed life. It was an amazing sight, strangely reminiscent of old battle pictures.

The farthermost line, now only a couple of hundred yards from the turmoil of the German position, had been reduced to a few shreds of its original formation. With a glitter of steel, its supports were ascending behind it, a single form, now on foot, turning from side to side as it plodded at their head: his horse had been shot under him. Then the figures in advance seemed to waver. Amid the din no sounds of cheering were audible, and in any case the distance was too great for us to hear. Forging ahead through the strewn figures of their comrades, this third line mounted higher and higher up the hill. Surely, here was the critical moment, for farther and farther they crawled, gradually enveloping the stragglers ahead. Only on them could our gaze remain. Elsewhere, the panorama became trivial.

In scattered groups they were now making for the enemy's wire, and, as if by magic, the French guns lifted beyond their objective. The drama had now apparently reached its height. Our excitement was intense, and our glasses were no longer so steady as before.

Yonder, detached figures were being checked by the wire, and a few moments later the French line, sadly thinned, was writhing along the obstacle. The firing must have been point-blank, for men were falling in all directions. In an agony of mind we began to realise they would *not* break through. . .

In despair, my eyes sought the lower slope for yet other reinforcements, and the sight that confronted them thrilled by its splendour. Here came the mighty climax, surpassing in effect one's puny imagination.

Like a stormy roller foaming up the shore came the French reserves, sunlight flickering on a hedge of bayonet points and flashing from their drums. On seeing those drums, I could have gasped; only the sight of them dumbfounded me. *Tambours battants, tambours battants!* God of Battles! Here came the *pas de charge!*

Visible through the splashes of smoke, this body rolled upward along the hill; in such a surging torrent must the Old Guard have mounted the slopes at Waterloo. Beside this, the art of Détaille faded into insignificance. Here was revealed the majesty of war. To be among these men, to hear their rattling drums, the clatter of equipment, and the cries of their officers—surely their echoes must stir the very tombs of the Invalides!

> " Et l'Empereur au sein de la mitraille,
>   l'Empereur viendra de nouveau."

Seething with a multitude of atoms, the raging tide swept onward and upward. Now they were flooding around the stragglers, sweeping them forward with their impetus. From the rise a short distance ahead figures were painfully emerging, the stabs of their rifle fire hacking through the haze that hung around.

Great as was this spectacle, it was rather by its significance that it awed one. As incoming waves sweep beyond their predecessors, so did the reserves surge into their comrades and carry them forward. France embattled hung poised for an instant amidst the smoke-drift, then, like a mighty breaker, tearing, boiling, and tumbling, it broke over the German line. From above its turmoil, its fringe of bayonets vanished as they were lowered to the charge!

From the German position burst a scattered flock of dark objects, running wildly toward the skyline. Beside me I heard a hiss of intaken breath. It was "mon Lieutenant," my host.

" Ils se sauvent !   Ils se sauvent ! "

In very truth they were; Bavaria had no taste for the "french fury."   Where the slope ran smoothly a while ago, there now lay swathes of dead; but it was not upon them that our thoughts dwelt, for above them, exulting in the enemy's position, the living remained in triumph.

" C'est fini."   My companion was deeply moved.

" No, monsieur ; not finished, only commenced."

" How mean you ? " he asked.

" We have seen a glorious incident, that is all."

But in my own mind, after what I had just seen, it seemed not only as if Rouget de Lisle lived again in France, but that, emerging from the struggle, Frenchmen would see before the end that " Day of Glory " of which he sang.

CHAPTER X

IN RESERVE

THE middle of the month of May ended a brilliant period for our allies. Within three days of the storming of the Loos–Béthune road the weather broke, and with this change a new form of tactical situation arose. Coinciding with the attack by their left, they had launched others against the Chapel of Notre Dame de Lorette and the cemetery of Neuville St. Vaast. On the following day, the 11th, Carency, defended house by house with the utmost stubbornness, became doomed.

On the first day of the battle, the 10th Army was supposed to have fired no less than 300,000 shells, but the bombardment on the 13th revealed no audible reduction of their artillery work. Tactically, the German line had been broken, but a sudden change in the character of the battle now appeared. Though shattered into particles, the enemy's forces still prevented any considerable advance, since, instead of dissolving, the defence rallied round a system of "strong points," a network through which it was found impossible for us to break. Thus the call on the artillery, which alone could reduce these *fortins*, became very great.

Now, more than ever before, the need was felt for guns and munitions. Though the French artillery had achieved an astonishing performance, such an effort was bound to end sooner or later by reason of limited supplies. The attack by the 10th Army did not close, however, before the surrender of Carency on the afternoon of the 12th. At the same time, the summit of the ridge, and with it the Chapel of Notre Dame de Lorette, was swept clear of the enemy. Ablain, now a blazing pyre, followed suit that night. All the high ground west of Souchez had been torn from the enemy together with some 5,000 prisoners.

Simultaneously with the French attack of Sunday the 16th, our Army again opened an offensive, which came to be known as the battle of Festubert. Our artillery preparation began on the Saturday night, and, in view of our weakness in guns, three groups of French 75's lent us their assistance. The infantry attack was launched at dawn, and in this the 2nd Division, to which the 4th (Guards) Brigade belonged, was partially involved. Together with the Indian Corps, it was responsible for the northern sector, while to the south, the 20th and 22nd Brigades were operating in concert, their respective points in the line being represented by the Rue du Bois and the Rue d'Ouvert. Meanwhile the 2nd Division was advancing from Richebourg.

At this time, I was transferred from the battalion with which I had been serving to a sister battalion, which also formed one of the units of the same brigade. It was in billets around a farm in the locality of Locon, and seemed to be in expectation of going up to the line to relieve another unit; but, as news of the action was very scanty, everything remained in a state of uncertainty.

Those battalions of the 2nd Division which were engaged had taken two lines of trenches, but the Indians had been held up. The centre had reached the Rue de Cailloux, and had advanced even farther, until brought to a standstill by heavy fire from a flank. On being reinforced, it had gained a point north-west of La Quinque Rue.

6

Presently, rumours began to circulate to the effect that, as in the case of the French 10th Army, the 2nd Division was encountering heavy opposition from isolated "strong points." Great stories were told of the bombers of the Grenadier Guards. The fate of a company of Scots Guards, though sad to contemplate, caused us to realise that the old spirit of the Brigade was still alive. Left in an advanced position with both flanks "in the air," this devoted band had repelled attack after attack, until, enveloped on all sides, it had been overwhelmed. Only when the ground passed once more into British occupation a few days later did the full heroism of their end become known. The bodies of these gallant men were found facing in every direction, ringed round with swathes of German dead.

A day or two after my arrival at the farm, a large movement of troops took place on the road running past our billets. Here I saw the Canadians for the first time. The story of their stand in face of the first German gas attack at Ypres had made their name renowned throughout the Army. Many and diverse were the types of men within their ranks, but all were hardy fellows, animated to an extraordinary degree by a hatred for the enemy. The ghastly fate of one of their sergeants no doubt kindled in them a far more personal animus than was to be found in the majority of home battalions, by whom "Fritz" was regarded with an intermingling of contempt and good-humoured irony. Germany, by crucifying its Canadian prisoner at the time of the second battle of Ypres, aroused among his comrades the fires of inextinguishable hate. "Fritz" was rapidly becoming in the eyes of British soldiers the "Blurry Hun," who, so long as he remained armed, was to be exterminated.

Rumours of our future movements were shortly ended by the announcement that the battalion would take over a portion of the newly won ground that very night. The engaged portions of the 2nd Division were to be relieved. Among these, the Irish Guards had lost heavily, seventeen officers being hit while their battalion was executing a night attack on the *fortins* ahead of it.

Once more ensued the bustle of preparation for departure, servants hurrying backwards and forwards in a burst of activity. In the dimly lit mess-room of the farmhouse, the Commanding Officer propounded the arrangements for the disposition of the various companies, including in his remarks some observations on the character of the recent fighting. From the large farmyard outside, the murmur of the men's preparations for the march filtered through the open window, and before long, a clatter of hoofs and a rumble of wheels announced the arrival of the mess-cart. In the kitchen adjoining, servants hurried with the task of packing up for the road, accompanying their efforts with a continuous rattle of odds and ends.

By and by, the council of war having ended, one by one the officers strode from the room and vanished into the darkness. The flashes of electric lamps marked their way through the glutinous and evil-smelling perils of the yard outside.

Another half-hour found companies falling into their places in the order of march, while the sound of an officer's voice rose occasionally above the steady beat of the rain. Underfoot the mud was bad, but one learnt with a sense of thankfulness that the march up to the line would be by road ; even the stony highway would be a luxury in comparison with the cross-country tracks. Up to the communication trenches the going would be very heavy, but as my company—"Number 4" —was to be in reserve, we should not have very far to go through such places.

Ahead of us a voice gave the order to advance, and

the preceding company moved off, followed a moment later by our own. Soon the steady tramp of feet sounded dully upon the road, and shortly after the order " march at ease " had been given, dull points of light, hovering in the ranks ahead like glow-worms, showed that the men were lighting up their cigarettes. Thus, trudging stolidly through the rain and darkness, our march proceeded in much the usual way, and not until we had accomplished several miles did any unusual event break the monotony of our progress. Glowing by moments on the horizon, the glare of Verey lights indicated as usual the direction of the fighting line.

We were brought to a standstill at last by a warning from ahead that the column had halted. Word soon came down the line that the men were to fall out and ease themselves of their equipment. A battalion, so we learnt, was halted in the roadway in front of us, for the enemy, feeling for the road, were shelling a wood that stood several hundred yards away invisible to us in the darkness.

It was above an hour before we received orders to fall in once more. Huddled at the side of the road, enveloped in their soaking greatcoats, the men at first had beguiled the time with snatches of song and fitful laughter, but as the delay dragged on and the rain continued without interruption, their spirits, like their clothes, became more and more damped. The battalion in advance, profiting by a cessation of the shelling, next resumed its march, but we, struggling into our equipment which by then was stiff from rain, had received almost immediately a counter-order. The shelling had been resumed. A groan, embodying all shades of blasphemy, arose from the shadows beside the road.

> " I wanter go 'ome, I wanter go 'ome ;
> I'm fed up with this blurry war ;
> I wanter go 'ome."

In such manner did the irresponsible vocalist give utterance to the feelings of the platoon. Our pipes had long grown cold, but somehow, in the dark, little satisfaction is to be obtained from smoking. Moreover it was growing chilly, and many of us were stamping about the road in order to counteract the effects of the damp air.

At last a subdued murmur arose from the darkness ahead.

"Fall in there, I tell you, and get that kit on. I suppose you wants me t'come and dress you ? " The raucous voice of a sergeant arose, ending with the inevitable non-commissioned humour regarding the sort of " dressing " someone was likely to receive at the speaker's hands. The company ahead was moving off, but still no order had reached us. Evidently the battalion was about to proceed on its way with intervals between companies ; this, in order to minimise risks from shell fire.

Word now came for us also to be getting ready, and within a couple of minutes we were plodding forward once more. No shells approached as we made our way along the side of the wood, for either the enemy had ceased their fire, or had turned their attention elsewhere. The illumination from the direction of the line was now growing steadily nearer. Once again the " toc-toc-toc " of a machine-gun reached our ears. With the frequent halts, the last mile or so must have taken us an hour to accomplish.

Now we were pushing slowly along a sodden country lane, now halting beside a row of slender trees, whose leaves whispered in the darkness overhead. A slight breeze was just perceptible in the air, blowing from the direction of the enemy and bearing to us the sounds of rifle shots and the occasional boom of a distant gun. Our march in full order and with greatcoats had warmed us up again, so caps were doffed for a moment's refreshment. By this time the rain had ceased, and the moon was struggling to appear through a rift in the clouds. Far overhead, a bullet moaned upon its invisible path.

"Too much foresight, Fritz."

A snigger greeted the remark ; then, once again, we were splashing forward through the mud.

CHAPTER XI

THE END OF FESTUBERT

THE position of " Number 4 " lay in a portion of the third line, which ran a short distance in front of the remnants of a village. After a daylight inspection, it proved to consist of barricades rather than properly excavated trenches, because, owing to the water-logged condition of the ground in this area, no digging could be done below a couple of feet in depth. Still lying about were considerable quantities of German and English equipment, especially in the continuation of our line beyond the company frontage, where three hundred yards or more of unoccupied trench separated us from the flanking companies, which, like ourselves, were in reserve.

Day had only just commenced when the enemy began to send over a few shells, but as these burst rather high, no damage was done. Among these there presently appeared a few high explosives, their black smoke rendering them easily distinguishable. Profiting by an interval in the firing, I set off to ascertain the cause of a most abominable smell that polluted our neighbourhood, and before long, guided by the direction of the wind, I discovered about a hundred yards in front of our right flank a couple of cows, obviously dead many days, since their skeletons were plainly visible through their sagging hides. These, I presumed, were the cause of our discomfort, but as they lay in the open, nothing could be done. The unsavoury breeze continued to enfilade our portion of the trench for the rest of the day.

On regaining my shelter shortly after breakfast, I became aware of a renewed bombardment, and going out to watch, could see a series of explosions spouting up from various points in our front-line ahead. Evidently they were getting a warm time of it. Half an hour later, several louder detonations occurred where I judged our second line to lie. Fragments of timber and earth, flying in all directions, indicated that the enemy had obtained direct hits on our position ; no very difficult feat, as our trenches had been lately occupied by them, and no doubt they knew the range to within a yard. One could not help hoping that they would leave our line alone.

Unfortunately this was not the case, for by and by a series of crescendo wails approached through the air, followed at once by several loud crashes overhead. Pieces of shrapnel droned round about, several whacking into the hurdle revetments. Everyone sought cover on hearing their approach, and the trench became apparently deserted. From the shelter to which we had hastily retired, it seemed as if screeches and explosions filled the world outside. There, missiles were thrashing the mud in a regular cascade, and every time the sound of an approaching projectile reached the ear, you wondered whether *this* would be the one destined for your own person.

Evidently the enemy did not think us worthy of high explosive, for the steady hum of shrapnel bullets and time-fuse common shell continued for about three hours. The reply of our own guns, if any, was inaudible amid the noise outside. It seemed to us in our shelters to be a very one-sided contest.

The monotony of the situation was interrupted presently by the abrupt arrival in the doorway of my shelter of a large splinter of shell-case, which had rebounded off a hurdle outside. Curiosity and ignorance prompted me to pick it up in order to examine it, but at first touch an oath escaped me, for although it looked harmless enough, it proved to be almost red-hot. Wounds from shell fire, besides being terribly mangling, now took on an additional aspect to my mind.

At last the barrage ceased, and some of us wondered whether an attack was to follow, though, so far, no sound of small-arm fire was audible. Emerging from the shelter, I discovered that very little material damage had been wrought along the front occupied by the platoon, and, what was better still, no casualties had arisen. This shelling had been distinctly heavy, but now one realised how little damage may be done to entrenched troops by shrapnel fire alone.

Shells were still bursting in pairs over the village, and there was little left of the shattered tile roofs that I had noticed earlier in the morning. Among the mangled foliage of trees loomed gaunt skeletons of roof timbers, together with crumbling walls of farm buildings. These husks of former habitations were at last being demolished entirely, as, flying high within a cloud of pink brick-dust, whirling beams and a con-vulsive spray of broken tiles were constantly visible.

Presently, while watching this spectacle, I was approached by my platoon sergeant bringing news from the remainder of the company across the road. Our Captain—known to his messmates as " Baedeker " —had just returned from a visit to the front line, where he had received a slight scratch from a shell splinter ; up there, several casualties had occurred, chiefly from high explosives ; also several hits in the trench had been made.

After midday, the gunfire having quite subsided, I went up to the front line to view the effects of the morning's bombardment. A number of slight casualties were coming back to the dressing station located in the village, while farther along the communication trench lay several stretchers, whose loads, covered from head to foot with ground-sheets, told their own tale. Here and there along the front line, progress was checked by great landslides of earth and torn sandbags, marking the spot where a shell had overthrown our parapet. The men were all seated in the shelters and had evidently received orders to remain there. Lying about in numerous spots were clusters of shattered rifles, British and German, many without a butt, a few twisted into weird shapes by the force of an explosion. Burst packs, German entrenching spades, "hair brush" bombs, and fragments of grey uniform ; tins, twisted bayonets, and boots, lay scattered in all directions : here was the flotsam and jetsam of a modern battle-field. And everywhere, glueing the whole medley of litter into a boundless pudding, stretched the mud of Flanders.

I had not proceeded very far through this wilderness before the arrival of another shell a short distance behind me caused me to stop ; apparently there was to be no peace for the front line that day. Another shell followed a few minutes later, so I decided to run the gauntlet of any further fire and to regain the com-munication trench by which I had come.

Most of the afternoon passed amid a constant harassing fire of shrapnel, in whose manner of arrival there seemed to be some sort of artful method. A solitary shell would burst harmlessly in the air at a fair height, and a few minutes later, when the unwary might be supposed to have emerged to see the results of its explosion, a Whizz Bang would flash below the drifting smoke of the first and scatter its hail of missiles around. This trick, however, was too well known to the majority of the men to meet with much success.

Toward evening, during a lull of some duration, the work of evacuating the dead and wounded began.

The latter were no longer " walking cases," for the
reason that all men of this category had already made
their own way back in the course of the day.

It was a sad procession that threaded its way presently past our reserve trench.   The supply of ground-
sheets had run out, so it was often upon terrible
sights that we gazed as the stretcher-bearers filed
slowly past.   Here was other wreckage of war : human
beings, many still conscious and nauseatingly repulsive in spite of their first-aid dressings.   These, often
soaked by blood, served only to emphasise the mangled
wounds which they concealed, but did not hide.   In
spite of the care shown by the stretcher-bearers, an
occasional groan would escape from the wounded
man whom they carried.   One fellow, borne by
unconscious, kept up a continuous moan until
out of earshot.   Fine upstanding fellows only a few
hours before, these pitiful wrecks were now hideously
injured carcases : " *Kanonen Futter.*"   Then in due
course, swaying limply to the motion of their reeking
stretchers, wrists tied across their breasts to prevent
their arms from falling over the side, came the
dead.

.   .   .   .

Toward dusk, our attention was arrested by a sudden
outburst from our own artillery.   About a mile away,
over on our right, a series of violent explosions arose
in what appeared to be a German trench.   Soon the
enemy's guns were retaliating, and shells descended
into the village once more.   They were endeavouring
to find our batteries, but in this they were unsuccessful, for the volume of our shell fire continued without
interruption.   Earth, sandbags, and pieces of timber
were soon flying madly in a kind of devil's dance.
Something out of the ordinary was afoot; this was
no normal " evening hate."   By and by, it became
known that a small local attack was about to be

launched in that direction ; the Canadians, so it was said, being under orders to take a trench opposite their line.

Darkness was rapidly obscuring the landscape, but it was not long before the attack was opened. The noise of the guns had swelled to a heavy orchestral effect, when, suddenly chiming in, first as a staccato *motif*, then swelling upward to a sullen dirge, an accompaniment of machine-gun fire emerged above the din. The British were over the top.

Now the sound of small-arm firing rose to a minor pandemonium amid the full-throated clamour of the guns : the Germans had manned their parapet and were pouring forth a " mad minute " of rapid rifle-fire. Then, by slow degrees, the volume of small-arms grew less.

For an hour or more the artillery continued their activity, but no more machine-gun fire was audible. Our opinions were confirmed within a short while : once again Canada had " made good."

That night, the battalion was relieved by the 7th (Territorial) Gordon Highlanders. Sturdy fellows these, as they appeared after nightfall filing along the communication trench past our position. Within an hour of their appearance, we, the last company to be relieved, were moving off through the darkness. Our stay at Festubert had been short, but nevertheless full of incident.

On the same night, the whole of the 2nd Division was withdrawn from the line. The battle of Festubert might now be said to have ended.

One of the lessons of the battle was the importance of adequate artillery preparation. The comparatively meagre gains of the British Army at Festubert and La Quinque Rue were largely due to insufficiency in this respect. In every branch of supply the enemy were showing themselves superior. Our guns had failed to cut the wire ; but through this, by prodigies of valour, the attacking infantry had forced their way, taking in various places no less than three lines of trenches, though at great cost. Thereupon, arising from too limited supplies, they were subsequently bombed out of a large portion of their gains, or, in some cases, shelled out by German batteries that could not be silenced.

Considering its duration, casualties, and the numbers engaged, this battle would in any other war but this have been classed among the major actions of the British Army. However, though lacking those geographical results commonly associated with a victorious engagement, substantial advantages were not wanting. Our chief object had been gained. Our allies to the southward had benefited in no small degree by the stubborn retaining-action fought by the British troops on this sector. Not only had the German Command been prevented from drafting reinforcements of men and guns from this portion of the line, but reserves, hurried up by motor transport and designed to stem the tide of the French advance, had found themselves flung into this subsidiary battle to the northward. The gain in ground, judged by later standards, might be thought trifling, but, at the time this action was fought, Festubert represented the largest advance made by British arms since the commencement of trench warfare. The enemy's losses had been heavy ; their lines had been occupied on a frontage of several thousand yards ; and though grievously deficient in all classes of material and men, the British Expeditionary Force still maintained a high spirit, wherein confidence in itself and the future was very noticeable.

CHAPTER XII

THE CIVILIANS

THE remaining days of May passed amid those un-
eventful doings incidental to rest in billets and sundry
moves, but the commencement of the new month
brought with it a change of locality ; for at that
time the 2nd Division took over from the French the
sector that ran in front of the village of Vermelles.
Thus it came about that the 4th (Guards) Brigade
found themselves, about June 1st, marching along
those dusty roads to the southward which converge
on Noeux-les-Mines.

The change of surroundings came as a relief to the
eye after the monotony of the country north of the
La Bassée–Béthune road. True the same dull plain
extended southward, but even slag-heaps were a change
from everlasting rows of poplars. In that direction,
now only a few miles distant, the horizon was bounded
by the rising spurs and bold outline of the Notre Dame
de Lorette ridge.

Upon our arrival, Noeux-les-Mines struck us at
first somewhat unfavourably. We were the first
British troops to enter this district, and no doubt
the inhabitants regretted the departure of their fellow
countrymen. A sense of uncertainty as to the new
administration about to be installed in their midst
was responsible perhaps for the half-hearted welcome
given us. We were foreigners, and these worthy
people were at first inclined to mistrust all such folk.
Besides, our first measures, necessitated by our different

view on the question of hygiene, were not entirely conducive to popularity.

Fortunately, a counter-impression was not long in making itself felt. If the municipal *bourgeoisie* and the working classes of this mining town looked askance on the inconceivable eccentricity of our sanitary arrangements, they were not long in appreciating the strict discipline and good behaviour of their English visitors. These, moreover, disbursed unusual sums on a variety of commodities, which ranged from copious quantities of beer to coloured picture-postcards of unimpeachable patriotic sentiment. Trade, like the traditional gourd, increased in a night. " What could one think of a race whose *poilus*' wealth ran into varying quantities of *billets de banque* ? Was it credible ? "

So, as one day succeeded another, the opinions of Jacques Bonhomme and, more important still, those of Madame his wife, underwent considerable readjustment.

During the morning shortly after our arrival, the town became subjected to long-range shelling by the enemy. Whining and moaning through the air, the projectiles gave us a short warning of their approach, during which some dash for cover was generally possible. Before long, the officers' mess, which had been installed in the *Mairie*, was disturbed by a loud crash in the road near by. As the interval between the arrival of these unwelcome attentions was sufficient for a hasty investigation, a number of us set out to the scene of the explosion.

Some way down the cobbled street, a litter of tiles and broken glass first attracted our attention ; then a number of soldiers and a few civilians gathered rapidly round a house from which wreaths of smoke were slowly ascending. On our arrival there, we discovered a scene of utter havoc. The roof had vanished completely, and, now stripped bare, shattered rafters were exposed to view. Fragments of window panes glistened everywhere round our feet, together with splintered frames, while, hanging like a local fog, filling the street with its white obscurity, a cloud of powdered plaster and lime hovered overhead. Already, as we approached the gaping door, a party of figures emerged, bearing in its midst a shrouded body. Hasty remarks in a subdued tone were exchanged by civilian bystanders. " It was indeed Madame, killed instantaneously." Following this procession came the form of a burly sergeant of the Guards, carrying in his arms with grotesque care a nondescript bundle. In response to a volley of inquiries he could only smile and pull aside an outer wrapping. " God be praised ! The little one was alive and untouched ! " Thus for one poor soul did the Great War end, and for another be said to commence.

The comments of this unfortunate old woman's friends are better imagined than described. Appearing hurriedly from neighbouring doors, these filled the air, not with loud lamentations as might be supposed, but with an atmosphere of sullen contemplation far more eloquent by its implacability and by reason of what it left unsaid.

The evening of this day ended with scenes of a very different nature. It was June 4th, and in a brigade that counted among its officers a large number of Old Etonians a proper celebration was imperative.

Nearly seventy sat down to a great dinner prepared at the *Mairie*. No stranger scene could ever have been enacted within its first-floor hall than that which took place that night. The company, from the Brigadier down to the most junior Ensign, represented the larger portion of officers then serving with the Brigade. After the customary honours had been paid and the inevitable speeches ended, the gathering joined in a mighty effort and gave forth the impressive anthem, " Floreat Etona." No doubt the passing townsman paused a moment beneath our windows, speculating on the identity of this unfamiliar though obviously national song of *les anglais*: a mistake that those present may be pardoned for considering excusable.

Our entry into a new sector brought with it further opportunities for studying the attitude of the civil population towards the war. The inhabitants of this locality were no longer small farmers or business folk, like their neighbours to the northward, but for the most part coal-workers; for Noeux-les-Mines lay upon the fringe of the French Black Country, which extends from here to the east beyond Lens. Mobilisation had robbed the district of all its able-bodied manhood, and the remaining men, now thrown out of employment, were engaged by the French Government on sundry labours of a military character, such as the maintenance of roads and the digging of newly designed trenches in the neighbourhood. What little farming survived was now done by womenfolk, and all the women required were forthcoming, their ages ranging from about twenty to fifty. Young girls cared for the children and poultry, superintended generally over the home; matrons, no longer fit for labour in the fields, tended the vegetable gardens and the family cows, or supervised the housework of their grand-daughters. One could not fail to perceive that everybody had work to do of some kind, work which was necessary to the community, performed, as I have said, almost entirely by women.

Because men were not very frequently seen, boys seemed by reason of their sex to be conspicuous. These, sunburned by hours of toil, and clad in a varied assortment of well-worn clothes that often comprised a pair of cast-off French or English puttees, would be encountered on the road toward evening. Their pensive demeanour when in the presence of a body of troops had in it something pathetic. Perhaps they

7

thought of the few years ahead when they in their turn would become eligible to wear uniform.

Here was no want of realisation of the war. Rolling over the country-side almost every hour of the day, the voice of the guns reminded these people of the menace in which they stood. The sounds of battle were with them from dawn to sundown, and even of a night the reminder would continue as their windows rattled uneasily to the concussions outside. A few miles distant from their homes lay the great army of the invader. Who could say whether or not his advance had been checked ?

Frequently, in conversation with these country-folk, one was confronted by this question, to which, as an Englishman, only one reply could be made.

" And the war, will it soon end, think you ? "

Memories of " business as usual " would spring to one's mind. " No, not yet, certainly another year. Soon you will see the Grand Army of England."

" And we shall win, monsieur ? You have no doubt of that ? "

As this question came one day from an old woman, an inspiration born of a moment's glance across the landscape presented itself. Pointing to where the fields glowed beneath a carpet of poppies, daisies, and cornflowers, I, in turn, put a question in indifferent French.

" See there, madame, can you doubt your eyes ? "

The poor shrivelled old creature gazed a while in silence, and slowly it seemed as if a gust of latent youth surged to her face, though her voice, when she spoke, came only in a whisper.

" Ah, monsieur, you are right ; the land lies beneath the Tricolour. Assuredly the soil is speaking. C'est la voix de la France ! "

And perhaps at that moment there came to the pathetic old dame a vision of promise such as centuries before had surely visited another humble soul in the golden fields of Domrémy.

It would be absurd to suggest that the whole of a people could be transformed by their sufferings into idealists of this kind. Very varied were the types that casual events brought to our notice.

Lying within the battered area of Annequin stands, or stood at this time, a group of farm buildings still inhabited by an old farmer and his wife. This locality, as many will know, was well within range of the ubiquitous German Whizz Bang. Here, one summer evening, the company found itself in battalion reserve, the officers' mess being installed in an outbuilding across the road. To cultivate the acquaintance of the owners was always a desirable course, if for no other reason, because according to their interest in us did our comfort or discomfort grow. Accordingly, I entered the farmyard and was at once confronted by its master, who was engaged in throwing scraps of food to some pigeons.

After we had exchanged a few commonplace remarks, I became aware for the first time of Madame's presence in the doorway of their living-room, which, as in all houses of this class, performed duty also as kitchen. It was not long before I had confessed a moderately intimate knowledge of her country, whereupon I was presently invited to partake of a glass of that remarkable fluid which is honoured in so many parts of France by the title of " beer."

There is one infallible road to favour with such kindly souls as these. If the absence of wide-eyed children bars the way, a few complimentary remarks upon the household belongings are certain of appreciation, especially from the lady of the house.

" Madame, permit me to admire your fine stove."

My hostess smiled benignly.

" It is a good stove, my lieutenant. When new, it cost 300 francs ; but the trouble necessary to keep it clean. Oh! la la!" This with a truly Gallic gesture of the hand.

"Why should that be, madame?"

"Why, on account of the coal. Ever since the war it has been of an abominable quality. The mines were shut down, and no more good coal is procurable; now, we burn slag. See the ashes that it makes." Here I was permitted a view of the cinder tray. "That makes a dust of which to choke!"

"It is the fortune of war," I replied with mock gravity.

"Ah, the war! Monsieur may have noticed the barn outside?"

Monsieur had indeed, for a shell had stripped it of its roof to a lamentable extent.

"It is surely dangerous for you to continue here?" I inquired.

"Certainly, but what would you? We have nowhere else to go. We are here: we rest here."

"My wife and I, we are of accord," interrupted my host. "They may kill, smash, and burn, but those creatures shall not turn us out-of-doors." Something in his tone arrested my attention.

"This war which they made is a terrible thing," I ventured. The old man gazed out on to the ruin of his farm buildings, then he quietly removed his pipe.

"Three sons had I, monsieur. One was killed at the Marne." No man could surpass the quiet dignity of his tone. "Another fell at Rheims; and François writes from the trenches in Alsace. You have seen that which is left of my property here; we sleep in the cellar at night for fear of shells. No! we did not make this war, but we shall endure it."

Meanwhile, Madame had busied herself quietly about some household matter, but now continued her husband's remarks in tones free from all passion.

"You in England do not know what war means; is it not so, monsieur? But I, for one, do not com-

plain. Many there are in these parts who have lost
all and everything; who are we that *we* should complain? But see here that which they have done,
which is truly disgusting."

Her gesture indicated the window. In it a pane
had been pierced neatly, a spray of cracks radiating
from its centre like a patch of frost.

"A bullet from a shell did that a few days ago."

"Most fortunate for you, madame, that the damage
done was no greater?"

"Ah, but we can take care of ourselves!" she
exclaimed indignantly, "but see you what those
alleboches have done!" My attention was directed
to the door of a wooden cupboard in a corner across
the room. One of its panels had been split by a
shrapnel bullet, and with an abrupt movement the
old woman now threw it open.

"See! here is something truly monstrous," she
cried, pointing to a black alpaca jacket hanging inside. "My window and my cupboard are not sufficient. No! those unclean pigs must need rip the
sleeve of my husband's best coat; is there no limit
to what we must support? And I, who have so much
to do, how can I, monsieur, find time to repair that?"

From the tattered jacket before me, my thoughts
flew to her sons who would never return, and noting
her indignation over this trifle, I marvelled greatly.
Here before me, beneath a shabby bodice, beat the
heart of a noble woman.

CHAPTER XIII

A NEW SECTOR

The trenches occupied by the battalion in this new sector lay about a mile to the east of the ruins of Vermelles. Held lately by the French Army, they differed in several respects from those recently left by the 2nd Division. Well-constructed dugouts were numerous, whereas the British had been obliged to dispense with them to a great extent owing to water-logged soil. The ground here was higher, and therefore better for digging. Moreover, a good supply of timber evidently had been obtained by the late occupants, so that many dugouts, besides being well built, were even furnished with rough tables and shelves. A large portion of their material had come from the timber depots formerly required by the mines. The trenches themselves were wider than ours, but though this fact was responsible for greater comfort, the consequent loss of cover might have been a serious disadvantage. Happily our stay in this part of the line was a very peaceful one.

On the whole, the wire defences were good, especially along the front line. At that time, the British had not adopted the French pattern of telescopic wire, which, on being drawn out, forms a cylindrical obstacle. Thus shaped, it requires no uprights to keep it in position. The support line was hardly wired at all. The reason for this, according to French officers themselves, was the difference between our method of defensive trench fighting and theirs. The tactics of " stand-your-ground-at-all-costs " preferred by us found little favour with our allies. The latter reduced to a minimum the strength of their front-line garrisons for the reason that casualties from shell fire and infantry attacks would thereby be lessened. In the event of hostile attack, when it became probable that the oncoming waves would reach their objectives, the garrison fell back from the front line along the communication trenches. This practice must have called for great judgment on the part of their officers.

As soon as the enemy entered the front line, a strong counter-attack would be launched immediately from the support position, over the top and down the communication trenches. Much value was attributed to the fact that the enemy would be under the disadvantage of fighting in unfamiliar surroundings, whereas the counter-attack would know every yard of the ground. Also, the retreat of the invading force would be hampered by the necessity of its having to climb out of the trench and pick its way through the remains of the entanglements. Great success was claimed for these tactics. They afforded an opportunity to the French to indulge in their temperamental liking for the offensive, and were usually attended by comparatively light losses.

The position in which we now found ourselves was half-way up a slope. In a slight hollow behind us lay several gravel-pits, and beneath their banks a number of dugouts had been excavated. These points proved to be useful as company headquarters and store dumps. Each side occupied ground which was " dead " to the opposing force.

The fields in front of our parapet sloped up to a ridge about three hundred yards away, behind which lay the enemy lines, about another four hundred. The place was very beautiful. Above the tall grass there rose a mass of poppies, marguerites, and cornflowers : millions everywhere you looked. One wondered if they sprang from the graves of departed French soldiers, a last homage from them to the country for which they had fought and died. Or was it the handiwork of La France, the Sower, who, some dark night, unseen by the eye of man, had stridden over their last billets spreading this gigantic shroud over their shattered forms ?

No Man's Land, represented by this ridge, was in places as much as seven hundred yards in width, and presented fine opportunities to night patrols, of which both British and Germans constantly availed themselves.

There occurred during this period one of those instances which serve to show how varied are the risks of such work.

On one occasion, my platoon had emerged after nightfall into No Man's Land for the purpose of digging an advanced trench, and work had been in progress about three hours, when a message reached me that a patrol had gone out from one of the other companies. The moon shone brightly that night, so that objects were quite visible about thirty yards away.

Scattered out about seventy paces in front of my diggers was a screen of double sentries with a corporal on either flank.

As I strolled to and fro supervising the work, I noted how brightly the moonlight was reflected upon the long grass. The work was proceeding in a satisfactory way, everyone understood his task, so I decided to visit my men out in front. Hearing my intention, Sergeant Buck, my platoon sergeant, asked leave to accompany me in order to guide me from one post to another.

Now it so happened that I had not remained at the first group longer than a couple of minutes, before a figure approached, carrying a rifle at the trail. He bore a message informing this post of a suspicious movement in the long grass near whence he had come :

they were to be on their guard. I decided to investigate this report in person and set out in the direction of the next outpost with Sergeant Buck following behind.

On arrival there, we found the sentry keenly on the alert. He insisted that his attention had been arrested some short while before by a suspicious swaying in the grass midway between him and the next group beyond. As nothing occurred for several minutes, I resolved to cross to the next group, which happened to be on the extreme right flank, so, with a warning to the sentry, I again set forth, moving as quietly and as low as possible.

Barely had we covered half the distance between the posts before half a dozen dim forms arose slowly from the long grass, which grew here to a height of about two feet. Sure enough, they were in the very spot indicated by the sentry whom we had just left. Instinctively I drew my revolver, and then recollected with a feeling of dismay that Sergeant Buck was unarmed. The mind works quickly at such a moment. For my own person I had no special concern, for I had six rounds, but the sergeant's dilemma was of a very different sort. Had they seen us ? Perhaps not. I motioned to my companion and we both " froze " in a crouching position. If they were Germans, to move farther would result in risking him to their fire. The corporal's group that we were making for could not be more than thirty yards away, and I imagined I could just see their heads. Meanwhile, the enemy had extended to a couple of paces and were moving at a slow walk in that direction.

If we waited, I, at any rate, might be able to create a sudden diversion on their flank. I told the sergeant in a whisper of my intention, but, as apparently we had not been seen, he suggested that we should make a short rush in the direction of our outpost. This we did, going to cover once more after about ten paces.

The corporal's group was there, and had evidently sighted the party in front. I decided to join up with it without further delay.

Arriving within a few yards of him, I called softly to the corporal in charge. Simultaneously, one of his sentries challenged the strangers. All three covered the advancing line of men, which now was hardly twenty paces distant. Then, receiving no reply, we all made ready to fire.

" Who are you ? " a voice cried suddenly from their midst. That was an old trick, I thought. Many German officers and even N.C.Os can speak English.

" Halt ! " cried the corporal. For an instant the line hesitated ; then it came on, and I recognised with a thrill that the approaching figures wore the flat forage cap of the German Army. Quickly I ordered all to withhold their fire until I gave the word.

" Halt, or we fire," I shouted.

" Don't shoot ! Who are you ? " came the reply. Now a few yards only separated the parties, and I motioned to my men to get up in readiness for a rush.

" Are you English ? Who are you ? " someone repeated from their midst. I did not fire ; why, I could not say. I believed them to be the enemy, and yet, some instinct warned me that they might be our own patrol. Bayonets gleamed at the " on guard " position in anticipation of a hand-to-hand encounter ; a glance revealed numbers of bombs hanging from their belts ; most of the party were gripping revolvers.

" Who are you ? " asked the corporal once more.

" Who are *you* ? " came the retort.

Now face to face, we named our battalion, and seeing a big fellow holding a bomb in readiness, I covered him with my revolver.

" Thank God ! " gasped a voice, hoarse with emotion.

They must be friends ; I advanced and scrutinised

them. Their flat forage caps were merely English ones reversed !

They had lost their direction after two and a half hours' patrol of the enemy's line. As they had wandered towards us, the sound of our digging had reached them, so, believing it to arise from an enemy working-party, they had stalked through the long grass in order to bomb it. The discovery of our sentry group had held them up, until they had decided to investigate in full force.

No more apt comment on the possibilities of such an episode could be made than that which I received from my corporal a few minutes later. "My God ! sir, to think that I had taken my first pull in readiness'! "

CHAPTER XIV

" DEBOUT LES MORTS ! "

" O vieux drapeaux ! Sortez des tombes, des abîmes !
Sortez en foule, ailés de vos haillons sublimes,
Drapeaux éblouissants !
Comme un sinistre airain qui sur l'horizon monte,
Sortez, venez, volez, sur toute cette honte,
Accourez frémissants ! "

THE village of Vermelles, mentioned in the previous chapter, possessed in those days a magical aspect. Its memory will seem ever mysterious to me, for I never saw it except by night. Time and circumstance may rob it of its appeal; daylight may dispel its impressiveness ; but to us, to whom it was permitted to see its gaunt ruins amidst a pall of gloom, its memory will remain ever great.

Upon the frieze of Gabriel's wing at Versailles, there is carved in large Roman letters this inscription :

" À toutes les gloires de la France."

I, like most visitors approaching the outer court, had not failed to remark it, and, for some reason, this fleeting recollection of a happy day before the war came uppermost in my thoughts the first time that the battalion marched through Vermelles. In that moment, the shell-tortured wreckage assumed an aspect of true grandeur that Time can never dispel. No need of the carver's artifice nor need of formal dedication here ; Vermelles herself *is* one of the glories of France. Even in the darkness of that night her proud title was apparent, surpassing the stones of Versailles by virtue of its poignancy. Grander for all time than any monument raised by man, this insignificant village deserves to rank with such hallowed spots as Thermopyle or the Farm of Hugomont. For through its straggling streets and medley of small gardens, in and around every building, from *château* to cottage, had resounded the strife of Titans!

The village had been stormed several months before. Upon a day of wrath, followed by the dark winter hours of a livid night, French Territorials had fought desperately for its possession. Like an eddying tumult of waters, these true sons of the people had returned again and again to the attack, bursting their way by slow degrees through one stronghold after another. The German garrison fought with all the martial courage of their race, dying literally where they stood, rather than yield their trust. These were the days before "fortress" methods had been fully developed, yet every house became in its turn a citadel, every room a battlefield.

So stirring an action could not fail to make irresistible appeal to Frenchmen, and it was from my neighbours near the La Bassée road that I first heard something of its story.

To a brigade of Territorials, older men of the French reserves, fell the honour of this episode. Familiarity with their comrades enables one to picture them : many of them past their prime, true *pères de famille* of those working-classes from which they were mobilised. In their day, these men had done their service as soldiers of the Republic, and had entered the Reserve at the expiration of their term of duty, becoming veterans who had seen no war, the cast-off refuse of an army at peace.

Advancing slowly toward the western outskirts of the village, these men had been checked by the furious resistance of the enemy, who, loopholing the walls

of the *château* grounds and converting every vestige
of cover into fire-positions, presented a formidable
barrier to their farther progress. Slowly but inevitably the tempest of gunfire drove back the defenders from one post after another, and where the
barrier bent, there surged forward the tide of the
French advance. Several hours later, the enemy
were rallying round the *château* itself, whence they
poured forth a torrent of fire from window, door,
and crevice. Then the guns played upon the buildings, which gradually crumbled beneath a shattering
deluge. Presently the ruins were enveloped by the
attacking waves ; battering rams forced an entry ;
and then followed a mighty incident of this furious
day.

Firing point-blank through the breach, a German
machine-gun spread death and havoc through the
clamouring mass. Like Paladins, these Territorials
sprang into the gap in order to use the bayonet. Reinforcements surged across the threshold ; bullets
rained into their ranks at a few yards' range, rifles
resounding loudly within the building, and the revolvers of the German machine-gunners spitting forth
a gust of fire. But France would not be denied.
Where one man sank to the floor, another strode over
him, bayonet athirst, shots flying wildly through the
rooms as he emptied his magazine from the hip.
Whirling overhead into the press of defenders went
bomb after bomb. The air grew hazy from smoke
and crumbled plaster, and through the fog of battle
gleamed the rending flash of rifle and of hand
grenade. Hell was unleashed. Who can imagine the
pandemonium as firearms mingled with the shriek
of stricken men ? The Huns were at bay, but their
proud courage was outmatched by these " fathers of
the people." Fighting madly, the defenders were
compelled to withdraw to the floor above, whence their
deafening fusillade was renewed. Floor boards were

wrenched up, and through these gaps the garrison fired
into the rooms below. No man could live in face of
the sleet from the staircase, yet the hated *alleboches*
should be routed out by hook or by crook ; rather rend
the entire *château* to pieces than abandon the half-
won position. It was then that one inspired mind
was able to grasp the situation.

The scene of this terrific conflict was in the great
hall. A *mitrailleuse* was brought up. Streams of
bullets tore away the floor joists along the sides of the
ceiling. Soon, above the din was heard the rending
and cracking of timbers, quickly drowned by an
exultant roar from below as the mass above them
began to splinter and give way. Who can imagine
the feelings of the defenders as they began to realise ?
Then—down on to the reeking floor thundered
the ruined ceiling, bearing with it the yelling mob
above, who slithered, cursing, to the hall below. A
dreadful combat ensued. The *fantassins*, baulked
hitherto of their prey, sprang forward into the cloud
of dust, stumbling over the corpses and wreckage
that lay around. Bayonets plied their awful work,
some snapping, others plunging home ; clubbed
rifles whirled amid the smoke-rack ; and above all
rose the clamour of shouting men. Locked grimly in
their death-grapple, figures swayed among the heaps
of debris, panting and tearing at each other in furious
frenzy. Improvised weapons smote and parried, for
rifles had been lost, bayonets were now bent and
useless. Men seized on anything that came to hand.
Here was a monstrous contest : hand-to-hand and
to the death. . . .

It is upon record, that as the final storm of fighting
swayed through the hall, the figure was seen of a
French soldier, eddying Hector-like through the press,
dealing smashing blows with a terrible mace of bronze
—the statuette of a beautiful girl—snatched from the
bloody wreckage !

To these fathers of families, sweating, shouting, and smiting, it must have seemed a delirious nightmare. What deeds were done that day, what thoughts rushed madly through their minds? One wonders what it was that animated them, that gave strength to their arms, and encouraged them to dare all. So must have fought the French of old, when in their ears rang the battle-cry of she who inspired them: "Amys, Amys, soyez de bon courage! À moi, à moi, France et Sainct Denis!"

At last, crowning a galaxy of horrors, came an outbreak of fire. Those few of the garrison who surrendered were hustled away, the wounded extricated from the shambles, and the rest left to the flames. So, as in the days of Troy, did the heroic dead vanish in the heart of a funeral pyre.

Meanwhile, outside the *château*, devastating the gardens and houses of the outskirts, the battle had raged with equal fury.

But a time came at the end of the day when the entire village echoed to the shouts of Frenchmen, and the last remnants of the defence clung despairingly to the farther edge. From this, a final charge hurled the Germans headlong for nearly a mile, to where they were now entrenched. French bayonets gleamed red in every corner of Vermelles.

With tales of this great episode in mind, our passage through the ruins of the village seemed an event. It was nearing midnight when we reached the jagged walls that flanked the road. Standing black and weird against the lighter sky, these were now plunged in profound silence, disturbed only by the rhythm of the marching column as its feet rang sharply upon the stones: "tramp, tramp, tramp, tramp."

What with the fatigue after a period in the line, and the night march over bad roads gaping with ruts and shell holes, I was lapsing into a half stupor derived of monotonous and enforced motion.

How hideous the place seemed! On either hand,
gnarled and twisted against the stars, loomed the
silhouette of riven rafters, while tottering walls gaped
in such a way as to challenge the law of gravity.
When, in the moonlight, portions of brickwork were
clearly visible, pock marks of bullets were noticeable all over them. Here, a gate pier had been
flung down into the roadway; there, where an oath
from the ranks ahead warned me, lay a shadowy shell
hole. Between the crumbling walls, the sound of our
march step swelled ever clearer, rebounding from the
pavé road and echoing from the ruins: "tramp,
tramp, tramp, tramp!"

Dürer alone could have portrayed the malignant
hideousness of the scene. Its fiendishness could be
felt. Strewn around was grim, silent, and petrified
devastation. Here, of a truth, was the Abomination
of Desolation. Now and then came the faint murmur
of a night breeze stirring through the ruins. Vermin
inhabited this rubble heap which had once been a
village; their rustling would occasionally reach the
ear. To a jaded mind it seemed as if the place
must be haunted. Surely, lurking amid the tumbled
heaps of litter, pervading the surrounding air, guardian
spirits must be brooding over the glorious past?

> "O Drapeaux du passé, si beaux dans les Histoires,
>   Drapeaux de tous nos preux et de toutes nos gloires,
>   Redoutés du fuyard,
>   Percés, troués, criblés, sans peur et sans reproche,
>   Vous qui dans vos lambeaux melez le sang de Hoche,
>   Et le sang de Bayard,
>   O vieux drapeaux! Sortez des tombes, des abîmes!
>   Sortez en foule, ailés de vos haillons sublimes,
>   Drapeaux éblouissants!"

In response to the thought, the ruins seemed to stir.
Though our footsteps rang loudly on the furrowed
roadway, and the tramp of marching men rebounded
from the tottering walls, these now seemed to raise

8

their echoes above the measured cadence on the road. Imperceptibly the everlasting sound forced itself into one's mind, banishing fatigue and craving for sleep: "tramp, tramp, tramp, tramp, tramp!" Its rhythm suggested the opening beats of drums. Then the wreckage, vibrating with our march, appeared to spring to life, and the very stones of the place to throb out the "Marseillaise"!

So at last we came to the farther side, and here we found signs of human occupation. A shattered hovel had been made passably weather-proof, and through its open door we could see into a brightly lit interior. There, the scene afforded such contrast with my previous thoughts as is only to be met with in war. With his back toward us, head and shoulders sharply defined against the candlelight, sat an officer at a gimcrack piano : the tune, once popular at home and now the requiem of Vermelles, was the "Merry Widow Waltz."

But this sharp transition of one's thoughts was shattered a few moments later.

I had stepped slightly to the side of the road to see whether the men were keeping straight in the ranks. Suddenly my foot caught against an obstacle, and recovering myself, I looked down to see what it was that I had kicked aside. It was a wooden cross uprooted from a wayside grave.

The tinkling and sentimental tune was no longer audible. Vermelles lay behind, but all its great associations came flooding back to me. That night, to one jaded mind at least, the ghosts of the *Grande Armée* had passed in review ; but now, the pomp and glory of victory was tempered by this last impression. With the thought of those Territorials who had paid the price, something of beauty crept into one's memory of this place. We had traversed a battle-ground, rightly famous in the annals of France, but sanctified for all the world.

CHAPTER XV

" THIS sort of thing is lasting too long, sir."

Sergeant Buck brushed the earth from his shoulder which the exploding grenade had spattered there. As he said, things were ceasing to be quietly tolerable. A steady and accurate fire of rifle grenades would have been more or less endurable in a good position, but here, in front of Cambrin, dugouts and traverses were practically non-existent.

" Whist, whist ! "—we ducked low into the bottom of the trench—" Whist, whist !—whoop, bang ! " Down the line, about twenty yards distant, an orange sheet of flame dispelled the darkness ; then followed a shower of earth.

" How far do you reckon we are from their line, sir ? "

" Difficult to say until we can use a periscope. The officer whom we relieved this evening said about fifty yards on an average."

" That means this place is going to be rather warm, I reckon, sir. They are pretty close in some places."

" What bombs have we, sergeant ? "

" Three boxes of Mills in the platoon, and a few rifle grenades ; but there's more at the company store."

" You know what the Captain said just now about our action in case of an attack ? "

" Yessir. Easier said than done, if I may say so. There's two traverses in the whole platoon frontage, and the trench is L-shaped, as you have remarked, sir, enfiladed each way; but it seems to me we could stop them advancing up that communication trench we entered by?"

"Yes, from there we have a straight shoot. Number 16 Section is all right, but it's this part on the left that seems weak."

Indeed, the portion of the company front allotted to the platoon was anything but encouraging. The re-entrant angle was awkward, to say the least of it, while cover was only afforded by a few flimsy shelters. Of the wire in front we knew nothing in reality, having only the rather vague description of our predecessors to depend on, since at present it was unsafe to venture out on an inspection. Although only our first night "in," we had already suffered three casualties.

Daylight revealed further deficiencies in the line we had just occupied, and the sergeant was not long in confirming my own suspicions.

"This here parapet is hopeless, sir—wouldn't stop an air-gun. Also the snipers' loopholes are impossible. I don't know how long they have been like it, but most of them are clogged by fallen sandbags. I call it cruel."

"We shall have to get to work on the place as quickly as possible; but first I'll see what the Captain has to say. Don't start on the parapet until I give definite orders. The men can do what is necessary to the fire-step, and if you can get hold of any sandbags, a few men from Number 15 Section can be filling them; but see that no one shows that we are at work. No earth must be thrown into view on top of the trench."

"Very good, sir."

It was to inspect this preparatory work that I set out after breakfast on a visit along the front allotted to my platoon, taking with me my periscope, which was attached to a shooting-stick.

In daylight there was no doubt whatever of the bad condition of the trench generally. The parapet in many places was not bullet-proof, and practically all steel plates used for snipers' posts had been allowed to fall out of position, or become obstructed by sandbags. Traverses also would have to be built. This was a larger programme of work than we would have time for, but it could be completed by our successors. The close proximity of the enemy would not allow more than a few men to work at a time.

Through the periscope I could see their parapet, in one place about thirty yards off, though farther to the right, the distance approached nearer to a hundred. Apparently their line formed a considerable salient toward our position.

The morning passed gradually, but their rifle grenades still worried us off and on. Fortunately these were easily visible in the air, giving us time to dodge them, so casualties were few.

Apart from the loss of two more men in the platoon, the most annoying fact was the constant sniping of our periscopes. By noon none was left, all having been smashed by good shooting from opposite. Mine remained in my own keeping, so a solitary one was borrowed from another part of the company front. It was useless to expose sentries behind an inferior parapet at so short a range, therefore these kept watch as best they could by means of pieces of broken mirror stuck in the parados.

By the afternoon, I think, nearly all ranks had arrived at the conclusion that in our portion of the line the enemy possessed a complete mastery. Our stock of bombs and rifle grenades did not permit of a sufficient retaliation being made to their frequent fire, nor could our snipers find adequate positions for annoying them. But I was far from realising how comfortably secure the enemy considered himself, until

just after teatime. Walking toward my small dugout,
which was just large enough to accommodate myself
and an extremely bold and attentive rat, I came
upon Sergeant Buck seated on the fire-step, gazing
fixedly into a " vigilant " mirror fastened by him in a
cleft stick on the parados.

" I'm very sorry, sir, indeed—your periscope stick is
broken." This I had lent to him half an hour before.

" How was that, sergeant ? " I asked in some
surprise.

" Cut in half, sir, before I had put it up five seconds.
I never saw such a shot."

A man standing by handed me the broken halves.
Sure enough, when joined together, the stick revealed
a bullet hole in its centre, about half-way up it.

" You were exposing it too much, I am afraid. No
need to show more than the top mirror. I'm sorry,
sergeant. It was useful at times, but it cannot be
helped. Have you any idea where the shot was fired
from ? "

" Yes, sir, I'm waiting for him. I'm very sorry
indeed," he added. His concern was evident.

An instant or so later, just as I was in the act of
turning away, I noticed him jerk forward his head as
if he had located something in the mirror. What
happened next was done in a moment : a most remarkable performance in its way.

Grasping a rifle that leant beside him against the
parapet, the sergeant leapt to his feet, thence to the
fire-step where he had been seated ; then, flinging the
rifle across the parapet, he fired a snapshot, paused for
a second, and ducked. Almost before I had realised
what he had done, he was standing beside me in the
trench, a broad grin upon his face.

" Nabbed 'im ! I've been waiting for *him*—got a
notion he broke your stick." A delighted chuckle
escaped from one of the men, who had jumped to the
" vigilant."

" The sergeant 'as given 'im the knock-out, sir. I can see the bloke all right ; proper stiff 'e is."

There, reflected in the mirror, I saw the head and shoulders of a German fully exposed across the parapet opposite, about thirty yards off. One arm, I noted, was flung across the top of the sandbags. Indeed it was a wonderful shot. Sergeant Buck beamed with joy, and my words of congratulation seemed to banish from his mind any lingering recollection of my loss. Like wild-fire, the news of this performance sped down the trench, and as it went, an idea came to me.

" Send off for a box of Mills, sergeant ; tell them to run like mad ! "

" Sir ! " came his instant reply. A moment later a man vanished down the trench toward a bomb store.

" We are going to improve on this occasion. I've got five casualties to square."

He now saw my idea, and his grin reappeared once more.

" Tell Corporal Thomason from the officer to double along here." Thus he anticipated my plans. Another form vanished at his bidding, whereon I returned to my place at the mirror. Rapid footsteps soon announced the arrival of the bombs and of the Bombing Corporal.

" Stand by, corporal, with these fellows. You all understand these things. Chuck together on the word, straight to your front over those near sandbags —range, thirty-five yards."

One by one the safety pins were extracted, and the four took up their stand in readiness to throw.

" See that you all have room behind you," I ordered.

About five minutes later I fancied the body moved slightly.

" Throw ! "

My voice was followed by the clicks of the released bombs as they flew into mid-air. Then came a pause, ended by a volley of loud reports. One had fallen

short, another had gone over, but two, I believed, had
landed right into the German trench. " Fritz " still
lay where he had fallen ; apparently Heinrich and
Hans had ceased to drag him in.

" Get ready again."

As I watched in the mirror, a queer idea occurred
to me. " Fritz " seemed strangely exposed.

" What could you see when you fired, sergeant ? "
I called over my shoulder.

" Most extraordinary, sir. He was standing there
a-showing himself down to the waist : I saw his
ammunition pouches. Looking around quite quiet
like, he was, sir—taking the air, so to speak."

" They seem to find things pretty comfortable over
there ! "

" Looks like it, sir. Anyway, one of 'em has gone
to sleep all right."

A chorus of sniggers was his reward.

Though a second attempt was made to drag it
down, the body remained where it was until nightfall.
To judge from a sudden gust of bullets that struck
our parapet, some damage must have resulted from
our bombs. I may have been unduly optimistic, but,
as I proceeded to my dugout an hour later, I fancied
that some of our account had been paid.

But greater things than this were being planned
elsewhere. The first inkling of further action on our
part was given me at dinner in our company dugout.
All day, Baedeker had been occupied with much observing and visits to Battalion Headquarters. Then
came his announcement, " Send all your rifle grenades
except a dozen to Number 15, and be ready to store
six boxes of Mills. To-night we are going to have a
row." That night, surely enough, we had a very considerable row, into which the men entered with enthusiasm. Had there not been thirty casualties in the
company ?

About 10 o'clock, several explosions denoted the

arrival of more rifle grenades from over the way.
Accordingly our bombers commenced work.

Soon, beneath the glare of a Verey light, a veritable
pandemonium arose. Bullets banged into our sandbags or ripped, screaming, overhead. Along the
enemy parapet flickered a line of flashes, mingling
with the yellow gleam of exploding hand and rifle
grenades. Drifting slowly over their line, smoke
clouds from our bombs trailed white and mysterious
in the light of the rocket flares.

Presently things became quiet once more, but the
enemy was too annoyed by our sudden activity to
allow the night to continue in such fashion. The
whoop and crash of falling rifle grenades recommenced,
accompanied this time by " hair brush " bombs.
Now, our orders were definite. The night became
filled with tumult.

Amid a gleam of bursting bombs and a continuous
rattle of rifle shots, the contest broke out afresh.
Here was something new in war pictures. All down
the shadowy trench stooping figures darted to and
fro, throwing from every point, for in that way it was
harder for our men to be located. Once a bomb had
been hurled, the bomber ducked down and skipped
away to a fresh position, dodging blindly past the
explosions near our line. Along the trench where
the next platoon was in position, a battery of rifles
with wired triggers was firing salvos of grenades into
the darkness.

At first the duel was hotly contested, but before
long it became evident that, along those portions of
the trench where the distance allowed our throwers to
operate, we were out-ranging the enemy. Many of
our men had no great difficulty in throwing a Mills
forty or fifty yards.

Toward morning they abandoned the fight, but
we, determined to give them a lasting impression,
continued our volleys at varying intervals. The

lines were too near one another to permit their guns to retaliate. If they chose to cease fire, that was no reason for our doing so. About dawn, however, after what must have been for them a night of misery and havoc, our bombs became totally used up. There remained only a reserve supply in case of attack. Our company alone had thrown 300 that night. In the middle of 1915 that constituted a very large number, for munitions were limited, and all material was precious in comparison with those copious quantities which we were to enjoy later. Seldom has the New Army known what it means when supplies run short and one has to endure patiently all that the enemy sends over.

Nevertheless, on this occasion, even at a risk of having to await replenishment, we had given him a lesson he was not likely soon to forget. By daybreak his line must have been reduced to a shambles. Whatever the loss inflicted, the fact remains that for the remainder of our stay we were unmolested. On this second morning we might have breakfasted upon the parapet.

CHAPTER XVI

DURING our period in the line at Cambrin, rumours began to circulate of great changes affecting all Guards battalions serving in France. Much talk was to be heard concerning the formation of a Guards Division. The arrival of two battalions of Grenadiers, one Coldstream, one Scots Guard, one Irish, and a battalion of the newly formed Welsh Guards, would bring up our effectives to three brigades when the 1st Coldstream and 1st Scots Guards had been transferred from the 7th Division, with which they had been serving hitherto.

In addition to forecasts relating to our own future, we now began to hear stories of the impending arrival in France of the first divisions of the New Army, which for almost a year had been in process of formation and training at home. Their appearance was awaited eagerly, and much speculation arose as to their abilities. Perhaps it was only natural that some scepticism should be indulged in. We had no doubts of their ultimate value, but many feared that they would fail to reach the standard of the existing Expeditionary Force before the next year.

For all that, the news of their coming imparted a certain amount of enthusiasm, since at last some prospect appeared of the British Army's entry on a rôle more in accordance with its old traditions. Hitherto we had been compelled to play a subordinate part beside the formidable armies of France ; the future now showed promise of things more worthy of Great Britain. Compared with the achievements of the French, our doings appeared puny, however gallant their execution. Already many of us were inclined to the prospect of another two years' war, and for several months past we had looked longingly for some evidence of the development of our own national power.

The wave of depression that had seized on the Press and public at home found no echo in our midst. The sterile results of Neuve Chapelle and Festubert were coming to be understood, and this knowledge served only to goad us to further efforts.

In these days we were in expectation of a great German offensive. The Galician and Polish retreats had slowed down, and there seemed every likelihood of a large transfer of enemy troops to the west. We were ready for them. Weeks of economy in ammunition had followed after Festubert; reinforcements had arrived; and much entrenching and field fortification had been accomplished; so we felt confident of repelling any attempt to reproduce on our front the tactics of Mackensen. They had failed in October and November of the previous year; they seemed unlikely to succeed now. Altogether, a big offensive by Rupert of Bavaria would be hailed by ourselves with satisfaction, for it would prove more costly than ever, and the question of numbers was felt to govern the ultimate fate of the war.

During these days, a certain revival of their artillery activity appeared to justify our expectations. Our lines were shelled in ever-growing frequency.

At this time the company was in support, about three-quarters of a mile to the east of Cambrin village. Here the platoons were split up as garrisons to a series of redoubts, each capable of independent action and defence.

The communication trenches in this position were rather elaborate. Constructed during the winter by the French, they were paved in many places by neatly laid bricks taken from the village in rear. Behind these *boyaux*, as the French signposts called them, lay a considerable hollow dividing the trench system from the village, and consequently this was often bombarded by the German guns. Occasionally some very good shooting was made. I remember one evening during our last " relief " in this position no less than two direct hits in the path, and several newly made craters beside it. Firing by the map, their gunners would have seriously harassed any parties approaching or going down from the lines. Their 'planes seldom came over, so their fire was no doubt laid by direct observation from the ground. For this purpose, the tall chimney stacks around La Bassée provided them with excellent facilities. It may be a matter for some surprise to the civilian to learn how great is the precision of modern artillery. Again and again, from several thousand yards, their field-guns scored hits on the sandbags of our parapet or parados. Spade work was our principal occupation at this period,

A shovelful of earth thrown up in a thoughtless moment was sufficient to draw down on that spot a couple of shells. Work had to be carried out with great care. Soil freshly excavated from new work had to be covered by grass or old sandbags ; otherwise, its fresh colour would have been observed from the air, and retribution would have followed.

Out in No Man's Land, about fifty yards in front of our first-line trench, lay the smashed and scarred remains of the aeroplane which had been shot down a couple of months previously when we were near Whizz Bang Villa. For some reason, it was often made a target for their rifle grenades. Possibly they suspected it of concealing a sniper's nest. We encouraged them in this belief by constructing a sniper's loophole in a direct line behind it ; he fired through its framework, and the direction of his shots soon became known to them. By night, in anticipation of a possible raid on the wreckage, we took steps to provide a warm reception for the bolder spirits from the position opposite. In this manner we constantly attempted to fool the enemy. Every day some new contrivance would be tried in the hope of thereby inflicting loss, or promoting a waste of ammunition on their part.

Trench warfare had not reached the height of development that came later. To us, the nerve-racking attentions of " Minnie " were still unknown. Snipers were our chief source of annoyance. Moreover, our trenches were well built and not yet liable on their completion to demolition by trench mortars. If life in the trenches was somewhat more peaceful than later on, it was certainly more constant; except for occasional rests of eight days, the battalion spent all its time in the line. But our limited number of troops resulted necessarily in few " reliefs," so the wear and tear on all ranks was correspondingly greater.

The prospect of a long rest behind the lines still seemed as far off as ever. Only one comfort was afforded us : leave to England had opened. True this hardly bore out the talk at home of an impending German attack, but leave might be expected to be stopped at any time. Something of the unutterable boredom of stationary routine entered into us ; at this rate of progress, the war would last ten years.

Meanwhile, in London, the controversy concerning Compulsory Service still dragged on. To us, the whole question would have been ridiculous had it not at the same time filled us with so much impatience. Out in Flanders, politics seemed trivial in comparison with our military prospects of the following year.

CHAPTER XVII

THE battalion was in billets at Beuvry, near Béthune, when rumours which had been current for some little while proved to be true : the brigade was to go into the line north of Givenchy.

The positions destined for our occupation did not enjoy too good a name. According to all accounts, they were breastworks rather than trenches. The approaches to the support positions were exposed to sniping and shell fire; "reliefs" were said to be costly on occasions; and other disadvantages were alleged to exist that were hardly compensated for by the fact of the enemy's being several hundred yards distant.

Therefore, about the end of July, after a fatiguing night march from our billets, we found ourselves groping our way into our new sector. Though bullets had droned overhead during most of our progress along the willow-flanked communication paths, by good fortune no one had been hit. This time, the company was to occupy a front-line position, with two platoons in support. As one of these happened to be mine, and no work was required of us that night, I was soon able to retire to an exceedingly uncomfortable dugout. There one enjoyed the rare luxury—for the trenches —of a complete night's rest.

On the following morning, we were all somewhat dismayed to find a total want of accommodation for the company mess. To continue for an indefinite

period in such dismal surroundings was unthinkable ;
eating our meals for several days on end in a crater
was hardly an attractive prospect. Accordingly,
Baedeker and I began to erect a large dugout
capable of receiving at least half a dozen persons.

Fortunately, in the secluded spot chosen, we were
able to work free from observation, for a mound of
earth, burst sandbags, and sundry trees screened us
from the view of the enemy. We worked for ten consecutive hours, taking a brief rest for dinner. Some
assistance was given us toward the end by the officers'
servants, for by then we had grown very tired. The
roof timbers were in place by midnight, and all that
remained to be done was to put down sheets of corrugated iron and to shovel on a couple of feet of soil.

In the middle of this final operation, a salvo of
Whizz Bangs flashed in the darkness some hundred
yards away. It was one of those spasmodic efforts
on their part by which the enemy frequently sought to
disturb our night's rest. Spreadeagled on top of the
roof, I awaited the coming of the next salvo, hoping
fervently that it would not be shifted towards my
position. By good fortune it came from beyond the
first explosions, therefore I took advantage of the pause
to scramble down hastily to a more sheltered spot.
So far as the dugout was concerned, work for that
day had ended, but I now learnt with dismay that it
was my turn to keep watch in the front line. Already
it was time to be going ; my " relief " would not be
due until four in the morning.

Seldom had I known so tiring a night as that which
followed. To keep awake, I was compelled to walk
up and down the company front the whole time, for
whenever I sat down for a moment's rest, an irresistible drowsiness stole over me.

The first gleam of dawn began to appear about
3.30 a.m. In half an hour more my watch would end,
though the " stand to " would keep me up for another

forty minutes or so. That morning, the approach of daylight seemed interminable, but at last I was able to return to my dugout, where I instantly fell asleep.

Desiring to profit by the spell of fine weather, we devoted ourselves later on to the completion of the dug-out, where, though the main structure had been finished, various details remained to be carried out. A large divan, capable of accommodating four persons, was constructed in a corner; then a sideboard and a cupboard for food were voted necessary, not to mention a window, and a door into the adjoining kitchen. Much criticism, not entirely free from derision, was levelled at our headquarters by stray visitors from the other companies; yet we did not fail to remark that they were well content to become our guests for some time before proceeding on their ways. Before long, "Number 4's" mess attained celebrity, which blossomed into fame, when, returning to it a fortnight later, we found the roof in imminent danger of falling on our heads.

Soon, a most disconcerting discovery made in the vicinity of our kitchen filled us with dismay. It was the company cook who first aroused our suspicions. His misgivings proved only too well founded. Investigation on our part disclosed the fact that within a few feet of our larder lay the body of a German soldier, half buried, or rather half dug up by rats. Copious supplies of chloride of lime together with the attentions of a fatigue party soon rectified this nuisance; but it was some time before we could definitely assure ourselves that no lingering smell hovered round our dwelling.

As a matter of fact, this episode was only characteristic of the entire position : gruesome relics of the winter and spring battles abounded on all sides; Germans, English, and Canadians still lying where they had fallen. To burn was easier than to bury them, so, awaiting a favourable breeze, we instituted

9

various cremation parties. On the enemy fell the consequences of these episodes, for we knew his predilection for gas attacks.

Since the enemy indulged only in intermittent shelling, and that at fixed times of the day, this position proved to be fairly quiet. The trenches, though largely of the breastwork variety, were good, having numerous traverses and passage trenches in rear of the fire-positions. Dugouts abounded, but these were flimsy contrivances only proof against shrapnel.

We had not passed many days in this new sector before orders came through that the battalion was to endeavour to bring in a prisoner. There was to be no actual raid, but efforts were to be made to ambush an enemy patrol at night. It happened to be my turn to undertake this task, so accordingly orders were given me for my guidance.

As the wilderness between the lines was intersected by numerous ditches and abandoned trenches, in places there was some uncertainty of the exact whereabouts of the enemy's lines, though their position generally was known to lie some six or seven hundred yards off at the foot of a ridge. By day, their sandbags were partially visible, but considerable doubt existed as to the nature of their defences.

The party destined for the patrol was to be a small one, and therefore it became necessary to pick special men for it. Sergeant Buck begged to accompany me, also the Bombing Corporal. Besides these, I decided to take two others, both tried men, who never ceased giving trouble to the company except when they were in the line. They were certainly wild fellows, but though their conduct sheets contained some lurid reading, I counted them while in the trenches among the leading spirits of my platoon. Together with a third, also a boon companion in petty crime, they represented an inimitable alliance of vice and virtue.

Having examined the locality as closely as possible

by daylight, I disclosed my plan to the sergeant. Our
first act would be to make for their wire and explore
it for some distance, after which we could form some
idea of the ground and obstacles, and so choose a place
in which to lie in waiting for a passing patrol. Each
man of the party would provide himself with bombs,
a bandolier, and a rifle ; bayonets would be worn in
their puttees.

In order to regain our position with the minimum
of risk, it was necessary to note carefully any landmarks that would guide us in the dark. These existed
in sufficient number, for in many places blasted
willow trees stood forlornly along the ditches in front.
About 10 o'clock, everything still being quiet, the
party, headed by myself, crept down an old sap and
crawled forward. Behind us the sentries had been
warned, so that our sudden reappearance might be
expected at any time.

It was an unusually dark night for the time of the
year, and a gentle breeze stirred the wild barley and
weeds that spread away into the darkness. Behind
me, I could hear the stealthy movements of Sergeant
Buck and an occasional whispered word. Before we
had covered a hundred yards I came upon a gaping
black line just on my left. This proved to be a
ruined communication trench formerly belonging to
the Germans. One by one we lowered ourselves into
it, as there was no use in going over the top when
a convenient road lay ahead of us. Crouching in
this evil track, where every kind of rotting obstacle
lay under foot, we stole forward with ears strained
for any sound in the night. It seemed a long time
before the shadow of our first objective loomed through
the darkness.

Here we halted a moment to allow every man of the
patrol a good look at his surroundings, for on our
ability to recognise landmarks our safety might
ultimately depend. From now onward, we might

expect to meet with enemies at every dip in the ground, therefore I determined to get out into the open where we might obtain a wider field of vision. Everything seemed deathly still; every whisper of the tall grass suggested the disturbance of some passing form. Our fingers lay on our triggers, and like prowling animals we listened for a warning. In No Man's Land you can hear before you can see. Gradually working our way forward in the direction of the enemy, we came upon a ditch and a group of three willows. We were keeping a good direction; another couple of hundred yards should bring us close to the German wire. There, we should have to move slowly and with the greatest caution, lest we should jangle a wire and thereby raise an alarm.

It seemed an endless age before we came to our next halt. Fortune proved unkind. We had hoped to find a working-party out in front, but the night air brought no sound with it whatever. For the first half-hour a perfect stillness had reigned over the opposing positions. On our side, this was intentional, because we did not wish for any firing or noise.

Suddenly a thin trail of fire spurted up ahead of us. Almost simultaneously we subsided into the grass, freezing into immobility. Over our heads the flare sped onward toward our lines, illuminating the ground with myriads of dancing points of light. For a minute we waited, then, all being still, we slowly crawled forward once more.

The pistol flare had been fired at no great distance from us. Every minute now, we might expect to come upon an obstacle. Presently, after another short advance, our movements were arrested by a motion from the sergeant. "I believe that's wire just ahead, sir," he whispered.

One by one we took stock of it. It seemed as if he might be right.

"You crawl forward to reconnoitre. Don't wave

to us ; it might attract attention. Their trench can't
be far away."

The phantom whom I had bidden stole forward
cautiously, our gaze following its shadowy course
toward the unknown object. A minute later the
fellow reappeared.

"Wire and stakes, sir, not thick. I thought I
heard the click of a shovel somewhere ahead, but
can't be sure of it."

"If you are right, they must be working in their
trench ; otherwise we should have discovered a
covering party out here. How far did the sound
seem to come from ? "

"Less than a hundred yards, sir, I should think."

Here was a possible piece of information. No one
puts out a thin entanglement at that distance, unless
stronger wire lies behind it.

Ordering the party to keep together, I crawled forward, a bomb ready in one hand, revolver in the
other. The scout was right : an indifferent line of
wire lay before us. Many of the stakes had become
loosened by the rain and weather, or so I judged, for
I dared not put much pressure on them for fear of
making a noise.

Crawling, crouching, listening, and groping softly,
we explored this wire for the best part of an hour.
In some places there were gaps, but through them
we did not venture, since our orders forbade any
conflict with the garrison. It was now approaching
midnight, so, having patrolled what I imagined to be
several hundred yards of entanglement, I decided to
lie up somewhere and hope for the appearance of a
hostile patrol. A sudden attack at close quarters,
followed by a dash into a neighbouring ditch, seemed
a possible line of action. If a prisoner was to be
brought in, we must make good our escape with the
utmost speed.

Accordingly we chose our place for our ambush near

a gap in the wire; later on, someone might emerge through it. From time to time, as we lay in our place of concealment, I looked at my watch, which I had taken the precaution of keeping in my pocket. Luminous dials have their advantages, but they can be dispensed with wisely in No Man's Land. Twelve-thirty came, then 1 o'clock; still no sound was audible save an occasional rifle shot far away in the distance, or the comet-like trail of a Verey light.

Conforming to my orders, I decided not to wait any longer in person. I had taken them out, shown them how to get home, and had given them full instructions. Sergeant Buck could be trusted to deal with any situation that now might arise, for he revelled in, and was well known for work of this nature.

Therefore, after examining my luminous compass, I warned him when to expect the dawn and crawled off into the darkness on my homeward way.

Without the sense of companionship afforded by the party, the night seemed more still and mysterious than ever. To hurry forward would result most probably in my losing my way, though with a compass I was confident of striking our line at some point. Proceeding as quickly as possible, I gradually retraced our course to the solitary willows; the party should have no great difficulty in regaining them, I thought. Coming suddenly upon a shell hole amid the grass some hundred yards or so farther on, I threw up my revolver at a dark object lying at the bottom. It did not move, and presently, smiling at my hastiness, I went forward to examine it. My enemy proved to be a couple of large rolls of rabbit wire. How they got there remains a mystery.

At last I recognised at a little distance on my right flank a line of willows. The old communication trench by which we had come should be somewhere in that direction; I had only to find that to make my way back. Sure enough it was the trench, so I stepped down into it at a point where it was half filled with earth. A rustling sound, at first suspicious, soon explained itself : the old trench was now infested by rats. Soon the reason was only too obvious. By and by, as I picked my way over various obstacles, my foot descended upon some hollow object that commenced to give way. Turning it over carefully with my boot, I saw it was a *pickelhaube*, which, on examination, I found to be in good condition. On it I could feel a large metal badge, Here to hand was a souvenir ready for the taking.

Presently I began to recognise my surroundings. Our saphead should be fairly close now.

How close, I did not quite realise until, turning a bend a moment later, I espied a wall of sandbags blocking the trench some twenty yards away.

" Halt ! "

I did so, remarking at the same time an almost imperceptible movement above the parapet.

" Who are you ? "

" Officer, No. 4 Company."

" Advance."

Stepping forward, I presently observed a rifle moved from the sandbags.

" All right, sir. We were expecting you, but one can't be sure."

The next morning I learnt from Sergeant Buck that the party had waited until nearly daylight, but nothing had been sighted.

    .   .   .   .

Many were the summer evenings one spent wandering from point to point behind these trenches. I say " behind," for in many places no parados existed, the rear traffic-trench being entirely open to the country that lay behind. Only in the fire-bays themselves was cover provided back and front. It was during such a stroll round the line one evening that I learned from the company sergeant-major some details of his experiences during the great march from Mons the year before. The subject arose through my observing we were at the anniversary of the retreat.

"So it is, sir, to be sure!" Then, after a pause, "A lot of water has run down to the seas since those days."

For a minute he continued gazing to our front. Around us our front line straggled across the scorched wilderness, while overhead the sky was growing crimson from the setting sun.

"I don't believe average folk at home have any idea of that retirement, sir," he continued by and by. "We marched all day and sometimes on into the night. It was the Reservists, newly mobilised chaps, who suffered most : they weren't fit. Why, sir, I saw some fellows as had no soles left to their boots by the end—marched clean off, they were. There were cruel sights to be seen in those days!"

"How did you get on, sergeant-major?"

A short silence followed my inquiry. Apparently he was debating how much to tell me.

"Well, sir, I don't deny that I used to be mighty glad when we cried halt for the day. I carry a good bit of weight, as you see, and that added to a full kit and the August heat beat me."

"It was like this," he continued after a pause, "the first few days were the worst. The boys were beginning to abandon their rifles and were falling out. Of course I tried to stop that, but our discipline was almost cracking. Some went down for the full count whilst stepping in the ranks. You may have some idea of what we were up against when I admit that I had to heave away my own rifle at last. It was either that or falling out."

I glanced at his face. Coming from him, that was indeed a grim admission. Bull-necked and massively built, he appeared a magnificent specimen of a man.

" After that, I got on better, but it was my last effort. I remember going down into the roadside. Presently someone turned me over with his foot and a voice whispered : ' He's gone, too. The cart will collect him when it passes.' Then I don't recollect anything more until I came to. I was lying on the bodies of some other chaps in a cart—dead they were, sir—and I was thought to be the same. The driver nearly had a fit when I sat up." Here he chuckled and next drew my attention to the sunset.

Viewed from behind our parapet, this seemed more arresting than almost any I had ever known. The afternoon's cannonade had died away, and the only sound to be heard was a lark swelling out its evening song far overhead. Gradually the sun dipped, throwing into dark relief the splintered wreck of a farmhouse roof, and sinking, it turned the whole sky to green, orange, red, and gold. And as deep purple clouds rolled over the spot where its orb had been, it seemed as though, having beaten down upon the land all day and having sucked up every particle of moisture from the ravaged country, the sun was gathering to itself the very blood from out the soil, bearing it away to Paradise.

CHAPTER XVIII

THE LAST OF A GREAT BRIGADE

ABOUT the middle of August our stay in the Givenchy position ended. Rumours which had been growing more and more persistent were at last confirmed officially : the days of the great 4th (Guards) Brigade were numbered. No more should we be associated with the 2nd Division. Units of the New Army were arriving almost every day, and as a spearhead to this vast citizen force there was to be formed an entire division of Guards.

The last days of the brigade were spent in the neighbourhood of Béthune, where it was arranged that the massed drums of the Grenadier, Coldstream, and Irish Guards should give a farewell display.

The *Place* in the centre of the town, usually thronged with soldiers and civilians, presented a strange appearance on that summer's afternoon, for, with the exception of "The Drums" drawn up on parade, its cobbled expanse was empty. Standing many deep on the surrounding pavement, a great concourse of British officers representing many units was present, and amid this khaki mass the French service dress and the familiar tabs of British staff officers were everywhere noticeable. Every window and balcony overlooking the spot was crowded with expectant townsfolk.

Les gardes anglaises had been familiar to them for several months, likewise to our fellow units of the 2nd

Division; thus our mode of farewell to them was looked upon with some expectancy.

Clanging melodiously over the tumbled roofs and gables of the old-fashioned square, the ancient bells of the Belfry Tower gave forth the hour of parade. Promptly the senior sergeant-drummer strode smartly across to the Brigadier, came rigidly to a halt, and saluted. Permission to commence being given, he next returned briskly to his position in the centre of the square.

With the echoes of the old-world chime ringing overhead came the sound of men springing to attention. Drums and fifes in ordered formation now answered to the sergeant's sign. Barely had the eddying notes of the clock melted away among the surrounding houses, before a sullen roll swelled from the massed side-drums, punctuated by the heavy concussions of their larger fellows. Then, with a crash of notes, "The Drums" stepped out, fifes pealing joyously and drumsticks rioting amid their ranks. Across the square they marched, revelling in the martial swagger of their drill; sticks rose and fell with machine-like precision; so may they have swaggered forward at Oudenarde and Fontenoy.

At length, turning upon a fixed point, the ranks faced about upon themselves, drummers threading through fifers and emerging from a coiling mass into their first formation. And so, back across the square.

The end of this opening tattoo was greeted by a loud outburst of applause from the crowded windows. Next, after a brief "stand easy," the old façades echoed once more to a lively march, and then in turn followed the strains of the " British Grenadiers," our own "Milanello," and "Hieland Laddie" of the Scots Guards; but it was perhaps the merry air of "St. Patrick's Day" that pleased our allies most. Resounding sonorously from the neighbouring walls, these time-honoured tunes rolled and swelled in our midst, and one could not but think of that fateful night when the streets of Brussels were filled with these very sounds as the British strode forth to Waterloo. They may not be great music, they may not claim famous authorship, but to us present these march tunes, executed with the old precision of our ancestor battalions, made their irresistible call. We, like the French, had our great traditions. Louis XIV and the Guards of his Household had met us; Masséna, Soult, Joseph, and their Master had felt our fire, the gallant Ney our steel. To those who had eyes for them, these burnished side-drums seemed as pages in our country's history, scroll upon scroll setting forth the mighty achievements of the Brigade of Guards. Here for a brief hour about the old-world town hovered the spirit of England.

At last, mingled with the fading echoes of the soldier hymns of Marlborough and of Wellington, there crashed forth the opening bars of the " Marseillaise." In honour of this, those present came to the salute, and thus we stood as the National Anthem ended the parade. Our farewell tattoo was over. Quickly, the sleepy old town resumed its wonted calm, and the ghosts of the past, who walk by day in times of war, vanished once again.

.   .   .   .   .

The next morning, the brigade took the road that runs to the north-west. At an early hour, long streams of transport threaded their way toward our starting-point. As the battalion awaited its turn to join the column, a skirl of bagpipes was borne back to us from the road ahead; the Irish Guards were already under way. Soon, in our turn, we were marching into the high-road; behind us in the distance we could now hear the drums of the Grenadiers.

The memory of that march is still fresh.   One after another, each battalion's music broke the still-

ness of that summer morning, drawing the attention
of labourers scattered in the fields, and throwing
into a clatter the placid streets of those villages
through which we passed.

Stretching away up and down the road there
crawled an endless multitude of khaki. Interspaced
along the dense masses of our front-line transport
were cookers, limbers, and mess-carts, rolling along
through a bank of dust. Away in the distance could
be heard the throb of a big drum, presently stilled ;
then banged the nearer clamour of our own. Hour
after hour the great pageant wound across the country-
side, and uniforms and equipment grew white with
grime. At the hourly halts, packs removed, dark
patches of sweat showed where the loads pressed heavily
on our backs and shoulders.

But the discomforts of our march were overlooked,
for we were " out," and some weeks of rest lay ahead
of us. Back in the rolling downs over toward the
sea, we should find friends newly arrived from England,
come to attend the birth of the Citizen Army. There,
for the first time, the Old and the Young Armies were
to meet. It was a gathering of the clans such as our
forefathers had never seen. Slow to awake, but
gathering momentum like an avalanche, the tide of
Britain's manhood was bursting its Island bonds at
last ! Our dream was proving true. Some day in the
future the men of the Empire would spread over the
lands of northern France ; then would our country
in the eyes of her allies come into her own.

Every week brought news of fresh arrivals. Pouring
across the Channel, as a hope to France, and a dreadful
joy to us, came horse and guns, ammunition and foot,
men of war of every kind, the Great Experiment.
What breed of men were these ? Would the New Army
withstand the hosts of Germany ? We wondered.

The New Army ! God grant they prove themselves
another New Model ! For in this land of French

Paladins, only Ironsides could carry the arms and the name of England.

Shortly, according to rumour, they would have an opportunity to prove their worth. Storm clouds were rolling up when September opened, and on all men's lips were words of the coming conflict. But to myself fate ordained no part in the doings of those great days. A week before the first bloody battle of the Guards Division, I was crippled by a commonplace accident, and the stirring rumours of the Battle of Loos reached me as I lay in hospital at the Base.

My first glimpse of the war had ended, and with it had come a certain disillusionment; but, on the other hand, signs of a change in our fortunes were not wanting. To the Allies, and above all to England, lay the future.

PART II

DAWN

" Come the three corners of the world in arms,
  And we shall shock them.   Naught make us rue,
  If England to itself do rest but true."

CHAPTER I

Down on the horizon the shore loomed faintly in the evening glow: the sea was fast enveloping it in a rising mist. Tranquil across a flood of burnished sea, the bold headlands of Dover and the Kentish coast stood like ramparts against the sky. So must they have appeared these many centuries.

On either hand, gliding swiftly through the waters ahead of us, appeared the dark hulls of our Destroyer escort. No other warships save these were in sight, no sign of that mighty vigil which for five hundred days and nights had held horrors unspeakable from our homes. Invisibly, though with a sureness equal to Fate, Britannia mounted guard.

Behind us, boiling away into a milky path, the ship's course vanished into obscurity toward the north. Each yard was bringing us nearer to France and destiny.

The scene on board was one of curious contrasts. Here and there among the crowded throng of khaki, civilians, proceeding overseas for various reasons, were seated in sheltered corners. Upon a ship crowded both by officers returning from leave and others, like our own little party, rejoining their units, the appearance of smartly dressed ladies reclining in deck chairs seemed strangely unreal. One could not help wondering what might be their destination or reason for going abroad. Beside their fellow passengers, they seemed

10   129

to be an anachronism, weirdly out of place. Such a scene belonged to far-off days before the war.

From our position in the stern, we watched the last shadowy form of England fade into the horizon. When, and under what circumstances, might we see it again ? Thoughts of this nature, perhaps not unnatural, were presently banished however, for ahead of us lay the wide coastline of France.

There, conspicuous amid its vague surroundings, loomed the Colonne de la Grande Armée above Boulogne, wrapped in memories of a Great Age, a symbol to us in these days. But time had wrought its changes. Over these narrow straits, far across the inland hills, stretching southward over a front four times the length of that of the preceding year, lay our army in its hundreds of thousands.

Presently the long mole, so familiar in bygone years, lay near at hand. Motionless against its parapet stood a French sentry, the dying sun gleaming vividly on his bayonet. We were back in France once more.

Disembarkation was a matter of no great concern to us, as we were a small party of officers without the responsibility of conducting men. Upon the quay, an ever-eddying crowd of figures surged backward and forward in the darkness, hurrying hither and thither in quest of missing kit. Baffling inquiries met one at every turn, but these, like our fellow travellers, we disregarded after a time ; it was everyone for himself.

Puny youths darted in and out of chattering groups seeking a job as porters of valises as big as themselves. On every side arose a babel of execrable French and a clatter of steel-shod boots upon the cobbles. Far down the length of the quay a light shone timidly in the darkness, and toward it the throng of new arrivals was attracted by hopes of information. Before long, among a crowd of fellow seekers after knowledge, we found ourselves outside the A.M.L.O.'s office, where, after a seemingly endless delay, we were instructed to put up for the night wherever we could and to report ourselves next day. Then followed a stampede toward the neighbouring hotels.

Having become separated from our small party, I decided to shift for myself without further ado ; so, instructing my man to keep watch over my kit, I hastened to an hotel near by. There, to my dismay, the whole building was declared to be occupied, but as it was beginning to rain outside and the dinner hour was already past, I decided to share a garret with an officer of the R.N.A.S.

Our room proved to be clean, but with mention of that its catalogue of virtues ended. However, as a refuge for a solitary night, it might have been worse ; and by the time my kit had arrived, it began to assume some aspect of comfort. Down in the dining-room I discovered a gathering of fellow officers of every grade and regiment. The majority had almost finished dinner, and in doing so had, I presumed, exhausted the resources of the establishment, for it was a very indifferent meal with which one was presently served.

On waking the next morning, I discovered that the solitary window in the sloping ceiling of our bedroom had admitted a large quantity of rain, which oozed about the floor in the form of a large puddle. Evidently, though the window had been made to open, visitors were expected to keep it tightly closed.

After breakfast, I set out through a steady drizzle in an attempt to discover the whereabouts of my travelling companions. These I found presently in one of the hotels along the farther side of the harbour, together with several officers of the division who were returning from leave. Among them was a former messmate whom I had not seen since my accident of the previous autumn, and from him I heard the latest news of my old battalion, which, before long, I hoped to rejoin.

On our arrival at the station according to orders, we discovered no R.T.O., but in his place a corporal, who informed us that our train would leave at 3 o'clock. We should get dinner at Abbeville and breakfast on the following morning at Rouen ; our final destination was to be Le Havre. Why we had not gone there direct by sea, I have never been able to understand.

Arriving at Abbeville about 10 p.m., not only did we discover no arrangements for feeding officers, but we were prevented from leaving the station in search of food by the necessity of having to change our coaches and all our belongings. As there were no porters, and because as yet none of us had a servant, the task of finding our valises devolved on ourselves.

The scene inside the luggage van, had the darkness permitted it to be seen, would have been a wild one. A solitary candle, produced from somebody's haversack, provided illumination for about twenty officers, who, one and all, were endeavouring to find and remove their kits from out of a heap of baggage. It was a long time before mine appeared, for of course it had been buried at the bottom. By then, my companions had already left, but I knew the direction of our new train.

A few minutes later, carrying my valise, which seemed to weigh many tons, I discovered that the train had gone. For a moment I reviled my luck, but soon became aware of distant shouts in the darkness. A flash-lamp flickered some couple of hundred yards down the line, evidently a signal from my companions, so I set off as fast as I could, stumbling over the sleepers in pursuit of the wandering train. I was wearing winter outfit, and over all a trench coat, therefore, what with my burden and the warmth of my clothing, I seemed on the point of apoplexy.

By good fortune I at last came up with the rearmost

coach and hurled my valise through an open door. To one unused to such labour the strain of the last few minutes had been very tiring; I stood a few moments to get my breath before climbing up into our compartment where a place had been kept for me. Then, without any warning, the train started off.

Running alongside the door, I was just in the act of hauling myself up, when a figure appeared out of the darkness and a lantern was flashed on the side of the train. The next instant a strong grip seized my arm, and a voice began to shout at me in French. The train was a long one, travelling at no great speed, thus, since it was impossible to enter the carriage so long as the fellow retained hold from below, it became necessary for me to get rid of him. This incident, coming on top of our other disappointments, caused my last vestige of good temper to vanish. I jumped down and turned on the fellow.

" Désirez-vous mourir, monsieur ? " he cried, swinging his lantern excitedly.

Here was the same old officiousness; nowhere but in England may one jump on a moving vehicle.

" Of course I do ! " I exclaimed in my best French. " For what other reason do you imagine I have come to your country ? "

A sharp twist of my arm broke his grip, and a shove in the chest sent him staggering. An instant later I was careering after the tail end of my vanishing train, which lumbered along in the darkness some yards away.

Apparently my would-be rescuer was content to leave me to my fate, for I heard nothing more of him, but gaining gradually on the train, was presently hauled aboard by sympathetic companions. The episode had by this time reduced them to fits of laughter, in which I endeavoured to join, though with indifferent success.

The journey by rail round to Havre seemed destined

to go wrong at every point. At Rouen the next morning we discovered once again no facilities for feeding. There was nothing for it but to resign ourselves to a steady process of starvation until our arrival at Havre.

We did not reach that place until the afternoon. For thirty-three hours our party of four subsisted on one packet of chocolate. The train left us stranded with our kit in the midst of the wilderness of sidings and warehouses of the Gare des Marchandises. To procure a cab from the town outside took some time, but about 3 o'clock we arrived, starving and travel-worn, at the principal hotel. All agreed that a wash and no ordinary meal were necessary before making our way to the Base Camp at Harfleur.

There we proceeded toward evening, but this time our short journey was made in comfort, for it was a couple of taxicabs that bore us and our belongings up to the great canvas town which, together with many other features, formed at that date the main British base.

In the twelve months since one had first seen it, Harfleur Camp had been transformed. In every case the changes denoted improvements. What formerly had been an assembly of huts and quagmires now appeared as well-tended paths, roads, huts, tents, and even flower beds and rustic railings. The old Mess was now reserved for officers of the Guards Division, as was evident to all by our colours floating languidly from the top of a brand-new flag-staff outside. Inside, the ante-room and mess-room had become almost unrecognisable. Card tables, comfortable armchairs, book-shelves, writing-tables, and even coloured mural decorations in the form of caricatures lent an air of homeliness to the place. Around the officers' huts across the road now reigned an ordered cleanliness. Duckboards had been provided, also cinder paths. Grass-plots, adorned with the badges of the various

regiments of Foot-guards picked out in flowers, lay
where once had been a mass of mud. Even a sentry
box on the road near the officers' mess was not
wanting.

Havre itself, when visited the following day, afforded
similar contrasts with its forlorn appearance of the
preceding year. With the growing influx of British
troops, trade and a measure of prosperity had sprung
up. More than ever, the streets presented a picture
of strange cosmopolitanism. Everywhere British
uniforms were in evidence—Australian, Scots, and
English ; and sprinkled among them was a large
number of French and Belgian soldiers. Even Russians
were represented. The proportion of Frenchmen
wearing medals was remarkable ; almost every officer
of field rank wore the *Médaille Militaire* or *Croix de
Guerre :* the inconspicuous ribbons of our own decorations seemed hardly noticeable. Standing on point
duty at every street corner were British military
police, their scarlet cap-covers giving a splash of
colour to an otherwise sombre mass of khaki. Order
and organisation were conspicuous on all sides.

The party with which I travelled out from England
had not been at Harfleur twenty-four hours before
orders arrived instructing it to proceed up the line.
Much to my disappointment, I was posted to the
Guards Entrenching Battalion instead of my old unit,
for which I had applied. We were to start at 6.15 on
the following morning.

The journey up the line next day was really not
unpleasant, for a few hours' break at Rouen enabled
us to obtain both an excellent meal and a welcome
rest from the train. The weather was beautiful. All
through that day our long troop train crawled onward,
but by nightfall we were still many hours from our
destination, though in former days a traveller would
have covered the distance in a very short time.

Everywhere across the country-side were signs of

the British occupation. Cavalry billets, motor-transport depots, and other branches of the A.S.C. seemed to be spread far and wide. Scores of miles behind the Front our khaki uniforms were to be found, and this huge back-area, more than anything else, gave us an inkling of the magnitude of our forces now in the field. Only a few months before, this great stretch of country had been occupied by our allies ; slowly, but surely, the armies of England were taking over the whole of northern France.

CHAPTER II

THE landscape was bathed in the full glare of the afternoon sun when we at last detrained at railhead. A hot and dusty march of seven miles in full equipment and packs brought us to our encampment, which, we found, lay on the farther side of an extensive wood— the Bois des Tailles. This, on its southern side, stretched to the edge of an abrupt plateau whence a fine view of the valley of the Somme was to be obtained. The camp was concealed among trees, a few clearings affording parade grounds, for, being within four or five miles of the line, it had to disguise itself against the possible visits of marauding Fokkers. The duties assigned to this entrenching unit were of such a kind that its camp was a permanent one, but in spite of this, no provision for a regular water supply had been made. Throughout our stay at this spot, all ranks suffered from a shortage of water. Our scanty allowance had to be carried up by fatigue parties from the river below, and the very steep slope up the valley side made this a labour to be undertaken only in cases of urgent necessity.

The men's quarters consisted of a series of timber and canvas huts, each capable of accommodating about forty persons. The floors being only of hard-baked earth, some discomfort was experienced from the constant presence of rats. The whole place swarmed with them ; large colonies were discovered beneath the floor-boards of almost every officer's tent. Though situated amidst ideal surroundings, this encampment was hardly so pleasant as a casual visitor might have supposed.

During frequent spells of intense heat, its shade was certainly most welcome, but whenever a breeze sprang up, parts of the camp became highly unpleasant on account of the presence near at hand of horse lines belonging to a battery of R.F.A. Compared with the relative comfort of an average billet, the conditions here were fairly primitive.

The Guards Entrenching Battalion at this time had only been in existence about six months. Though performing the duties of a pioneer battalion, it was not attached to a division, save in a nominal sense ; its real purpose was rather an advanced reinforcement depot than anything else. From it, at comparatively short notice, drafts could be sent to various units of the division, and by this means over-crowding was avoided down at the Base. The number of reinforcements for the Guards, when drawn from these two sources, was considerable. By limiting the number of service battalions in each regiment, units were maintained at effective strength. Nearly all reinforcements passed through this entrenching battalion on their way up to their final destination ; thus it was that I found some dozen Coldstream officers on my arrival. Our strength consisted of three companies : Grenadier, Coldstream, and Scots Guards, each company providing drafts for its regimental units serving with the division. The Irish and Welsh Guards detachments were a separate body, though situated in our neighbourhood. Owing to a temporary preponderance of Coldstreamers, I was lent to the Scots Guards as their company commander, taking with me several junior Ensigns.

At this time, the work of the battalion consisted largely of road-making : either improving existing roads or cutting new ones. So, on the day following that

of my arrival, I went up with my company to the hill
overlooking Bray, where we were engaged in making
a loop road, which, running round the hill to the
northward, rejoined the Bray–Albert road on the lower
level. Our task had only been commenced a few days
before, and the work of preliminary excavation marked
out by the R.E. had not been completed. The ground,
as in most of this region, consisted of chalk at no
great depth, so our labours became the harder.

The summit of Bray Hill afforded a splendid view
of the surrounding country. Far to the north-east,
the land swelled upward in fold beyond fold, while on
the left, standing out against the sky, there ran a
bold ridge overlooking Carnoy and the valley beyond.
Clustered here and there in the far distance were
groups of woodland, grey in the morning haze, and
behind these, faintly visible, floated a German observation balloon.

As the day wore on, the men discarded their jackets
and shirts, for upon the open hill-side the sun beat
mercilessly. At intervals squads were dotted along the
excavation, some picking at the chalk, others breaking
and smoothing the bed of the road. Higher up the
hill, partly screened from view, another party worked
in a chalk quarry, while beside it stood a row of carts
in process of being loaded with material for filling up
the irregularities of the gradient.

By and by, one's attention was called to a distant
working-party of pioneers visible at work upon a railway cutting about a couple of miles away. Behind
them had risen heavy clouds of dust and smoke thrown
up by a series of heavy explosions, and following one
another at intervals of a minute, each appeared as a
vast mushroom in the air before the noise of its detonation reached us. They seemed to be heavy shell-bursts,
and I thought of the ghostly balloon yonder on the
horizon. Through glasses, this working-party could be
seen proceeding unconcernedly with its task. Evidently

the explosions were considerably beyond it, though the flatness of vision caused by the lenses had the strange effect of making them appear quite close to the railway.

Presently my ears caught a familiar sound of the previous year : " blup, blup, blup." Looking up, I perceived a trail of " Archies," like balls of cotton wool in the blue sky overhead. Even as one watched, others appeared noiselessly, prolonging the chain ; then came the faint sound of their explosion. Ahead of them flashed a sudden gleam as the sunlight was reflected from the swerving body of an aeroplane. It was German. Before long the sky was mottled with white puffs and stabbed with brilliant flashes as our " Archies " poured up their stream of shells. The intruder turned eastward and disappeared, chased out of sight by a relentless trail of shell-bursts.

At last, with the waning sun, came the close of our day's work, and back we marched to the Bois des Tailles, weary and sunburnt and very hungry.

Life under the steady routine of daily " fatigues " soon settled down to a monotonous existence, which from time to time we relieved by a day's fishing for perch in the backwaters of the Somme. In spite of a shortage of material for metalling its surface, work on the " New Road " progressed steadily. What metal was obtainable had to be brought from the neighbourhood of Corbie, ten kilometres distant on the road to Amiens.

The weather, which for the latter half of May had been extraordinarily fine, broke at last, and it was not long before the whole country-side was reduced to a sea of mud. Even in the Bois des Tailles our discomfort from this cause became acute, and many were the hours that we were compelled to pass in the damp misery of our draughty mess, or seated in our tents listening to the steady beat of the rain on the stretching canvas overhead.

However, the change in the weather was not per-

mitted to interfere with our labours. The rain to some
extent helped us to prepare the road for the final layers
of metal and sand. Each day witnessed substantial
progress, and disclosed, moreover, fresh gun positions
in the valley behind the Fricourt ridge. Dugouts
seemed to be burrowed almost in a night; fresh
bivouacs to spring into view within a couple of days.
Now, large numbers of men and guns were beginning
to appear, and with their advent came the voice of
Rumour.

So, amidst a world of digging, carting, and rolling,
and of growing gunfire, came the month of June,
bringing with it news from Verdun and the Trentino,
and whisperings of future events on this very front.

An Army Order had just been circulated prohibiting
our efforts to fish in the lakes and backwaters of the
valley, thus rambles across the country-side became a
favourite manner of beguiling our leisure hours. The
valley itself was exceedingly flat and picturesque, lying
as it did between abrupt banks of hills, which rose,
smooth and steep, like giant escarpments on either
flank. The summit on our side, with its crest of
woods, ran in a gradual slope for a couple of miles
down-stream, where it merged into the lower level
at a right-angle bend. Opposite, on the farther side,
meandered a series of undulating hills until, at the
end, they rose in a bold and solid cliff at the river's
bend. Straggling down the vale in a riot of fresh
summer tints ran clusters of verdure, linked together
by a solid bank of trees bordering the canal; for
here in this reach the river had been canalised, and
its gleaming course could be seen beside the trees
for a mile or more. The bed of the valley appeared
like a luxuriant garden. Stagnant beyond the northern
edge of the canal lay broad patches of still water,
homes for many a perch or marauding pike, haunts
for myriads of dragonflies; while adjoining the
eastern end of the hollow stood the scattered village

of Etinehem, and there, where a clump of undulating
tree-tops screened its river-side, the red-brick church
reared its slender spire.   Descending the opposite
slope crawled long dark columns of mules on their
way to water and a welcome roll in the backwater
shallows.   Down by the canal, forms of bathers glistened in the evening sunlight, scattering the sparkling
water, and higher up the reach, visible through the
tree-trunks along the tow-path, lay the squat form of
a French gunboat beflagged with a flutter of drying
shirts suspended from a line.   Dark shadows, like long
fingers, stretched themselves across the vale, intensi-
fying the gold of leaf and water where either was
caught by the sun's dying rays.   Far southward,
beyond the farther cliff, rolled an expanse of corn,
meadow, and woodland, merging by degrees into the
rosy haze of evening.

Now stirring the evening stillness with their drone,
great birds speed up from the darkening horizon.   It
is a flight of aeroplanes homeward bound after its
distant voyage into the unknown.   You wonder what
they have seen.   Following in the wake of her smaller
companions drives a giant form.   Her appearance is
unfamiliar to one lately arrived in France, for this is
a new battle-plane.   Slowly she emerges from the
purple background, approaches through the dusk
with increasing speed, and sweeps overhead, steering
westward.   Still poised above Bray hovers a French
observation balloon ; when that begins to descend the
day is ended.

Near at hand, beyond the Bois des Tailles, rise spirals
of blue smoke coiling languidly in the air : our neighbours the gunners are preparing supper.   Already the
valley below is shrouded in shadow, and the last red
gleam of sunlight is creeping upward along the hill.
In the silence of the evening comes the sound of mules
returning up the Etinehem road, the shouts of their
attendants echoing clearly in the stillness.   From the

village spire, now nearly lost in gloom, floats the sound
of bells.   It is the Angelus, and its mellow faintness
steals softly through the gloaming.   A distant howitzer
flings forth its booming note, which rolls away over
hill and vale until lost in rumbling echoes in the
distance.   Once more all is still; the Angelus tolls
on.   The French balloon is descending.

CHAPTER III

THE month of June had arrived, bringing with it floods of rain. Once more the camp in the wood became a mass of mud, and the roads veritable quagmires. Along with this spell of wet weather came a deluge of rumours. These had one point in common, namely, the prospect of a big attack by our army on this front, but beyond that, most of them were mutually contradictory. Apart from these, however, it was evident to all that something out of the ordinary was impending, for men and guns continued to appear in ever-growing quantities. Valleys that only a week before had been devoid of all occupants now began to assume an aspect of busy preparation. Huts and dugouts were being constantly erected, and the masses of materials assembled for the R.E. became exceedingly great. Horse lines seemed to spread themselves across every fold in the ground, and batteries to spring from the soil in every direction. Once again, as on the eve of Loos, we lived in an atmosphere of endless speculation.

Certainly, many signs and portents gave credence to our belief that great things were about to happen. The construction of new roads along specially selected routes seemed hardly explicable on any other grounds ; also, a new railway was being built across the country-side to the north of us. Though only a single track, it would be a valuable auxiliary to the permanent line down at our present railhead. Every ravine and hollow

behind the Fricourt ridge was being converted into a
battery position, and trenching and mining operations
were being pushed on at all possible speed throughout
the neighbourhood. Miles of wire cables were said
to have been laid in trenches seven feet deep, these
being joined up at certain points into a huge telephonic system.

About the beginning of June, F—— and I were
able to see for ourselves something of the preparations beyond Bray. He was in charge of a party
engaged on the construction of a special telephone
exchange.

After toiling through a slough of mud for several
miles, we arrived at last on the rear slope of the Fricourt
ridge, not far from Bronfay Farm. The dugout was
approached by a sloping passage, from which we descended by a sort of manhole into a chamber beneath.
The men entrusted with this work were all miners,
and the corporal in charge seemed evidently delighted
with his new duties, which probably recalled to him
his work in times of peace. The place proved to be
an enormous undertaking, as the depth from ground
level to floor measured no less than twenty-five feet.
There were two exits in case of need, which led from
the subterranean chamber. This itself measured nine
feet by fifteen, and the headroom beneath the steel
girders that supported the solid roof was rather more
than seven. Here, because at this depth there was no
illumination from above, operations had to be conducted
by candlelight. The entrance shafts were skilfully
arranged so as to afford as much security as possible :
neither opened directly into the room, but into short
passages adjoining it. Owing to the absence of daylight, I have no doubt that the place was lit subsequently by electricity.

The only point that struck us as unsound was the
question of the wire-ducts outside, but for these we
were not responsible. A number of these narrow

11

trenches radiated from the spot, and in consequence of
their depth, a considerable quantity of soil had been
cast up beside them. If not very conspicuous to a
hostile airman, they would have appeared sufficiently
prominent to anyone examining at leisure an aerial
photograph. One can only suppose that to disguise
them as ordinary communication trenches would have
entailed too much labour. However that may be,
there could be no question of the extraordinary pains
and skill devoted to this piece of work. Coming after
the puny dugouts known to me in the preceding year,
it was something of a revelation.

The ridge lay several hundred yards to the eastward,
and up this we made our way. The hill-side, covered
with an expanse of long grass, was perfectly open ;
but it was quite invisible to the enemy. At the time,
one of our airmen was being shelled, and many
fragments of metal came whistling down about us.
The odds against our being hit were enormous, but
the contemplation of that fact hardly sufficed to ease
our minds when an especially large splinter whacked
into the ground a few yards away.

F—— had been up here before, so I followed his
lead, wondering all the while what lay beyond the
skyline. Our trenches wound along the reverse slope,
but on the summit we should be visible to the enemy,
though at what range I did not know.

Topping the crest by and by, we obtained a fine
view of the valley beyond. Along this, at a range of
about a thousand yards, ran the straggling lines of
the German trenches ; our own we could see immediately below us. Over on our left front, we could
also make out a battered village nestling in the valley
among some gaunt and splintered trees. That must
be Mametz.

Sitting down in the grass, my companion told me
that there was no risk of our being fired on. Men
came up here occasionally for the reason that the

enemy never wasted ammunition on one or two stray
figures. I followed his example.

The scene in front of us was likely soon to be a field
of battle, therefore, as keen young officers, we fell to
discussing the various features of the landscape. From
a defensive point of view the village appeared very
strongly situated, and we both realised its power to
enfilade any assault against the main position on the
farther ridge. It was certain to be strongly held and
to be full of machine-guns, which, firing from concealed
points among the walls, could only be silenced by
direct hits from our batteries. We agreed that this
sector would require much preparation before infantry
could advance with any prospect of success.

After a while, returning into the valley from which
we had come, we met an Engineer who offered to show
us another dugout. It had only recently been finished
and was said to be well worth a visit. Indeed, like
the one we had just examined, it proved to be a
most astonishing place. This was reserved, we were
told, for a Divisional Battle Headquarters. Access
to it was gained through one of the reserve trenches,
and on arrival we found it to consist of a suite of
chambers. These lay at a depth of fifteen feet below
the level of the floor of the trench, which was itself
about eight feet deep. Each room communicated by
a separate staircase with the trench above, and each
was connected to the other by a doorway. The
centre one was destined for the General's own use;
opening off on one side was his bedroom, and on the
other lay the kitchen and servants' quarters. Every
apartment had boarded floors, and the walls and
ceilings were finished in a similar manner.

.   .   .   .

June 4th, celebrated the previous year at Noeux-
les-Mines, was again at hand. Arrangements had been
made for a dinner that should take place in Amiens,

and to this all Old Etonians serving in the 4th Army were invited. The prospect of a temporary return to civilisation, and the enjoyments thereof, induced many of us to face the twenty-mile journey. There, among a number of old friends and companions, I found my former Colonel with whom I had served the year before. Like many of the senior officers of the regiment, he now commanded a brigade. It was somewhat strange to renew old acquaintances in such surroundings. Familiar faces, seen last in the High Street at Eton or around "The Pitt" at Cambridge, confronted one in all directions. Memories, long forgotten, revived like returning echoes; a flood of conversation bore back many a reminiscence of former days. Everyone, save myself, seemed to be blest with an amazing memory. Doubtless that fact accounted for the large number of young Staff officers present.

But good things end all too soon : the time arrived at last for us to leave. It was not long, however, before we discovered that the motor which should have been waiting for us had absconded, leaving us at midnight in Amiens, twenty miles from our camp. After endeavouring to make use of a car that was bound for our locality, our party was compelled to abandon all hope of returning that night.

Our predicament was somewhat awkward, for military regulations required that all hotels should close at eleven. For this occasion, the establishment in which we had passed the evening had been granted a special permit. Nevertheless, we set out to test the possibilities of obtaining a lodging for the night.

One hotel after another remained coldly unresponsive to our summons. Then, in desperation, someone suggested the French police. With the aid of a solitary electric torch we groped our way through several streets, and encountered at last a couple of Municipal Guards, who showed us the way to a small flat. There, after filling up innumerable forms and losing the toss for a bed, I settled down for the night in an armchair. A pillow for my head, and a couple of chairs for my legs, afforded a passable substitute for a couch, and on these I had no difficulty in sleeping soundly.

Arriving at the station next morning, we discovered that no train left for our railhead until the afternoon. We set off, therefore, to the *Mairie*, where the office of the A.P.M. was said to be situated. Outside the iron railings screening the forecourt we found a large concourse of people awaiting some ceremony, and within the courtyard itself, formed in a three-sided square, stood half a battalion of French infantry. Our uniform gained us ready admission, and after inquiring our way from a corporal at the gate, we found the office we were seeking. The A.P.M. was out.

As our position on a first-floor balcony enabled us to witness everything on the parade ground below, we decided to await events before leaving the building.

Before long, a movement arose among the bandsmen in the centre of the court, and a moment later a French Staff car drew up at the gates beyond. From this a General alighted, accompanied by several aides-de-camp, and at his appearance the parade presented arms. Next, a brief consultation ensued, during which one noticed for the first time a number of civilians, men and women, standing among a party of wounded officers and men facing the Colours and escort. Suddenly, arresting one's wandering attention, drums and trumpets crashed forth the " Marseillaise." The crowd in the street, now grown to considerable dimensions, became agitated as men uncovered. Our party paid the customary compliment, much to the surprise and needless gratification of our civilian neighbours on the balcony. As soon as the last notes had ceased, the ceremony commenced.

One by one, those about to be decorated were called

out; then followed a summary of their deeds. As each figure walked to the centre of the parade, an aide-de-camp handed a medal to the General, who proceeded to pin it upon the breast of the *décoré*. Then followed the accolade and embrace, as is the custom in France, whereupon General and soldier exchanged salutes before the latter returned to his place on parade.

"Guyot, Charles Etienne, soldat du 107ième!" At the sound of his name, there lurched forward a crippled *poilu*. His crutches, shod with metal, beat time upon the paving to the recital of his gallant deed. Coming to a halt before the General, he endeavoured to raise his hand to the salute, then, unable to do so, he inclined his head toward his upraised arm. The movement was acknowledged by the General, who, accompanying his action with a smile, drew down the soldier's hand and shook it. A moment later, upon the one-legged soldier's breast gleamed the *Médaille Militaire*.

"Picard, Jean Grégoire, caporal du 135ième!" From the crowded railings arose a murmur of emotion, instantly suppressed, for already an upright figure was advancing to where the General stood, seemingly taller for having lost both its arms! The voice of the aide-de-camp alone was heard, as, with head erect, the terrible apparition went forth to receive its honour. Halting before the General and his staff, he drew himself up, stiff as a ramrod. It was the only salute the poor fellow could give. I shall never forget that moment. A minute later this broken relic of a man had entered the ranks of Napoleon's Légion d'Honneur.

And so they came and went, until at last, in response to the aide-de-camp's call, there advanced the hesitating figure of a girl draped in black from head to foot. Her husband's deeds were ringing in her ears as she stood before us all. He was one of those who had paid the utmost price. To her the General first gave his salute, then handed her the *Médaille Militaire* and

with it the *Croix de Guerre*. But as she withdrew
with veiled and drooping head, one realised from the
convulsion of her shoulders the bitterness of such
fame.

By and by, bearing aloft their Tricolour, and stepping
out to the strains of the " Chant du Départ," the parade
marched away through an avenue of spectators. These
in their turn dispersed before long, and the courtyard
of the *Mairie* became empty. Seeing which, a cloud
of pigeons swooped back from temporary exile and
resumed their placid occupation of this recent *Champ
de Mars.*

.   .   .   .   .

In the Bois des Tailles, we found on our return no
news of consequence. Burdened with a growing atmosphere of tension, the days of June sped slowly by,
rumour following rumour. Enormous supplies were
now rolling up to the Front by day and night. Already events were confirming our anticipations, among
which was the fact that our heavy guns had commenced to register their targets. With the certain
approach of Fate, a hurricane was brewing in our
midst.

CHAPTER IV

AMONG THE FRENCH

By the middle of June, the region about Bray seemed to have grown into a vast encampment, which included not only every branch of the British Army, but also our allies. Below our camp, the flats and roadway of the broad valley swarmed with gangs of French engineers busily constructing a light railway. In addition, several gunboats had crept up the canal, and there was now quite a flotilla of these craft moored along the embankment. Beneath their awnings, one could see large naval guns pointed upward toward the east. In many places the mottled tents of their troops had overflowed the barrier of the river, and were now scattered in ordered fashion upon the British side of the valley. The French were relieving us of the whole river sector.

About the 16th, I was sent with the Coldstream company, to which I had reverted, to aid our Engineers in constructing a new road in the woods near Suzanne. This village lay some three miles to the east of Bray, in a district occupied practically entirely by the French. The point of contact between the allied forces must have been close to our new road, because, working upon another parallel to ours, and only a few yards distant, there was a battalion of the 160th of the line. Our respective roads were destined for " up " and " down " traffic.

Never had I seen such a congestion of troops as

that along the Bray–Suzanne road. As far as the eye could see, hundreds of men in the familiar "horizon-blue" of the French Army were at work. Along the highway, which wound down the valley, there swarmed a mass of transport that must have been fully three miles long. Their coming and going was endless. Engineer waggons, pontoons, ammunition lorries, water carts, guns, and infantry, passed slowly on their way back-wards and forwards, but in spite of this tremendous press of traffic, I saw but few police directing it and few outward signs of organisation ; yet no confusion seemed to arise. Along the hill-side skirting the north-ern flank of the high-road, a brigade, at least, was occupied in widening the fairway, and among the trees nearer to our own work the figures of other fatigue-parties could be seen engaged in various ways. By-roads were being made to the numerous battery positions situated here in almost every copse and grove. The woods around echoed with clicking picks and spades.

Already staked out by the R.E., our road was fully prepared for our arrival. With a sublime faith in our powers for work, they had run it straight through a morass of mud, which lay stagnant beneath the shade of the wood. On inspecting the place, we found that, as a result of recent rains, we had to cope with a pond of mud having an average depth of eighteen inches. This ran down the bed of a disused road for about fifty yards. Accordingly we set-to with ardour, for three days only had been granted us in which to com-plete this task. By cutting channels into a ditch, we were able to drain off most of the water before many hours ; then the remaining mud was shovelled clear of the track, and the face of the old metal laid bare. On this we unloaded fresh stone chippings to bring the road to a level surface. Upon this again, the Engineers laid a wooden road as we completed each section of the way. But in spite of their repeated

assertions as to the importance of this work, they
seemed unable to provide us with much material.
Except for what we could find in the locality, there
was almost a complete lack of supplies; evidently the
French had seized everything. Small blame to them!

A walk through the wood revealed guns on every
side, both French and English, though ours were
markedly fewer. While patrolling up and down the
working-party, one had ample opportunity for studying
the appearance of our neighbours who were working
on the second road a few yards away. Their physique,
while not up to that of my own men, was nevertheless
good; many of them were powerfully built, though of
medium height. Their N.C.Os seemed very inactive,
yet little slackness was observable among the workers.
The lieutenant in charge was very young, but seemed
to have a knowledge of handling men. More than
once I had observed previously that air of mingled
familiarity and authority among officers of the French
Army. Either, French or British, is imbued with that
sense of discipline most natural to its national feelings;
but in one respect the *poilu* and Private Atkins show
similar characteristics : both are confirmed lovers of
mischief.

In the intervals of digging, either party would
rest awhile to watch the other's labours. After a
mutual silent contemplation, the more sociable spirits
proceeded to fraternise. A *pioupiou*, resting a moment on his spade in order to wipe his steaming face,
caught the eye of Private Jones ; whereupon, he
proceeded to whistle an almost unrecognisable version
of "Tipperary." This was interpreted by several
guardsmen as a signal to cease work, so the inevitable
water-bottle was produced. Private Jones, executing
an amazing gesture toward his allies, took his pull,
ending the ceremony with an eloquent wink.

"Eau-de-vie, hein ? " exclaimed the grinning Frenchman,

" Jerner ponce pas ! " cried the drinker, revealing an unsuspected mastery of our allies' language. " Eau-de-mort," he continued, tapping his water-bottle ; " are you compree ? No bon ! "

A roar of mirth greeted this observation.

" De qui êtes-vous, de la Génie ? "

" Non compree, ole cock."

" Votre régiment, alors ? "

" ' O Lor' yourself. We're the raygimong de Cold-stream Guards."

" Ah, vous êtes de la Garde ? "

" Wee."

" Play up, the Lily Whites ! " The inevitable interruption came from somewhere down the road.

" Qu'est-ce que vous avez là ? " continued one of the 160th, pointing to the ornate leather belt of one of the Englishmen. The object of his inquiry, in addition to wearing a pair of braces, had girt himself with a huge leather belt upon which had been fastened numerous regimental badges.

" Oh, sooverneers," he exclaimed, obviously gratified at being the centre of public attention.

The Frenchmen instantly became interested.

" Des Boches ? Vous avez tué tous ces gens ? "

A corporal interpreted to the puzzled owner of the belt.

" Non Boches, no blurry Allemans. Sooverneers anglais ! "

The mystification of our allies was complete.

" Mais, pourquoi les portez-vous ? " cried one in amazement.

The belted one, learning this question, seemed rather disconcerted. He wore them because all the " best boys " did so,

" They're for the girls, Froggy," chimed in the wit of the party. Apparently this was understood ; a grin overspread the faces of some of the Frenchmen.

" Tiens ! pour les amies. Bon ! Vous n'êtes pas fiancé, vous ? "

" 'E's arskin' 'ow many finances you 'ave, Bill."

Bill scratched his head and gave his belt a hitch, but at this point I noticed that our rest interval had ended. Moreover, the good name of one of my men was becoming dangerously imperilled ; so I blew my whistle.

Hardly had work been resumed before a sudden hubbub arose among the 160th. Dashing impetuously to and fro among the brushwood before the tolerant gaze of one of their sergeants, a party of men began chasing into the shrubs some object on the ground. Blows whacked right and left, and more than one of their number narrowly escaped injury. Presently, two long spades successfully smashed, the chief huntsman held aloft the mangled remains of a rat.

Hereupon, approaching from behind, came the young lieutenant. The others grinned in delighted anticipation, for the victorious one was already pronouncing a funeral oration over the victim.

" Charette ! get back to your work at once. I've been watching you." This was untrue, but no matter. " Who broke those spades ? " he continued.

As was to be expected, a guilty silence followed this inquiry.

" Corporal, I hold you responsible for those. See to it that your work is completed in time." Thus implicated, the corporal found himself charged with the task of finding the owners of the broken spades ; with that the boy officer passed on. The group of huntsmen resumed their digging. Two of them, displaying a suspicious diligence, had discovered a large stone over which they were absorbed. They were endeavouring to lever it up with picks.

But it would be a mistake to imagine that the French were anything else than strenuous workmen : their achievements as soldiers speak for themselves.

Yet the Frenchman, however much disguised by uniform, still remains an individual by reason of his
buoyant animal spirits. In some respects they are an
army of children, and it is largely due to this characteristic, together with the unquenchable good-
humour of the British soldier, that our respective
armies have become such fast friends.

Later in the day, I made the acquaintance of the
little lieutenant. After an exchange of a few commonplace remarks, I observed that his men appeared
to be good sportsmen. A twinkle came into his eye at
my allusion to a *Régiment de Chasseurs*.

" One has to be constantly watching them, monsieur.
With you it is no doubt the same ? They are fine-
looking fellows yonder."

"We have no finer," I replied. "They are our
Guards : all voluntary men."

" Ah, you surprised us there. But now you have
adopted universal service, is it not so ? "

" Yes, it had to come, and a good thing too. Have
you been long in this sector ? "

" No, monsieur. Lately, we were waiting behind
the line ; before that, we were at Verdun."

" Things must have been pretty warm for you
there ? " I observed hopefully.

" I should think so ! Eight days in the front line
under a deluge of shell fire day and night ; we lost
many men, of course. Food and water were only
obtained with difficulty on account of their barrages,
but our ammunition was all right."

" And the Boches ? " I inquired.

The Frenchman grimaced and clucked his tongue.

" Awful ! I cannot imagine their losses. We of the
160th caught them like this again and again," and he
mowed down a tuft of grass with his stick. " They
were brave men, nevertheless. We were told they
belonged to a Brandenburg corps ; now they belong
to the rats. You could see them coming on in solid

waves; and as they advanced, rank after rank seemed to melt away like smoke. It was our gunners that held Verdun."

"And yourselves," I added.

"Perhaps; we did our share, I suppose. At any rate, our *mitrailleuses* boiled again and again. Mon Dieu! you should have seen our targets!"

"Whereabouts were you?"

"Douaumont. It was hell. But they withdrew that corps before we left."

"You were at Douaumont? Were you there when that great counter-attack was made?"

He glanced at me and smiled.

"Yes, we were there."

"What is your division, monsieur?"

"The 20th."

But the story of Verdun and its epic associations was cut short: my sergeant stood by, evidently awaiting me.

"Good-bye. I fear I must be going. Good luck!"

"That's mutual, monsieur, of course!" So saying, he drew himself up and gave me a slight formal gesture of farewell.

In the evening, as the company, drawn up by the roadside, was waiting for the lorries which should carry us back to camp, we obtained another view of the Bray–Suzanne road.

Flowing in an endless stream, the same flood of troops and transport rolled on. As far as the eye could reach, the highway surged with men and horses slowly moving in contrary directions. Purring alongside a huge waggon-load of bridging materials came a Staff car; inside, seen through the fog of dust raised by the passing men, one noticed the gold-trimmed *képis* of its occupants. Then, from the clattering throng emerged a company of French infantry wearing the bright khaki recently issued to some of their army. In one's ears there hummed a multitudinous sound: the tramp of feet, the clatter of hoofs, the groan of labouring wheels.

Heralded by a deeper note, there next came a battery of 75's, and here, sitting lazily upon the lofty seats of the waggons or driving the teams, an extraordinary variety of types could be seen. Their chief characteristic was a total disregard for soldierly smartness, both in their persons and in their dress. Dirty and unkempt, their forbidding appearance was intensified further by the motley assortment of their uniforms. I could not help contrasting them with the smart figures beside me. No two seemed dressed alike. Here, amid a turmoil of dust, loomed a blue *képi* ; there, a grey-blue helmet ; yonder, a red *képi* ; and farther off a light-blue forage cap. Some wore dark-blue jackets, others a light-blue greatcoat. Almost every type of kit was represented. It was not a battery, it was a museum.

Grins of friendly derision appeared on the faces of my men, and small wonder ; for, unwashed, dishevelled, and clad in the refuse of a quartermaster's store, they seemed rather a gang of Operatic brigands than a body of disciplined soldiers. Even their teams presented as sorry an appearance, for rope was visible among the traces, showing where the harness had been spliced in rough-and-ready fashion. Bristling with their seven days' beards, these fellows wore the air of a gipsy caravan. But though their horses, too, were badly groomed, their guns were in perfect trim.

Beside one of these, an officer came riding along, puffing at a pipe. Evidently our presence among the French Army aroused the curiosity of these men, for, as they passed us, they turned to stare at the ordered line standing along the roadside. My sergeant's face was a perfect study : he was disgusted beyond words

But presently, as one gazed in amazement at their array, doubts began to form themselves. Were these fellows really what they seemed ? Perhaps not. Beneath the unkempt exterior of these Frenchmen, there lurked, I fancied, a spirit no less rugged. Many of them had an imperious glance ; several of the older men were noticeable for their granite cast of feature and unflinching gaze. Who on earth could they be ?

Here, sitting his saddle in nonchalant fashion, came a figure whose stained and threadbare trousers were stuffed into a pair of knee-boots strangely out of keeping with the horizon-blue service jacket clothing his massive form. Perched jauntily upon his tangle of black hair was a forage cap, while the flying embers of his clay pipe seemed to threaten his bushy beard with imminent disaster. His face had not been washed for several days, but in spite of that, its features attracted remark by their almost classic form. With head erect and eye for any man, he sat his horse like the King of all the Tramps. Thus he rode before us, straight from the pages of Rabelais.

With a jangle of harness and a sweep of upraised whips the battery came to a momentary halt : shouts mingled with the sound of stamping hoofs all down the column. Somewhere along the seething road a check had arisen. At this moment, an officer who had been eyeing us detached himself from the throng.

" Who are you, monsieur ? " he called, urging his horse toward me. " We don't often meet with the English Army."

" The English Guards," I replied. " We have been working near here."

" A hot business ! " he exclaimed, glancing at our sweaty faces, " but not so warm as we shall be having soon." His teeth gleamed beneath his dusty moustache as he laughed.

" And who are you, monsieur ? " I inquired, impelled not only by politeness, but by infinite curiosity.

" Artillery, as you see—20th Division."

Then, in a flash, my memory awoke.

" You are the 20th Division ! That belongs to the ' Iron Corps ' ! "

He smiled and nodded.

" Why ! " I thought, " *these* are the saviours of Verdun ! " I almost burst out laughing as I recalled my conversation with my little lieutenant, for the significance of what he said had not struck me at the time. The defeat of the Brandenburghers, and Douaumont, would be for ever associated with these men. *Corps de Fer !* The words themselves were now part of the history of France !

Then as the guns rolled forward once more the scales seemed to be falling from our eyes. The champing tumult of mud-stained horses, the swaying figures of swarthy men, the mass of curving necks and rippling muscles—this was the real panoply of war. Every aspect of the great picture seemed to suggest the passing of a frieze of ancient heroes. Here was the Parthenon sprung to life.

" À toutes les gloires de la France " !

One I had already seen : here, shouting and swaying past in majestic cavalcade, was yet another !

.   .   .   .   .

By and by, while our lorry was wending its way slowly homewards along the road to Bray, I fell to thinking of what I had just heard. The presence of this French corps, renowned as one of the "crack" units of their Army, foreboded great events for the future. For more than a week past, it had been evident that we had passed the realm of rumours. Before our eyes, great undertakings were in process of preparation, and now, crowning all, came the knowledge that in the great days ahead our allies would be acting in concert and in no negative fashion.

But amid all the surrounding bustle one could not remain for long wrapt in such thoughts. Nine hours before, we had passed along this road, but still the enormous volume of men and vehicles rolled on and

12

on, still the valley was choked with horse and foot gradually vanishing into a cloud of dust. Batteries of guns, proceeding at the general walking pace, were wedged between a long column of commissariat and a company of Engineers. Near at hand, a battalion of the line carrying picks and spades headed a convoy of motor lorries, and as these vehicles jerked forward at a marching pace, their engines throbbed in fits and starts above the ocean murmur of the advancing mass. Turning at last into another straight vista of road, we beheld the same endless scene. It was the passage of an army.

Entering Bray at last, we were directed by a British policeman on point duty to a special route through the town reserved for returning motor traffic ; otherwise, the congestion through the narrow streets would have been fatal. Here the streams of troops and transport, British almost entirely, caused the walls around to quiver with their echoes.

" Gawd blime, mate, look at *them !* " came a whisper from behind me. For a moment there was an amazed silence ; even the British soldier was impressed. Then came a storm of hoots, catcalls, and yells, plentifully spiced with the time-honoured epithets of the barrack-room.

Lumbering down the main road rolled a belching traction-engine, drawing in its wake an elephantine mass that rumbled beside the walls of the houses, almost filling the width of the village roadway. To one who had never seen such a piece of ordnance, the sight was almost incredible. Sweeping upward beside the roofs rose its massive barrel, and its giant wheels, huge and ponderous, revolved high above the doll-like forms of men on either flank. The earth quivered beneath its weight, and windows trembled at its approach. Behind it followed another and another behind that. A glimpse of these vast forms filled every civilian spectator with wonder. To the gaping townsfolk, it must have seemed as if the guns of the British Fleet had entered their midst, like a herd of mastodons.

Speculation on the destination and powers of these enormous howitzers still continued as we drew near the Bois des Tailles. At least the orator of the party knew his own mind.

" You blighters, just mark my words. Them blinkin' things is goin' to punch the Kaiser's ticket." Whereupon, in order to emphasise his meaning, he spat with faultless aim into the ditch across the road.

CHAPTER V

Now, in the last week of June, came a spell of glorious weather, and with it a final burst of activity. All through the long summer days, banks of dust clouds hung across the wide country-side where endless columns of horse and motor traffic flowed along the high-roads. Guns were rolling up almost every night, batteries of guns, scores of guns; and in their train flowed streams of ammunition, ranking from the modest 18-pounder to the food destined for the heaviest pieces. Each morning, the tracks of caterpillar tractors on the roads revealed the night's activity.

And as our preparations behind the lines increased, so did the enemy's gunfire, seeking out the clouds raised by the Allies' transport columns. Long-range shrapnel fire became frequent, woods and hollows being favourite targets; but beyond an inevitable series of petty casualties among men and horses, no great loss was inflicted. In the event of their shelling our encampment, orders were issued for us to refuge in an adjoining chalk quarry.

During these days of growing bombardment, the Bray–Corbie road was subjected to frequent shelling. It afforded one of the main routes of supply, and damage to it would have proved a serious matter; but though the enemy succeeded in smashing several craters into the ground in its vicinity, they did not obtain a direct hit on the road itself. Well-known landmarks of this sort became targets in ever-growing frequency, and in order to avoid them if necessary, and at the same time, to preserve them from an excess of traffic as much as possible, supplementary routes were cut in all directions. These were more of the nature of tracks, since their surface was left unmetalled, though rendered fairly smooth. The weather was now gloriously fine, the sun reducing the soil once more to the hardness of iron.

Throughout this week the Entrenching Battalion worked in desperate haste on such a new roadway. The nature of our task may be better estimated when I mention that in two days we prepared two miles of track, cutting through a coppice and a wood, and building along a hill-crest an embanked causeway. The most difficult part of our labours was the removal of roots of trees, which in many places obstructed the way. Of course, a few days' rain would suffice to convert this "X" road, as it was called, into the state of a quagmire, but so long as it was used for horse transport alone, it might be expected to render reliable service.

From our positions on the crest overlooking the Somme valley, a large expanse of open country lay visible to the eastward. There, wafted from the hazy horizon, the deep notes of our guns were clearly distinguishable as they flung back their reply to the enemy. Around us the atmosphere seemed charged with the myriad thoughts of an army. The crisis was at hand. One could almost hear and feel the hopes that were rising on every side. For the New Army, it was the time of its supreme test; to the men of the "Old Contemptibles," it seemed as if the dream for which they had fought and prayed so long was unfolding itself at last.

Then came the announcement of the day of days! A week of unprecedented bombardment would herald its coming, until, on July 1st, our line would leap to the attack. This spell of artillery preparation became known as U, V, W, X, Y, and Z days. Following upon Z, came " Zero Day," July 1st. Over a front of many miles, extending to the north as far as Gommecourt, our intended onslaught was known to be in readiness. Prolonging the battle southwards of the river, lay the French. Not since the Aisne had such a conflict been planned.

But even at this last period of our suspense, work of the greatest importance remained to be done, and to the Guards Entrenching Battalion fell one more task of pioneering.

Running north-east from the town of Bray toward the British ridge lay the Bronfay road, so named on account of the farm that stood beside it on the sheltered side of the crest. Here, on the first day of our bombardment, I received orders to take a working-party of Coldstream and Scots Guards.

By 8 a.m. we were ready to commence work. Our task was one of widening the roadway by several feet for a distance of three or four hundred yards. This route constituted the supply line of the local corps. Distant about three-quarters of a mile on our left front lay the Fricourt ridge, still veiled by a slight ground mist, while, in the valley behind it, lurked massed batteries awaiting their orders. Straight ahead, only a few hundred yards up the road, stood the farm buildings, now seething with orderlies and Staff cars. To the right spread the continuation of the ridge where it joined the French positions.

As, in the event of their shelling us along the open road, we should be entirely exposed, and expecting German counter-fire later on, I started off to find cover for my men. I had not been long absent from the party before, owing to good luck, I found a series of disused gun-emplacements, which would afford us all the cover we should require.

It must have been about an hour later when the time arrived for our guns to open; thereupon, punctually to the minute, a sudden salvo broke the stillness of the early morning. But my expectation of a dramatic outburst was grievously disappointed. The noise seemed trifling in comparison with the gunfire which had opened the battle of Festubert. After watching the batteries for a while, some of us came to the conclusion that the stories we had heard concerning our ammunition supplies had been greatly exaggerated.

From time to time, flying low above the green slopes, an aeroplane would speed up at a great pace from the eastward. As it swooped over the farm, a message fluttered down, and men could be seen running to where it was falling. Then, presently a car glided past us along the road, while on the track used by infantry, scattered bodies of men wearing full kit marched onward up the hill-side. They were reliefs going to the trenches.

For several hours our guns continued to thunder, firing in salvos of batteries ; but so slow and deliberate was their shooting, that for some considerable time it was hard for us to realise their activity was anything more than their usual daily routine. Many of us wondered when they were going to commence. However, as they continued with unabated precision hour after hour, one began to realise by and by the great quantity of shells they must have been consuming.

No enemy shots came over, no Fokker appeared to interrupt the progress of our work : the enemy remained ominously quiet. As it had seemed probable that we might come within the zone of their counter-battery fire, many had anticipated a warm time for the party, but in this also our expectations were at fault.

As the day wore on, one grew accustomed to the clanging reports of our guns, but toward the afternoon their methodical fire swelled in volume. According to reports, two hundred and fifty guns lay concealed in the valley, and now a large proportion of them appeared to have come into action. Certainly there were great numbers yonder, for we could see the streaming flashes of each battery as it fired over the heads of those in front of it. But though their noise rose at times to an impressive intensity, their output did not suggest a great bombardment.

The artillery programme, so far as we could ascertain, was planned on a scheme of progressive intensity. W, X, Y, and Z days would each witness a steady increase of power as larger and larger guns reinforced the bombarding batteries, until, on the final day, the enemy's positions would feel the full shock of the massed artillery of the 4th Army. First, their wire would be cut, then, lifting on to their front line, our guns would play on that for a whole day until the desired effect had been obtained, after which they would lengthen once more on to the support line. Meanwhile, our heavy pieces would spread devastation among their billets in rear.

If on their part our gunners were content with a steady output, our allies decided otherwise. On our homeward march to the Bois des Tailles, we had a fine opportunity for noting the effect of their bombardment. From the summit of Bray Hill, the sector opposite them lay in full view, disclosing a thrilling spectacle. The entire German position appeared as a seething wall of smoke, rent and splashed by volcanoes of black clouds and darting flame. Mingled with these, and exploding continuously, were sparkling gleams of shrapnel, while above this scintillating mass, billowing aloft to a great height, there ascended a heavy mantle of smoke and dust. But though an awe-inspiring sight to see, the scene was yet more wonderful to hear; for from the direc-

tion of this sombre canopy there pealed a sound
that filled the landscape with tumult, a tumult in
which our throbbing ears could distinguish the thunderous strokes of war.   The Battle of the Somme had
begun.

CHAPTER VI

BACK TO THE BATTALION

WITHIN two days of my visit to Bronfay Farm I found myself, in company with several other Coldstream officers, journeying to a very different region ; our battalions had vacancies for us at last. So, leaving the Somme, we passed by a devious route to the Guards Division. Thus, on the eve of the great offensive, we found ourselves after a voyage of thirty hours in the town of Poperinghe, where the party split up, each group proceeding to the camp of its respective unit.

I, by good fortune, had been posted to my former battalion, but amid strange surroundings the task of finding it was no easy one ; so, profiting from past experience, I visited the Headquarters of the division then occupying the town in order to verify the rather scanty directions given me by the R.T.O. There my suspicions were confirmed : my battalion had just moved to a fresh area. Before long, I was able to get into telephonic communication with the brigade, but only to be informed that my battalion was actually in the line, and consequently I should have to report at the first-line transport, which was situated a few miles north-eastward of the town. MacIvor, a newly joined Ensign proceeding to the same unit as myself, accompanied me.

There we spent the night, regaled with the news of the battalion by the Brigade Transport Officer, formerly a popular member of our mess.

The following day, MacIvor and I repaired to some neighbouring rest billets, where our battalion was

due to arrive that night. " D " camp, as it was called,
proved to be an assembly of Nissen huts situated
amidst some coppices not far from the Poperinghe road.
The place was intersected in all directions by duckboard pathways, and adjoining the road on one side
lay a large parade ground.

Our kits having safely arrived, I spent the afternoon
in visiting a sister battalion, which was proceeding
to the trenches that night ; there I found many friends,
with whom I remained to dinner.

My own unit was not expected to reach camp until
a late hour, so after waiting up some time I turned in.
Several hours later, at three in the morning, I was
awakened by the disturbance of their arrival, and
presently found my hut invaded by several former
companions. And thus I rejoined the battalion.

Many changes in our personnel had occurred during
my absence. Only one-third of the old battalion mess
had survived the interval of the winter, and the non-
commissioned ranks showed almost as great a change.
Our former company sergeant-major was now one of
the battalion drill-sergeants ; Sergeant Buck, my old
platoon sergeant and trusted help, was dead, killed in
a dugout by a shell which had taken off his head.
As my old company, " Number 4," was full, I commenced duty under a fresh Captain in " Number 2,"
where I found MacIvor. There, most of the N.C.Os
were strangers, but the company sergeant - major
proved to be a former platoon sergeant of my old
company whom I had known in La Bassée days. In
such fashion, one learnt from tales of either good or
evil fortune the fates of many friends or former comrades.

We had not been long in this new locality before
rumours began to reach us from the Somme. Down
there the great day had opened, but with what prospects
we in The Salient did not yet know. Ill news travels
fast : that from Gommecourt outstripped the rest.

The enemy had *not* been surprised, and there for the present we had failed. But by degrees, as more information came through, we began to realise the measure of our success. Mametz, apparently impregnable, had fallen to us like a house of cards, and Fricourt and Carnoy also. Along the southern half of our battle front the day had gone well, and still farther south the effect of our allies' onslaught had been dramatic. Reading in my Belgian billet of their great advance, I recalled to mind the hill at Bray and the mighty spectacle seen from it.

During the battalion's next tour in the line, I was at a Trench Mortar School. My course ended the day that the battalion came out. Their billets, to which they were returning that night, lay around a *château*, and it was there that I met them once again in the early hours of a summer morning.

Amid forlorn and dreary recollections of this region, the memory of this *château* stands out as an oasis in the desert. Goodness knows by what miracle so secluded a spot had escaped the enemy's attention ; we used to wonder if they intended it for a Divisional Headquarters when they should succeed in breaking through. At all events, the fact remains that we were in very tolerable quarters. The building was approached by a long avenue, behind which, screened by tall trees and a group of farm buildings, lay one of our 18-pounder batteries. The place itself had a hybrid appearance, not unpleasant with its picturesque turrets and high-pitched roof. On all sides were the ravages of two years' neglect. In many places the moat had become silted up, and the kitchen gardens had run wild. Through the grounds wound a complete system of defensive trenches. Dug during desperate days of early battles, these had remained for many months unoccupied, a silent proof of the stubbornness of the British defence lying a few miles to the north-east. Now they had come to be the unauthorised dumping-ground for sundry ration tins and other rubbish, which lay scattered in the foul mud at the bottom. In this shady retreat clouds of hovering mosquitoes held their revels. Walking among the trees, one would suddenly hear the piercing note of a whistle, closely followed by two more blasts, and see figures " freezing " where they stood in the men's quarters. It was the alarm against hostile aircraft.

Here in The Salient we were always overlooked, both from the ridges that enclosed us and from air patrols. Our positions, thus exposed to the enemy, frequently came in for shelling. We had only passed one day of tranquillity in this billet before I renewed my acquaintance with the trenches

.   .   .   .

Night had fallen before the " fatigue " of which I had charge arrived at the famous Canal Bank. Crossing by a timber bridge, we found ourselves in an open space hard by an R.E. dump. On all sides stood groups of helmeted figures, evidently other " fatigues " from the line, and presently among these scattered parties I found the Engineer officer I wanted.

An hour later found us plunging cautiously through a quagmire alleged to be a communication trench, our ears straining to catch those curiously familiar sounds which the trenches alone give forth at night-time. It is with a feeling of incredulous wonder that one returns to such surroundings after the relief of a few months' absence. For five hundred nights, the same old play of Verey lights, rifle shots, and splutter of machine-guns had continued without ceasing ; in no single hour of that time had the opposing front lines known complete rest. The idea was appalling. At this moment, I wondered whether at nights people at home were giving any real thought to what was passing in this dark and sinister wilderness. Away in London, hundreds were filling the theatres ; the plays would be in

full progress, perhaps the second act had just opened ;
and here were we, glued half-way up to our knees in
a slough of graveyard fluid, listening to a running fire
of rifle shots—and the same moon up there was looking
down on us all alike.

"Rat-tat-tat-tat!" A Vickers gun snapped its greetings, and a moment later came the moan of a wandering ricochet. In the distance, sounding dully through
the night, boomed a heavy concussion. That was
"Minnie" rolling forth her welcome at one's return.

In my position among the shell holes between the
front and second lines I fell to recalling some of my
memories of La Bassée fifteen months before. Various ideas were born of my surroundings. How many
Verey lights had been fired since I first saw one at
Cuinchy ? How many miles of trenches had been dug
since I last saw the line ? How many decomposing
bodies had contributed to the vile stench of the mud
around me ? How many promenaders had graced
Piccadilly that day, and what had been their thoughts ?
Like the Walrus, one's mind flew at times to Cab-
bages and Kings.

Dawn was breaking before all our work was done,
so we prepared to get clear of the lines before the light
should grow much stronger. Along the winding duckboards of the communication trenches our feet rapped
a hollow tattoo. The way seemed endless. It was
light before we regained the Canal Bank, and broad
day before we plodded into the drive that led to the
château and rest. We were all worn out, since though
the return march was only of moderate length, the
conditions up in the line had made any movement
there difficult and exhausting.

.   .   .   .   .

A few nights later, the whole of the battalion went
into the position of the Mortalje Estaminet, where the
state of affairs was much the same. There were hardly

any dugouts, the trenches were shallow, and traverses were often wanting for considerable distances. Here the clayish soil gave rise to a perpetual chilliness, because the whole country, even at this time of the year, was full of water. The place had been retaken only a few days previously by the Welsh Guards, and the work of consolidation had not yet been completed.

The frontage allotted to "Number 2" proved to be an unusually peculiar one; moreover, it possessed many weak points. A gap of some two to three hundred yards separated us from the rest of the battalion, the trench along that distance being impassable by day on account of the gaps blown into it by shell fire. Also, not more than one platoon was in real contact with the enemy, for the reason that, the trench being "L" shaped, only the shorter arm faced toward the German line. This lay about two hundred yards away, and was easily located at night by reason of several tree-trunks which rose stark against the sky. One tree, in particular, became noted for its sinister appearance. A solitary branch, snapped off close, stuck out at right angles from the shorn trunk, giving it the likeness of a large gallows.

On our right flank, the position formed an extensive salient intruding into the British lines; but into this the enemy had not entered. The Estaminet itself no longer existed, but its site, now represented by a few bricks around one of our sap-heads, remained in our possession. Owing to the disposition of the company, the greater portion of it was directly enfiladed by the enemy's guns—an advantage to them of which they availed themselves on frequent occasions. Still, things would not have been so bad, had the long side of our shell-swept line been provided with ample traverses, but only one existed; the remainder of this portion of the trench lay open to their artillery fire. Besides these drawbacks, a total absence of wire defences did not contribute to our peace of mind.

But in spite of bodily discomfort and harassing shelling, life here was very different from one's experiences in the past, and for a very good reason. If the enemy did venture to blow in our crumbling parapet, the means for a formidable retaliation now lay behind us. Time and again, in response to our appeal on the telephone, the air above our heads howled with the flight of an avenging bombardment. At last we had the guns.

At the commencement of our occupation of the Mortalje, a good example of the new era was afforded us. At the rear extremity of the company stood the shattered remains of a small brick building, known to us all as "Algerian Cottage." The origin of its name had become somewhat obscure, but it may have been a surviving memory of those days when the line about here was held by the French. The trench in its vicinity stood on rather elevated ground, forming a kind of keep, and it was in a narrow portion of this place that I had found a sleeping shelter. By no stretch of imagination could it be called a dugout. Here, on the afternoon of the first day, I was trying to obtain a few hours' sleep, having been actively engaged all night and most of the morning; but an unkind fate decreed that my rest should not be allowed to continue. I was wakened by the sound of heavy detonations outside. A sudden vibration shook my shelter, a deluge of dust descended from the ceiling, and for several moments heavy clods of earth rained on to the roof above my head.

To dart outside and drive the men to cover was my first care, but, alas! there was no cover worth seeking. From the ruins of Algerian Cottage spouted another volcano of fire and earth; shells were falling every minute, both over and short of us. The long stretch of open trench which separated us from Company Headquarters was being swept with shrapnel, so, as the noise of the explosions must be easily heard

there, I resolved to get as many men as possible into
shelter and to await what measures Headquarters
thought necessary on our behalf.

At regular intervals of about a minute came the on-
rushing shrieks of their shells, and instantaneously
one wondered whether *this* one would pass over as
before. If the enemy were to lift one barrage or
shorten the other, our chances would be gloomy, to
say the least of them. However, there was nothing
that we could do but bide our time patiently.

Crowded round the entrance of my shelter, and sitting
in huddled attitudes along the narrow section of the
trench outside, were assembled all those whom I had
gathered from the most exposed points. Though some
of us endeavoured to make light of the affair, our
manner was in reality nothing more than a pose. Some
of my companions remained stolidly glum, but others
ventured to cap my remarks, thereby spreading a
feeling of confidence, if not joviality.

For about an hour, the cascade of falling debris
continued to clatter about our ears. Outside, the men
were becoming cramped by their confinement; still
they never failed to greet a stray clod with uproarious
derision. By this time I had come to believe that
Company Headquarters were in ignorance of our
plight, but just as I was preparing to run the gauntlet
of the open trench, the longed-for relief arrived.

Like a swarm of giant bees, a sudden gust tore the
air above us, one salvo following another, and it was
not long before the enemy's guns were silenced.

As I turned into the trench to investigate the damage
to our position, a chorus of guffaws arose from the
direction of my late companions :

" Plenty o' blinkin' iron-rations for Fritz to-night."

" That's so, Jim, plenty o' grub waitin' 'ere, if he
wants it."

Yonder in the open fire-bay beside the solitary traverse lay a huddled mass. He, at least, would never

13

" grouse " or jest again. On him, flies were already gorging themselves. I knew the poor fellow, and as I covered his awful remains with a ground-sheet, a vague recollection of some matter concerning him came to my mind. Then I remembered : it was an increase of his allotment to his wife.

CHAPTER VII

MANY of us with the Army at this time were convinced that a new phase of the war could not be long delayed. One by one, beneath the hammer blows of the 4th Army, the German strongholds were crumbling; for down on the Somme a conflict had been opened that had, with the exception of Verdun, no counterpart in history. It was not a battle, it was a war in itself. Battle followed battle, and as the news of them spread across Europe the minds of men grew amazed.

In the Ypres salient throughout these weeks, we marked with ever-growing thankfulness the victorious progress of the New Army. Amid a holocaust of slaughter and convulsion, it was revealing its innate manhood. Theirs was that divine enthusiasm before which the materialistic force of Blood and Iron rebounded again and again. Invincible hitherto, the German Army was staggering. Signs were not wanting, even on distant fronts, of the strain to which it was being subjected: Verdun lapsed by degrees into complete quiescence, and here in The Salient their artillery fire also appreciably slackened. Now their men and material poured on a desperate pilgrimage to the "Somme Graveyard"; the ground lost must be "won back at all costs"; such was the language of German official documents circulated by our Intelligence Department.

After its last period in the line, the battalion had spent a few days at the *château*, following on which,

179

it had moved up again to the Canal Bank. Through many dreary months of war, this position had provided quarters for troops in support, and therefore its steep banks had become a gigantic warren of dugouts and shelters.

But though forlorn enough at times, it did not always appear so ; for, when bathed in the summer sun and thronged with men, it could seem quite animated and cheerful. Along a narrow duckboard path flanking its stagnant waters, groups of men sat outside their dugout doors, smoking, playing cards, or writing letters home. In some places, where lines of swaying shirts adorned the busy bank, you could see others engaged in washing their clothes. In the dugouts we were safe from the enemy's guns. The R.E. had constructed them, and right well had they done their work. Large circular vaults of corrugated iron supported the massive ceilings, and beds of rabbit wire afforded means for rest to weary infantry down from the trenches. Spanning the turbid canal in frequent places stretched slender foot-bridges, while spaced at rare intervals lay more massive ones for heavy traffic. These the enemy often shelled, hoping thereby to destroy our communications to the line.

Contrasting with the heat outside, our dugouts were dark and chilly, but these were trifling hardships in view of the security we enjoyed. Candles could remedy the one, and a woolly waistcoat the other. No longer were our meals peppered with descending dust whenever a high explosive landed in our neighbourhood ; our metal roof prevented that, though candles continued to shiver from the concussion. At times we were disturbed by the aircraft warning, whereupon we would vanish from sight like a cluster of nervous rabbits. Not that the Fokkers caused us the least apprehension. So rare and so brief were their visits, that curiosity alone would have urged us to stop to examine them ; but orders were inexorable. Within the depths of our shelters, the bursts of our " Archies " were inaudible, but we knew that they must be firing heavily. A few minutes later, in proof of this, there would come the signal " all clear."

Within the confined spaces of the embankment it was not possible to hold any parades, except the most necessary ones, such as kit or rifle inspection. These were carried out by platoons, which, lined up along the edge of the foot-walk, still nearly blocked the way to passers-by. However, kits could be inspected in the men's dugouts, so this was usually done. Life in this spot was made as easy as possible for all ranks, since what they specially needed was relaxation. These men were " the finished article ": young in the Service, but old in experience, the greater part had acquired the calm confidence of veterans.

By this time, one was able to form an opinion of the newcomers to the battalion. Loos had dealt generously with us—that is, more so than any other unit of the division—and since then, we had only suffered those miscellaneous casualties incidental to trench routine. A large number of tried and experienced N.C.Os remained, and many of the new ones were veterans of '14 returned from convalescence in England. These formed the backbone of the battalion. Most of the fresh drafts still maintained a splendid standard, and their average intelligence was perhaps higher than ever. The latent possibilities of each man, though subdued by the bonds of tradition, had become greater. Though many of us did not suspect it, the time was not far distant when this factor was to blossom forth.

．

A walk along the eastern side of the Canal Bank was well worth while to those who had grown familiar with shells. So, desiring one afternoon to explore the country, I set out, accompanied by another seeker after variety, along the paved road that ran parallel to the canal. Vanishing into distant perspective on either hand stood an avenue of tall trees, some showing their splintered trunks and lifeless limbs, others shimmering in the full luxuriance of their summer foliage. Some there were that had encountered the full blast of an explosion. These lay riven and gashed beneath their shroud of blackened leaves and tangled branches; the gaps thus formed in the ordered line of trees seemed like the missing teeth of a giant comb. The road, too, bore traces of the enemy's shell fire, for scattered in the ditches at its sides lay stones from the paved highway, and here and there gaped a shallow hole skirted by the tracks of many wheels.

Away to the south-west stretched fields and ragged enclosures, which, in those distant days before the war, had been under cultivation. Now they were left unheeded. In Man's absence wild flowers had thriven in abundance. Thousands had sprung up in the last twenty-three months, giving to the landscape an air of gorgeous disorder. Farther down the road, where the avenue took a slight turn in its course, we came upon a perfect riot of these. Mingled with their scent rose the sickly odour of decomposing flesh, wafted from the hastily dug grave of a horse. Presently, as we continued on our way, we noted above the trees less than a mile away a tall shaft of jagged masonry gleaming brightly in the rays of the afternoon sun. It was the bleached skeleton of the Cloth Hall tower of Ypres.

Yonder pile stood like a spearhead amid the surrounding landscape. Thus, as a petrified sentinel, it had remained since those epic days in October '14, marking the limit of the German onslaught against northern France. Clad in lonely grandeur, it seemed to proclaim to all the world: "Thus far and no farther." Here was one of the great memorials of the age, to which future generations would flock in idle curiosity. Doubtless preserved by a venerating people, it might endure through the next century, losing by degrees its eloquent appeal, until such time when it would be relegated by the tourist of the future to the category of a "beastly ruin." They, pitiful creatures, would reckon little of the countless dead for whom it had stood as a beacon of victory. To us whose perception had been aroused, the formal pomp of monuments seemed mean and paltry; to us, this shell-shattered pile glowed with all the glory of an Arc de Triomphe. Far from the cannon's roar, the Invalides and Nelson's Column, gigantically moribund, spoke of things they had never seen; but not so this humble fragment. There, every stone had vibrated to the concussion of a thousand guns; every crevice had felt the gas-laden wind of battle; every scar was a glorious ornament. Carved by the thrashing splinters of high explosives, designed by the God of Battles Himself, it stood triumphant above the realms of Art, another Wonder of the World.

And as we thus gazed upon it, our thoughts flew to that immortal "band of brothers," by whose toil and blood and sacrifice this monument had won renown. The Great Advance Guard of England! Here among these very hills and vales they slept, thousands of our countrymen. As yet, England was ignorant of their deeds, ignorant of that new St. Crispin's Day, when all along the slender front our forces bent and ebbed in the agony of fearful odds, enduring the onrush of half a million enemies. But some day justice will be done them,

> "And gentlemen in England now abed
> Shall think themselves accursed they were not here,
> And hold their manhoods cheap whiles any speaks
> That fought with us upon Saint Crispin's day."

.   .   .   .   .

Along the outskirts of the town we lingered awhile,

for there lay a world of eloquent desolation. Pausing before the shattered walls of bygone homes, one wondered for a moment where their inhabitants might be now—scattered far and wide across the northern lands of Flanders. On the walls you could see crumpled strips of befouled wall-paper, sodden and discoloured by many hours of rain. Here, protruding from a heap of bricks, lay a battered chair; there, surveying a devastated room, hung a life-size photograph of some departed inmate. The opposite wall had been pierced by a shell, and the floor was now heaped with brickbats and plaster. In a corner, the floorboards had been ripped away for purposes of fuel, and near by, face upward beside a flattened tin of stinking meat, lay an oleograph of the Blessed Virgin. Its tawdry frame, though warped, still stuck together; the glass had long since disappeared. In the gutter beside a fire-blackened doorway we noticed the filthy remnants of a cotton dress, dropped no doubt by its fleeing owner at the time of the great exodus. Cartridges protruded from the mud around it, trampled and pounded flat by the feet of casual wanderers.

Splattered with mud to half their one-storied height, across the roadway stood the gaping walls of a redbrick house. The window openings, gaunt and frameless, peered at us like the eye-sockets of a skull, while still stretched across the lintel of the door there hung a discoloured and bullet-marked board bearing the half-legible sign—" Boissons à vendre." Within, exposed to the sky and weather, lay a mass of filthy rags and dung. The old *estaminet* was now the hunting-ground of rats and flies, which, by their perpetual buzz, alone disturbed the deathly silence of the spot.

Hard by, in a patch of enclosed ground, the battered remains of a harrow were visible. Now they were red with rust and half concealed by weeds. On what fateful day had it last done service? Then, there had been no shadow of our calamity; the world was

gay, confident in the security born of its vaunted
civilisation. In what far-off verminous trench was its
owner now ?—or did he lie, a prey to the rats, stinking
in a hardened bed of mud ? Perhaps Fate had been
more kind, and, hanging from a crumpled scarecrow
upon a barbed-wire entanglement, his feet alone had
been eaten. There he might continue to grace the
mangled waste of No Man's Land, wide-eyed though
seeing nothing, open-mouthed though silent, dead but
uncoffined ? Looking upon those relics of longed-for
days, one was seized with a desire for devilish laughter.
What a lamentable fool is Man. . . .

Everywhere, in all directions, lay scattered the
brutality of war, the wanton destruction of inoffensive
things, the artificial bestiality of Man's own making.
If we had not called forth such doings, we had at least
to endure them ; a fate in some ways more iniqui-
tous. On the other hand, we should have had no
heart for the business but for this same outrage to our
feelings. Indignation, self-defence, and the desire to
live at peace, all these primitive instincts of humanity
bade us rise in opposition to this infamy and hurl it
headlong.

. . .

Shattering the mournful silence of the ruins came
the crash of an exploding shell. Another, bursting
close behind the drifting smoke, glinted for an instant
before its sound could reach us. The enemy were
shelling something yonder among the trees.

Ypres, though dead and abandoned, was still made
a target for their guns ; it was never safe to linger long
among its ruins. Therefore we retraced our steps,
keeping a wary eye open for any nearer approach of
their missiles, since these continued to arrive in couples,
landing with loud detonations among some poplars a
quarter of a mile distant. In such fashion had the
Huns displayed their activity for hundreds of days

past, and for hundreds of days to come they would no doubt continue in the same way. We paused to light our pipes, and then moved on.

Following a well-trodden track through the long grass, we came by and by to the canal, enclosed at this point between steep retaining walls of brickwork. In former days a system of lock-gates had evidently existed here, for we could see the remains of a huge timbered construction battered into splinters near the walls. That which faced toward the enemy had been hit repeatedly by shells, with the result that large cavities had been blown into its surface. However, the general structure seemed but little the worse for such treatment. Down below us, the stagnant canal lay placid beneath the sun, and an evil smell hovered around. Since the arrival of the summer weather, the waters had subsided, thereby disclosing the mass of putrefication which the mud contained. From these uncovered banks arose a foul miasma, around which myriads of mosquitoes played.

Proceeding on our way back, we skirted the western bank by means of a rough bridle-path, which in places wound in and out of clusters of brushwood growing along the top of the incline. Here, on the exposed side of the canal, shell craters were grouped thickly. Whenever no better target offered itself, the German gunners loved nothing more than a half-hour's shoot on to this track, and although the results obtained were hardly worth the ammunition expended, men and horses occasionally fell a prey to their sudden fire.

But this afternoon their guns were ignoring the Canal Bank. No warning scream sent us bounding to cover. Before long, the distant line of wooden railings and dugout entrances came into view on the farther side; and where a group of figures sat beside a large doorway, we recognised Brigade Head-quarters.

Crossing by means of a wooden foot-bridge, we at

last arrived in the lines, where groups of men carrying mess-tins proclaimed the hour of tea.

" 'Urry up there, Tom ! Grub's up ! "

It was, and possibly the mail also. We quickened our pace along the duckboards. Hope dies hard.

.   .   .   .

By the luminous hands of one's watch it was half-past eleven ; in another half-hour I should be relieved by one of the Ensigns. With this cheering thought I mounted the fire-step and peered around, tilting my helmet over my eyes to shelter them from the drizzling rain. Not a sound—not a thing in sight—only a few scattered stakes. These, set in a slough of mud and tumbled soil a few yards away, sloped at a variety of angles ; beyond them, enveloping No Man's Land in impenetrable mystery, drifted a nebulous wall of vapour.

What a God-forsaken wilderness ! If men must wage war, why couldn't they do it decently ? Lying in the trench beside me, in an ooze of mud, tea-slops, and filth, some of the company were seeking rest. From time to time, a grunt would arise as an uneasy sleeper wallowed afresh upon a glutinous ground-sheet. No, this was not soldiering, it was a life of pure bestiality.

A gun spoke distantly along the line—the shell would have exploded before the echo of the discharge reached us—probably some wretched devil had been hit. Far away, one could imagine the sudden cry of his comrades : " Stretcher-bearer ! stretcher-bearer ! " The thought came as a tonic. Fellow-men, British and French, were at this moment sharing this dismal vigil. Five hundred miles of sentries ! their number was inestimable.

Submerged in a war such as this, a solitary man seemed after all a very insignificant atom ; an animate one, it was true, but only so far master of its destiny as a fly in a jampot. Here we were, members of a

state of society that only a few months before had
prided itself on the scope it afforded to the individual.
Ours had been pre-eminently the era of " self-made
men." But what man makes himself ? Their claim,
or perhaps the claim made on their behalf, branded
their authors as fools ; for seemingly no man in this
world can make himself. True, many by dint of
continuous striving after a set idea achieved material
profit, but how many, once their object had been
attained, could truly claim to be men in the full
sense ? They were the very antithesis of Man : merely
automatons.

Behind me arose a noisy sound of sucking mud,
interrupting my parapet philosophy. A dark figure
cloaked in a ground-sheet emerged from the background,
breathing noisily, and clutching with grimy hands at
the streaming walls of the trench. It was the corporal
of the neighbouring section seeking his " reliefs " for
sentry-go.

" This is what I calls a perfectly blarsted night."

" Thanks. I was just thinking so myself."

At the sound of my voice the figure straightened,
letting its hands fall to its sides.

" Beg pardon, sir. I didn't know it was you ! "

" Don't mind me. A little glow of language is all
the warmth any of us will get to-night."

" I reckon that's so, sir," he agreed with a grin.

" When do you change sentries, corporal ? "

" I'm just for doing it now, sir."

" All right ; carry on."

The sound of his labouring footsteps slowly receded :
his hapless section lay in a shelter round the corner.
Once more the loneliness of the night descended on
me.

The bank of rainy mist shows signs of rising. Intently you strive to pierce the obscurity. As if in
echo of one's thoughts, and the result of an equal
suspicion, the fiery trail of a German rocket shoots up

from the darkness ahead. Darting upwards and towards us, it turns the fog below into an iridescent haze. Slowly moving shadows glide through a *danse d'apache* as, with romping and fantastic gait, they slide in and out of the shell craters. Tufts of grass, silhouetted a moment before against the bright oasis of light, grow slowly brighter as the illumination sweeps nearer on its course. Now the clinging dewdrops upon their points glisten like clusters of diamonds, and while one watches, they scintillate with the movement of the comet up above, flashing in the light like a woman's tiara. Then, as the flare swoops downward and nearer, you duck your head, for there are sharp eyes yonder watching for their prey. A gush of sparks accompanies the rocket's descent. Now comes the sound of its impact on the sodden earth, followed by an angry hiss. Beside one's face the edge of the sandbags fades in the dying light, and presently all grows dark once more as the night floods back, blacker than ever.

"That came from near the Gallows Tree." Instinctively with the thought, I peered intently in the direction where, a few moments before, the slender trunk had gleamed momentarily in the sweeping glare. No shot disturbed the brooding silence, no sound of life ; here in the night lay watchful Death. All seemed quiet—it was time to pass on.

Greedily the mud tugged at my feet as I proceeded heavily along the trench. Each step squelched loudly in the narrow way. Here and there, the fitful ray of my electric lamp revealed the oily surface of a puddle or the half-submerged slats of a slimy duckboard. Groping along a wider bend, I presently knocked against a yielding obstacle—something gave forth a muttered exclamation—it was a pair of legs. Mumbling and sighing, the uneasy sleeper settled himself anew. Perhaps for a couple of merciful hours his spirit had flown home to England.

By and by, from out of the darkness ahead came
the muffled sounds of a slapping spade. That came
from the working-party along by the new traverse.

Here, where the passage opened toward the scene
of their labours, lay the open stretch where the body
had been found when last time " in." To improve
that dangerous spot, men were now at work in the
shadows near by. There, in the dark, was the spectral
form of a stooping figure—*he* had fallen in such an
attitude ! But this was no ghost ; there was no room
for them in the trenches, they would have crowded
us out ; someone was holding open an empty sandbag for filling. Beyond, gliding to and fro against the
sky, a figure was at work on top of the new traverse.
New and clean sandbags loomed out of the dusky
trench : they would be finished in another hour.

" Corporal Adams here ? "

The figure against the skyline paused at the sound
of my question.

" Here, sir."

" How are things getting on ? "

" All right, I think, sir. We've got more sandbags
than what we need, and they're being filled as fast as
we can build 'em in."

" What about the cutting of the side passage ? "

" There's men on that, sir. No more room for others
to work just here. We're filling the bags from what
they dig out."

The new traverse was of massive construction ;
evidently the corporal was a master hand at this
job.

" You'll have to smear this side with mud before
you leave ; also the top. Get some tufts of grass on
it ; we don't want Fritz to know in the morning what
we've been up to."

" Very good, sir." The figure turned to receive
another sandbag and found it placed ready to hand.
" These 'ere things they send us now, sir, are some-

thing cruel." A punch and a slap accompanied the remark.

" How's that, corporal ? "

" They come in 'arf, sir, if you even look at 'em. We 'ave to leave enough to fold across the mouth ; you can't fill 'em right up."

A murmur of acquiescence came from the dark forms who stood around following our conversation. Apparently, many were completely absorbed by it.

" Now then, you fellows ; no need to stop work because I pay you a visit. Work's work all the world over, but at the Mortalje it's something extra special."

The corporal, hearing my remark, stooped abruptly in their direction.

" Hi ! show a leg there ! Grimwold, d'yer 'ear me ? I've been watching some of you. D'yer 'ear what the officer says ? Then shake yerselves up a bit ! "

Engrossed in his self-appointed task, he had *not* been watching them ; but that was no affair of theirs.

" Report to the officer on watch when you have finished, corporal. You must go up another couple of feet yet. Get on with the new passage at the side— and don't forget the grass."

Once more I continued the round, picking a course over the sprawling legs that occasionally barred the way.

Farther on gleamed a thin wedge of light deeply recessed in the side of the trench : it was the stretcher-bearers' hovel. A stuffy odour of stale food, damp earth, and sweat filtered past the split sandbags, which, nailed into place with cartridges, screened the threshold.

Down the trench arose a gurgle of wallowing duck-boards—another place that would have to be drained as soon as possible. Someone was approaching. A flash from my lamp revealed a pair of encrusted trench boots : it was my " relief."

Ten minutes later I crawled into my shanty, reflecting that for one night at least the rain would have driven the spiders away.

.   .   .   .   .

"This bit along here has got to be deepened." "The Captain"—our commander's *nom de guerre*— indicated the trench ahead. "Nothing must be thrown up, of course. You had better get a whole section on to it, sergeant ; you've got plenty of men who were not working in the night ? "

"Yessir, there's Corporal Bone's section."

"Well then, get them to work as soon as possible, and see that Corporal Bone understands what I've been saying."

The Captain paused a moment, as if awaiting further questions, then, satisfied that he had been understood, he turned away and resumed his tour of inspection.

"It's a rotten hole, isn't it ? " he continued after a while. "We must do what we can during the day to clean up the trench itself. All our time at night will be wanted for improving the defences. You tumble to it ? "

I did. The same idea had occurred to me the previous night. Comfort is all right in its proper place, but none but a born fool would seek it before security. Those flooded duckboards would have to wait until we had more wire out in front.

"Then you might keep a watch on Corporal Bone's lot. I'm going to turn in for a bit of shut-eye."

Bedaubed in a thick coat of drying mud, my companion turned off round a corner of the trench. Around his knees and ankles cracks indicated the top and bottom of his leggings ; otherwise, from thigh to toe he seemed a walking plaster statue.

It was perhaps an hour later when, among other points to be visited, I arrived at the portion of trench allotted to Corporal Bone. Midway along this sector, a short passage trench led into a large open space called "The Crater," wherein we kept a garrison of about a dozen men and a sergeant whose duty it was to provide reinforcements to the small post established on the site of the Estaminet. That, in its turn, lay at the end of an eighty-yard sap, which was in direct communication with The Crater. One corporal and two men formed a permanent post at this sap-head, and at night these were strengthened by the addition of a couple of bombers. Every morning at dawn, the enemy made a habit of throwing a few bombs at the Estaminet from a counter-sap of their own, situated about forty yards distant. Though ignorant of its precise locality, we had a fair notion of its whereabouts, but so far had refrained from getting the artillery to destroy it, as it never succeeded in causing real annoyance.

Our work of deepening the main trench was necessarily slow, for, as no soil might be thrown up by daylight, we were compelled to carry away the excavated earth in sandbags ; these would prove useful after nightfall. The air, as the work proceeded, became filled with the pungent smell of rotting canvas and filth, since the place had been made dry at some previous time by the simple, though short-sighted, process of dumping sandbags into the liquid mud. It must have been an awful spot ; buried in layers underneath the other we disinterred no less than three long lengths of duck-boarding. Their removal required strenuous efforts, and the men's faces, streaked and channelled with mud and perspiration, proved it.

But for the solitary explosion of a bomb, no sound was to be heard. The morning was unusually quiet.

"I wonder what that was ? " My remark was promptly answered by Corporal Bone.

"I expects it was a dirty one somebody has found and won't trouble to clean."

No doubt he was right. Though that summary

way of dealing with muddy grenades was contrary to orders, it was still the method most favoured by the men.

A minute later, without any warning, a sudden commotion arose along the trench, and turning to investigate it, I saw a figure wildly gesticulating before a dugout entrance. " Look out, you chaps ! They're coming in ! " he cried in obvious agitation. " Fritz is coming up the sap ! " For an instant, the significance of his words did not dawn on me. What on earth ailed the fellow ? Already he was striding to where one of his comrades had risen from sleep on the fire-step.

" 'Ere, mate, the blurry Allemans are coming ! I ain't codding yer." Then, seeing the working-party near me, he stumbled forward at a run, pouring forth a blasphemous warning.

I confronted him in the narrow way ; whereupon, for the first time he caught sight of me.

" What's all this hullabaloo, my good man ? "

" Beg pardon, sir, but they're coming in at the Estaminet. I came to warn the chaps. They'll——"

" How many were there ? and who sent you back ? " Quickly I glanced to and fro, making a mental note of the number of men within call.

" I dunno, sir. Most like a goodish number—nobody's sent me," he added somewhat lamely.

" Did you see them ? "

" Not exactly, sir."

" Good heavens, man, answer my question ! "

" No, sir, I didn't, but I 'eard them."

" Coming over the top ? "

" I think so, sir."

" Corporal Bone, tell your platoon sergeant from me to stand to arms at once. Warn the bombers round the corner to prepare for immediate action ! "

The next moment, rushing through The Crater, one left behind a group of figures leaping to their arms. Behind me, squelching heavily in the mud, followed an improvised orderly. Along the sap I floundered at top speed, steadying myself with one hand while with the other I pulled out my revolver. Gradually the narrow way grew narrower still ; without the use of one's arms, progress through the glutinous mud would have been impossible. At last there was only room left between the walls for one foot at a time. On either hand the slimy surfaces of the earth stretched upward, seeming as if they would presently grip us in their embrace. Then the bottom of the trench dwindled to the width of a cart rut, and at each step our feet were almost wedged tight. The way seemed endless.

The fellow had *not* been sent back ; what, then, did it mean ? The question seemed to be hammering my brain.

Turning a corner abruptly, I came face to face with the corporal in charge of the post. In the moment that followed, everything seemed as quiet as death except for the heaving of my lungs.

" What is it, corporal ? " The question came pantingly.

" They threw a bomb over, sir, and one of my men's missing."

" I've got him. What happened up here ? that's what I want to know."

" Well, sir, I can hardly say as to the rights of it. I was asleep at the time along with the chap what disappeared, and the bomb woke me up. When I had finished questioning the sentry here, I missed the other fellow."

" What have you got to report, sentry ? "

" Only that a bomb was thrown at us from the direction of that there sap-'ead, sir. I saw it spinnin' over and over ; it fell about eight yards short. After that, I heard someone splashin' down the trench wot you've come by, sir, and that's all I know."

" The other man was asleep with you, corporal ? "

" Yessir. The sentry was to wake us in half an hour, as his relief ended then."

The affair appeared clear enough in view of what they said. Roused suddenly from sleep, the fellow had jumped to wrong conclusions, and had acted promptly, but wrongly.

As suddenly as it had arisen, the alarm subsided, leaving the position free to resume its normal aspect of watchful stagnation.

CHAPTER VIII

NIGHT FATIGUE

" Diggin', diggin', diggin',
    Always blurry-well digg—in' ! "

" SHUT your ugly mouth, you !   What 'ave *you* got to grouse about, I should like to know ! "

The notes of an outraged hymn ceased abruptly, for the interruption from the darkness came from the company sergeant-major.

The aggrieved singer vanished into the night, stumbling heavily in the wake of his comrades, who glided like a string of phantoms into the obscurity.   At a short distance you could hear the occasional tap of a rifle against a water-bottle, otherwise, nothing disturbed the faint swish of trampled grass.

" Spade, spade, pick ; spade, spade—here, catch 'old !—think I'm goin' to stand 'ere all night ? "

The dawdler clutched his pick and darted out of range of further comments.   The rear men closed up, each, as he passed the sergeant-major, seizing a tool, and each in his turn melting in the shadows ahead.

" 'Oo are you ? " inquires the same voice presently.

" Reynolds, sir.   One, three, O, O——"

" 'Eavens !   I don't want to know your *name*, man ! You may be called ' Clarence ' for all I care.   What's your platoon ? "

" Number eight, sir."

" Good !   Catch 'old, and learn to give a straight answer to a straight question."

Soon the last platoon had drawn its tools at the dump and was threading its way in single file round ensnaring shell holes amid the long grass. Dimly visible in the light, outlines of heads and shoulders were constantly vanishing; above them, ends of spades jutted out like suppliant arms. So silent was our march and so slow, that we seemed like a procession of ghostly mourners. One noted with surprise the pallidness of hands and faces of those around.

For half an hour or more the column meandered onward. Beyond the skyline would gleam the fitful glare of a Verey light. Presently the rustle of some creature near at hand was drowned by the distant "toc-toc-toc" of a machine-gun, while overhead, the air became alive for a moment with long-drawn moans. Occasionally someone muttered an inaudible remark. Prowling forms showed up momentarily in the night and disappeared as silently as they came. They attract no comment, as we know that close at hand lie the dugouts of the battalion in reserve.

We were nearing the second-line system where the company was to carry out its "fatigue." Fortunately the ground was already familiar to us, and it was only necessary to check occasionally the passing landmarks. Here on the right ran a light railway line; if one followed that, all would be well. Then a dark mass appeared in the middle of the track: the ambulance trolley on which stretchers were run down by night to the dressing-station in rear. Now for a brief time it stood unused.

At last it seems that we have arrived at our destination. A shadow detaches itself from the darkness—"Yes," you reply, in answer to its question. It is the officer of R.E. who has charge of the new work.

"Then if you'll come along, I'll show you what's got to be done. Have you all got tools?"

A moment later, word was passed down for the platoon sergeants. "Platoon sergeants! Platoon sergeants!" The murmured call died away along the line. Soon, one by one, they came hurrying from out of the grey background; one by one, they reported themselves present, until they were complete. Then we moved off.

"I shall want two platoons for this job here," remarked the Engineer by and by. "It's to be a new communication trench, seven feet by two and a half. They'll have to start it about three and a half, to allow for the batter."

Fortunately I knew the meaning of the word— I nodded wisely. Next, I noticed that the line of the proposed trench had been already marked out by a few sticks.

"Sergeant Thurston and Sergeant Davis, this will be your job. Bring your platoons along and get them started."

"Sir!"

The pair vanished, and we proceeded on our ramble.

"Here we are," exclaimed my companion, stopping again before long. "I want the rest of the company brought here. I can explain what the work is while your sergeants are fetching them."

Thus, with the least loss of time, the company was put to work: one half on the trench, the other on two large dugouts.

.   .

Stooping and heaving, swaying and panting, figures around one seemed to animate the gloom. Dull thuds of picks punctuated a murmur of conversation. Standing aloof, yonder loomed the upright silhouette of a sergeant superintending the work of his men.

"Now then, Jepherson, m'lad, we can't spare you. You'll be for the Medical Officer if you works so 'ard." His watchful eye had detected a lounging figure in the act of sniggering at some pleasantry of his neighbour. Now, the fellow began to scrape his spade assiduously, and that finished to his satisfaction, he spat ostentatiously on his palms.

" Wot I should like to see is every one of 'em shoved in a sap-'ead." A lurking shadow near at hand emphasised his words with a heavy swing of his pick.

" I reckon that wouldn't suit their ticket, mate," a comrade replied. " They're all blokes of ' national importance.' 'Oo's goin' to cheer at the pictures if they 'ave to join up ? It can't be done."

" Pictures ! Blimy ! That reminds me of the rotter wot I met when I was on leave. Did I ever tell you 'bout 'im ? " The speaker heaved up a heavy clod of earth and paused to ease his back.

" The bloke as tried to pinch yer fags ? Yes, I 'eard of 'im from Tug."

" 'E 'ad some lip, an' no mistake. Why ! You could 'ear 'im explainin' the soldier parts to the bit o' fluff by his side, swankin' away like a ruddy sarjint-major, jawrin' about ' The Front ' all the time ; ' grand sport,' and all that sort o' blab : you know the stuff ! "

His companions swore by way of answer, and hurled a shovelful of earth on to the bank.

" ' Grand sport ' ! " echoed the voice, then it was choked by a fiendish laugh. The speaker paused to wipe his brow with a grimy hand and to open his shirt, for even at midnight their arduous labour caused all to sweat freely.

" What's the good o' worryin' about it, mate ? We can't do nothing," observed his fellow.

" That's true ; but, you know, a bloke can't 'elp thinking about things sometimes."

At this profound remark, I moved to where another group worked steadily in a shallow excavation. This was one of the new dugouts, already sunk to nearly two feet, for the soil was easy to work and did not clog the spade.

Here the men toiled in silence, taking it in turns to break up the ground with a pick or to shovel it out. There, one was heaving up great scoops of earth with astonishing vigour, and in consequence, tiring himself rapidly. Anyone could see that he was a new hand at this job. Yonder, putting his weight into his efforts besides using his arms alone, worked an old soldier. His body straightened and bent in a slow rhythm, never ceasing and never hastening. By watching these men thus employed, one could almost guess their length of service from their aptitude as navvies.

The night was mild. The party worked accordingly in their shirt sleeves, leaving their jackets with their rifles a few paces distant. The moon, peering fitfully from behind a gliding veil of clouds, gleamed with special intensity on their grey shirts, and in contrast, the occasional spurts of light from the direction of the front line seemed paler than usual. Abruptly, toward the east, the night was rent by a sudden fountain of red flame; then came the sound of a detonation. "Minnie" also had work on hand that night.

"Oh, Christopher! If there ain't another one come! I'm getting as raw as a cook-house carcass." A neighbouring phantom had ceased work for a minute and was peering closely at his palm,

"Spit on yor hands, you fool; didn't they learn you that at 'ome?"

"Not likely! It was shinin' yer brass, an' yer bloomin' teeth, an' such-like fallals. I always did say they wanted the skin off a feller; since I come out, I knows it."

"Garn! what's the good of talkin' silly? Blisters is yor own fault; I don't get 'em."

"All right, Rhino, you needn't start puttin' it over me like that. You 'aven't got yer stripes yet, you know."

"Nor bloomin'-well likely!" chimes in another figure.

" An' what the bleedin' 'ell do you know about it, Mister Swabface, Esquire ? You can take it from me it ain't for lack of oppertoonity I ain't a corprul. Don't I remember the Capting at 'ome offerin' me the stripes, and don't I remember refusin' of 'em ? The Capting he sez to me——" but a splutter of guffaws drowned his further reminiscences.

" Oh, cut it out, 'Aig, old sport. You makes me cry ! " A comrade seemed about to explode with suppressed mirth ; others chuckled contentedly.

" All right, mates, 'ave yer little joke," growled " 'Aig," slamming his pick viciously into the earth. " Blurry lot of 'yenas ! "

A sombre form, attracted by the general titter, appeared on the bank of the upturned earth near at hand.

" Time to close your mother's meeting down there ! I'll do all the talking for to-night. Get a move on, all of you ! " It was the platoon sergeant, who, doubtless recognising my presence, and wishing to avoid my intervention, hurried into the breach.

Then it all happened in a moment. Even as I turned in the direction of the rest of the party, I saw the sergeant leap down beside the workers.

" Cover ! "

The shout seemed to be echoed simultaneously from several points in the darkness. The next instant I was prone upon my face, tickled by the long grass into which I had cast myself, my ears humming with the screech of bullets. Swish, swish, swish ! Nearer they came in a crackling crescendo, until they lashed the air overhead with their strident reports. Swish, swish—would they miss ?—one's lightning thoughts seemed to harmonise with their rushing sound as they swept over to the farther flank. A moment later, their death notes swelled louder once more as they traversed backwards across our position. Damn the fellows ! why couldn't they leave us alone ?

Working as we were many hundred yards from the front line, it was impossible that they could have either heard or seen us. This was merely a little speculative night-firing.

A third gust of bullets, sweeping over our heads, passed whining through the night. You could hear their prolonged wail as they receded in the distance. Abruptly the machine-gun ceased fire.

For several long minutes no one stirred. Like rats we lay in hiding, awaiting further events ; but as time slipped by and none came, we began to raise our heads, furtively, and with straining ears.

Lying close to the ground, one was filled with a sense of utter loneliness. The world now seemed strangely still, and overhead the stars appeared to mock at us. Sudden squeaks near at hand betrayed the presence of field-mice. They at any rate were unconcerned at events : amid Man's wars they held high revel. My thoughts pictured Man the overlord. *He*, we had been taught, was the supreme triumph of Creation. At this moment the idea seemed infinitely humorous.

Then, near-by in the darkness, someone coughed and spat. Presently, rising with ears alert for the first sound of alarm, one passed word along to resume work. Chances had to be taken, if the work was to be finished by dawn.

A muffled clatter of iron arose as the men picked up their tools whence they had thrown them. Subdued voices merged once more into the thud of digging.

" I wonder what Fritz's game is, a-pepperin' away like that ? " The speaker, a huge fellow judged by his outline, paused after a spell of heavy picking. His neighbour, in the act of shovelling, turned his head and sniggered at the rest of the party.

" 'Ere's our Tich 'oo doesn't know there's a war on."

A snort proceeded from the direction of the Great Tich.

"Just a bar or two from the ''Ymn of 'Ate,' I guess," he resumed presently.

"'Ymn of 'Ate be damned!" replied another, pausing to scrape the earth from his spade with a filthy hand. "'Ere, you chaps, can you keep a seecrit?"

In spite of his air of mystery, few paid any visible heed to him, but no doubt many ears were cocked in anticipation. His comrades' silence evidently implied assent, for, as he resumed his shovelling, he proceeded:

"This is between you an' me an' the company cooker. My ole woman, wot's a lady 'elp at Mrs. Asquith's, she tells me that things is very bad with the Allemans. They *do* say in Downin' Street as 'ow the Kaiser 'as signed the pledge: sort o' makin' another start, you know, the usual 'umbug; 'opes to get a clean sheet outer St. Peter. Well, conseequently, Fritz's rum ration ain't wot it uster be, an' no doubt their M.G.'s got a dud deal to-night. Are you compree, monsewers?"

Once more a cackle of merriment proved that they were.

．　．　．　．　．

Glancing at my watch, I discovered that already we had commenced another day. It was nearly one o'clock; if necessary, we should work for another two and a half hours. The men still continued to labour steadily, if more silently. Fatigue was beginning to make itself felt. Still, in another hour we ought to satisfy the R.E.'s requirements, for the soil was easy and the men had worked well. By now, their shoulders were almost level with the ground.

"Beg pardon, sir." One of the platoon sergeants was approaching. "About that man you gave permission to fall out—he hasn't returned yet."

" The chap with diarrhœa, sergeant ? "

" Yessir, Drake, Corporal Finch's section."

" Perhaps he has wandered off to another squad? It's pretty dark."

" Begging your pardon, sir, he hasn't ; I've looked among the other squads for him."

" It's very strange.   How long have you been looking for him ? "

" A matter of half an hour, sir."

" He's been away a long time now," I observed after a pause.   " What on earth can he be up to ? "   The sergeant remained silent.

He seemed to be chewing the cud of deep reflection.

" If I might make so bold, I should say he has cleared out."   His tone was emphatic.

" Well, we can't waste time over one man, we've got to keep the others at it.   Put him in the report. He will turn up sooner or later, and then the Captain will deal with him."

" I reckon he has gone off home, sir."

" Perhaps you are right, but it's no good bothering about him now.   He will be dealt with later."

" Very good, sir."

I had not proceeded far upon my way before another figure accosted me : the R.E. lieutenant in charge of the work.

" I knew you would get the work done," he exclaimed amiably.   " The Guards always do somehow, but I did not count on this.   You will have completed the seven feet in an hour and a half ; do you think you could carry out a bit of camouflage afterwards ? "

" Curse the fellow ! " was my thought, " they are all the same."

" That's hardly in our line, you know," I replied.

" Oh, it's quite easy, really.   I've got one or two sergeants here who could explain matters to your N.C.Os."

" My orders did not specify any particular work,

they merely stated that we were to remain until you had finished with us. The men have dug for nearly five consecutive hours, and, as you have noticed, when they dig, they dig ; they don't scratch around like a crowd of hens."

" It will only be another half-hour extra, and in any case you will get away before dawn," he urged.

" That being so, we will do what we can in the time."

His object thus attained, the Engineer proceeded with his tour of inspection ; but this sudden addition to the night's work was ill received by the men when later on it became known to them.

.   .   .   .   .

As most of the party had finished their digging, they were enjoying a rest on the mounds alongside. Suddenly a corporal and a file of men bearing rolls of rabbit wire appeared. One by one, these were cast heavily to earth, their bearers puffing and blowing with somewhat unconvincing ardour. In turn, they were followed by scattered groups carrying turves of grass which had been carefully preserved, while others arrived with additional tufts cut in the vicinity. But for the murmured commands of the N.C.Os, all worked in silence, as a gradual depression had descended on most. But though apathy had made its appearance in the last hour, the men's curiosity began to be aroused by the work on hand.

" Wot's the game, mate ? " one inquired of another. No sooner had he spoken than the inevitable Authority hastened to explain matters.

" It's cammerflarge, old cock, that's wot it is."

" 'Ow d'yer know ? " asked a bystander dubiously.

" 'Eard Sarjint Ackroyd jawin' to Corprul Bull."

" Well, but wot is it ? "

" Wot's wot ? "

" Cammerflarge, you mug."

" Why, cammerflarge is cammerflarge, stoopid."

" Wee wee, mossoo, but wot does it mean ? "

" Aren't I a-tellin' you ! It's cammerflarge ! Ain't King's English good enough for you ? "

" Never 'eard as 'ow it was English," replied the other.

" If it ain't English, wot the devil would it be ? "

" Thort it was French, p'raps—I 'aven't ever 'eard the name, anyway."

The other snorted in contempt.

" French ! Oh, Lordy, no ! It's Egyptshun or Algebra, that's wot it is ! Wot for should the sarjint jaw French to the corprul ? You're talkin' through yer neck, you are. It's chaps like you as gives me the fair 'ump, and makes the war last so long." And with that he turned away in disgust.

But though their stupidity prevented them from understanding that " cammerflarge " meant precisely what it did, events soon brought them enlightenment.

Acting under the direction of the R.E. sergeants, small parties began to bury one end of a wire roll under a heavy bank of soil. Secured in this manner, it was unwound across the pit and cut to a suitable length. Then this end was buried firmly. By repeating this process, it was not long before a covering of wire mesh extended all over the dugout. Ample supplies of grass had been collected while this work was in progress, so that a few minutes sufficed for roofing the pit with scattered handfuls. Then the turves were placed over the newly exposed soil in order to disguise our handiwork.

The men, ever ready to enter into what they considered a new game, responded with growing interest. The mysteries of " cammerflarge " were now as clear as day. None had any difficulty in recognising in it a familiar friend, a " fake."

Shortly, as the finishing touches alone remained to be done, a large proportion of the fatigue-party commenced to collect the tools. Our work was nearly over.

Defined as dark clusters in the dusk of the early morning, some were visible putting on their jackets and equipment, while here and there strode an occasional corporal urging on his laggards. A final look round remained to be carried out, so a few who were already dressed were sent in search of stray equipment and to see that nothing should be left behind. From the direction of the assembling platoons arose a murmur of conversation punctuated by sudden laughs and exclamations ; everywhere one could observe that air of sudden animation which comes with the finish of a long night " fatigue."

Strolling casually along the ground bordering the scene of our labours, I could note the strange whiteness of the grass in the moonlight. Everything appeared in monotone, suggesting an etching to an extraordinary degree, since the illusion was borne out, not by appearances alone, but by the profound silence. Nothing moved : the world was asleep.

Ah ! Sure enough, someone was leaving his kit behind ; though how it could have got there, goodness only knew.

My eye had encountered a dark object nestling half-concealed in the long grass. But as I advanced on it, idle curiosity grew to surprise, for, lying close beside it, something long and white lay distinguishable in the moonlight. It was a bare arm.

Stooping lower, I discovered the back of a close-cropped head, and beyond it, the trunk and sprawling legs of a body ; so approaching my lamp to within a few inches of him, I flashed on the light. It revealed a grey flannel shirt, a leather belt, and the top of a pair of trousers. Then, as I directed the ray upwards to the head, something dark and glistening appeared within the patch of illumination. A second glance showed that it was blood.

Now, in response to my shout, a swish of feet approached from the company.

A glance around gave me some clue to the affair. The body lay heading in the direction of the newly made dugout, face buried in the grass, one arm tucked beneath it. It was not quite cold. A bullet entering his back had apparently passed right through him, as a smear of blood had oozed on to the top of his shirt, and the grass below was sticky to the touch.

Beside me, two figures had come to a halt: one was the company sergeant-major.

"Sergeant-major, a short while ago I gave an order for Drake to be put in to-morrow's report. You can cancel it."

"Is that him, sir ? "

I nodded.

Against his case we might write " Explained," for he had already gone to his Captain's " orders."

15

CHAPTER IX

To those accustomed to the speed of railways at home, our journey would have seemed without doubt a tedious affliction ; for us it was an enjoyable holiday. We who had passed through the toil and discomforts of a period in the line were neither critical of the slowness of the train, nor indifferent to the scenery. To sprawl upon upholstered seats, to gaze upon an ever-changing landscape, to feast our eyes on well-kept houses, sign-boards, advertisements, and, above all, women-folk, all these came to us as a rare treat ; for they were tokens of that pleasant world which we had forsaken, and in contrast with what we had lately experienced they seemed surprisingly fair and restful. Thus the battalion was filled with a mood, almost a holiday mood, to which we had long been strangers.

Far away to the eastward, receding every moment, lay the vast line of battle with all its sinister associations. No longer should we hear the dull reverberations of the guns, since we were gliding now into a new country untouched by war, passing farther and farther into the half-forgotten realms of peace and rest. The miry trenches, the night "fatigues," the stench of decaying bodies, the whirlwind rush of shells, the hazard of patrols and snipers, all these recollections were falling from us and vanishing into a confusion of jumbled memories.

Along the train arose from time to time the strains of a mouth-organ : the men were voicing the feelings

210

of all. Hour after hour the heavily laden train wound slowly through the country-side, until, toward evening, we drew near to the town of St. Pol. There, accompanied by a clatter of couplings and clank of buffers, the waggons slowed up. The R.T.O. appeared, attended by the familiar figure of the Staff Captain of the brigade, and we realised that we had reached our detraining point.

Shortly, as word was passed down by the Adjutant, the waggons seethed with activity and noise. Officers, bearing their equipment, tumbled from the compartment reserved to them and mingled with the hurrying forms of the N.C.Os, who were already urging their platoons and sections to " show a leg." From each van arose a babble of voices, mingled with a clatter of rifle-butts, water-bottles, and mess-tins.

" All change ! "—" Slough Junction, change for Windsor ! " These and other witticisms penetrated the hubbub of disembarkation.

Squeezing and jostling within the sliding doors of their waggons, the men began to descend like a noisy landslide. By ones and twos they reached the cinder track, swelling the torrent of khaki forms that was tumbling on to the rails down the length of the train. To and fro through the crowd, figures darted in quest of some missing article of equipment. " Anybody seen my gas 'elmet ? "—" 'Oo's sneaked my entrenchin' tool ? "

Presently the missing objects were discovered among a litter of empty bully-beef tins and uncleanly odds and ends upon the floors of the vans. Order began to emerge from chaos. Hurrying backwards and forwards, shouting orders here and there, company officers marshalled their platoons. Like a long disjointed snake, the battalion began to piece itself together, section by section and company by company. At a short distance, Lewis gunners were gathering around a freight waggon ; farther off, a group of officers' servants struggled with stores of rations and company mess kit.

Then, at the word of command, each platoon became an agitated swaying line as it sprang to take up its dressing : the companies were falling in.

One after another, platoon sergeants reported " all correct," emphasising their words with a resounding salute upon their rifle-butts ; platoon commanders in their turn reported to their captain, who called his company to attention.

" Company ! pi—le harms ! "

A murmur of movement arose as the front rank turned about. The men now made an avenue between which rifles became piled like small pyramids.

" Look up there, you ! "—" Over to the front with that pile of yours, Gregson." Thus the platoon sergeants as they busied themselves in correcting the alignment.

Soon, all being satisfactorily arranged, the order came to stand clear, followed shortly by that of " off packs," for word had come through that the men were to fall out. Picquets were posted at all the exits of the sidings in readiness to check stragglers, and points such as goods-sheds were put out of bounds. Lying prone in the dust, heads pillowed on their packs, the battalion reclined in a hundred attitudes, the majority soon puffing at cigarettes. By degrees, patches of blue tobacco smoke arose, and the air became burdened with a hum of voices and frequent outbursts of bantered chaff. The holiday mood, interrupted for a while by the requirements of discipline, had broken out anew.

However, at various points along the stationary waggons, scenes of bustling activity proceeded without interruption, as now commenced the harder work of unloading the battalion transport. Roped firmly in position upon the open trucks stood cookers and mess-carts. These were quickly unlashed and made ready for the gangs of transport men. Creaking and groaning, they were soon lowered down the inclined platforms by human buttresses of struggling men. Above the confusion floated the raucous directions of the superintending transport sergeants. Amid a swirl of panting figures a cooker rumbled to the ground, clattering ponderously, and swaying its slender chimney threateningly above the perspiring heads of its straining escort. An ironical cheer from the reposing platoons greeted its safe descent. So, beneath the summer sun and a growing pall of white dust, the performance was repeated again and again.

Presently a new sound mingled with the general noise. In reply to the cries of transport drivers, a drumming of hoofs arose : a frightened horse was endeavouring to rear in the confined entrance of a horse van. A judicious admixture of patience, muscle, and persuasive blasphemy met with its due reward. Where one bold spirit had ventured, others equally nervous decided to follow ; horses in ever-growing numbers appeared in the medley of the station yard. The scene began to resemble a village fair.

By and by, stalking through the forms of men, animals, and vehicles, came the battalion sergeant-major, bearing a message to all companies from Battalion Headquarters : arrangements were being made for giving the men their tea ; the battalion would parade in an hour's time.

Hereupon came a fresh outburst from the sergeants. These, hurrying to and fro, sought their section commanders, who, in their turn, " told off " their parties for the cookers. The men, already in the best of spirits, greeted this intelligence with noisy approval. A general stir and rattle of mess-tins indicated their preparations.

Meanwhile the company servants had not been idle. Down by some derelict trucks they had contrived to light a fire. Tea would be ready for the company mess in about a quarter of an hour.

The officers of the battalion, strolling about the
station yard, exchanged rumours as to our destination.
The ignorance of the Adjutant was palpably feigned,
but we were too wise to press our desire for knowledge.
Within an hour the battalion would embark in a
convoy of motor lorries, beyond that, our future lay
shrouded in mystery. With dismay we learnt a few
minutes later that our valises were to follow on the
wheeled transport. They *might* arrive toward midnight; on the other hand they might not. While proceeding over to the company servants to ascertain our
prospects of a dinner, we prayed for a comfortable
billet. From them we learnt that almost all the food
for the journey had been consumed; consequently we
should have to wait the arrival of the mess-cart.

" Tea will be ready in about a quarter of an hour,
sir."

The cook, by the announcement of this satisfying
prospect, sought to divert attention from the subject
of his misdeeds.

" But I was told that a quarter of an hour ago ! "

" Very sorry, sir. We couldn't get no water from
the cooker; they'd used it all for the men's teas. As
it was, I had to get it m'self."

The cook, grimy and unkempt as usual, assumed an
expression of unctuous rectitude. And so the old
farce went on : promises and hopes alternating with
hints of others' shortcomings and the speaker's own
martyrdom.

By the time the men were swilling down the last
dregs of their tea our own meal was announced to be
ready. By some occult means that one wisely refrained from investigating, a large packing-case had
been conjured up and draped with a fancy covering
of American cloth. The clan whose tartan it professed
to reproduce was presumably the MacIroquois. Upon
this was arranged an assortment of battered enamel
ware, and a venerable teapot, dating approximately

from the early Iron Age. This, raising a lordly spout above the clustered cups, seemed like some extinct species of hen marshalling her young. Tins of jam, butter in a doubtful scrap of paper, and a hunk of ration bread, composed our one and only meal for the remainder of the day.

Half an hour later the battalion fell in once more. The presence of motor lorries rendered the joy of the men complete.

One by one, the companies moved forward through the gates of the station and halted in the road outside. There, drawn up in a lengthy vista of canvas roofs, lay a straggling line of lorries, into which the men were presently packed under the eyes of their officers and their company sergeant-majors.

" This way, Vauxhall! All aboard, please ! "

Once more the irresistible pleasantries were speedily forthcoming, only to be as speedily repressed by the harassed sergeants. Hauling, hustling, and straining, the men, heavily encumbered as they were, proceeded to clamber into the conveyances, most endeavouring to occupy a seat upon the tail-board at the back, but from there they were driven inside in order to make way for those behind.

At last, after much squeezing and rearrangement, all were safely aboard ; officers took their places beside the driver; and the battalion was ready to move off. This it did a few minutes later, accompanied by a whirr of gears and gusts of reeking air from the exhausts of the preceding motors. Quickly St. Pol turned out to view this phenomenon, for along the foot-walks stood men, women, and children, in every pose and expression of astonished interest. Presently the town had been left behind, the last military policeman had received our broadside of wit, and we were thundering through the swirling dust flung up by the column ahead. We must have seemed a strange procession.

Here, as everywhere in France, long avenues of trees bordered the high-road. To us who had become accustomed to the dreary flatness of The Salient the country seemed open and agreeable. Wide views were disclosed from time to time. The waning sun was already low in the heavens, and across the distant landscape the approaching evening was spreading its purple mist. Like rungs of a ladder, shadows of flanking tree-trunks stretched across the white high-way ahead, leaping strangely up the side of a country cart as it crossed their track. Far and wide shimmered the mellow glow of a declining summer's day, bathing with its radiance the vivid cornfields, and glistening from the rugged bark of nearer trees. On the other hand, the rank grass of the ditches wore a dull coat of thick dust. In the wake of the swiftly moving column the air was dry and choking. Already the men on the tail-board of the nearest lorry seemed turned to stone: caps, faces, jackets, and boots appeared to have been whitewashed.

Presently, toiling wearily upon their way, a battalion of the Scots Guards hove in sight. Men, horses, and limbers were likewise thickly powdered, from out of which, scarlet hands and faces shone beneath a lacquer of streaming sweat. Here at the tail of the rearmost company the step was maintained with difficulty, and envious glances were turned up at us as we slowly came abreast. Yonder, tethered to a cooker, strode the forlorn figure of a soldier under arrest, his heavily laden escort tramping beside him. Many of the men were carrying their caps in their hands in a vain endeavour to refresh their streaming heads, and their hair, matted with dust and sweat, gave them an old-time air of Georgian Foot-guards. A minute or two later, above the dull rumble of our wheels, we heard the throb of drums and the wail of bagpipes, to whose notes the grimy platoons marched steadily forward with the resigned air of a herd of cattle.

Theirs had been a long march, for the brigade of which they were a part had travelled afoot for many hours that day.

Hour after hour these high-roads had witnessed a great migration. By battalions and brigades, by marching or by motor, the Guards Division was pouring southward through the land.

CHAPTER X

BENEATH the pallid light of the moon, the earthen walls, sandbags, and sleeping men seemed to be fashioned from a single substance: a mass of monotone. Splashed in as if by a scene-painter's brush, dark shadows lay beside the traverses and dugout doors. Numbers of bayonets, fixed on rifles that leant against the parapet, appeared like scratches on a photographic negative, and, in contrast with these, inky spectres moved slowly in the moonlight, their helmets seemingly covered with snow, their faces obscured by shadow. Rembrandt himself might have been pleased with such a scene.

As the myriads of flies had gone to rest, abandoning for the time being the human wreckage in the vicinity, the night was now still. From the fire-step of this front-line trench one could see many a grisly tenant of No Man's Land. Yonder, the body of a corporal had lost its feet, eaten away by rats, and beside an up-turned pack the moon shone luridly on a skull. Within a restricted range of vision, appalling relics lay strewn among the grass and wire entanglements, huddled and stretched in a score of different attitudes. Smitten down side by side, two fellows lay stark and rigid, the one wearing upon his face a frozen grimace of agony, the other a placid calm.

Here, only a few short weeks before, a grim tragedy had been staged. The occasion was the memorable 1st of July; the scene, the left flank of the British

218

attack. Down on the Somme the tide had surged forward triumphantly, but here it had been otherwise. Broken and mangled, dauntless men of the New Army had vainly crossed this intervening stretch of No Man's Land, and also the ground beyond. Rifles, bombs, helmets, and packs were still scattered in wild confusion among the dark silent bodies. A close scrutiny revealed something of the order of their formation, for here and there we could make out eloquent details of individual equipment. Traces yet survived to bear testimony of those frenzied moments. Clutched in a mortifying hand was a canvas bucket containing Lewis gun magazines : the carrier had been shot in the act of clearing the parapet and lay sprawling in a heap where he had fallen. Among the equipment cast aside were rusting rifles, their magazines charged full, their bayonets still sheathed. These bodies had evidently belonged to the supports. Thus shrouded by the gloom, these relics still awaited burial. The place was a Golgotha, a charnel-house, amidst which, even at this moment, one could hear the sounds of trench rats as they revelled at their ghastly work.

Then a step in the trench behind diverted attention. It was Sergeant Gill, of the Lewis guns.

" Good evening, sir. I'm thinking things look pretty quiet to-night."

" Let's hope they will continue so, sergeant."

The vast swarthy figure stepped up beside me on the fire-step and sniffed the air.

" Streuth ! " The involuntary remark was cut short by the sound of a hearty expectoration. "Them stiffs are horrible, sir ! "

A silence fell between us, broken at last by his hoarse whisper.

" There's a deal of harm comes from them pore chaps, sir ; one can 'ardly figure the amount. It's a wonder to me we don't all catch a fever. These trenches must be swarming with microbes and bacilluses. A bullet's all right—I've no objection, scientifically speaking, to that sort of thing—but swallowing dead men's germs is 'orrid. Lice are all right, too ; but microbes are different."

" Where have you found out all this, sergeant ? "

" Oh, I'm a reading man, sir, in a way of speaking. I'd done my time with the Colours and was a Reservist before the war."

" What was your job ? "

" Engineer's foreman at Birmingham."

" And that's why you took to the Lewis guns, I suppose ? "

" You're right, sir. Machinery is my job."

" I've noticed your South African ribbons," I observed. " What service did you see out there ? "

" Modder River, Bloemfontein, and various places. That was a cushy show, sir, and no mistake ; though we had our share of casualities.

" It's a strange thing how some chaps pull through," he continued by and by. " Some don't seem to have any luck at all, others don't seem to be ever without it. Look at me : there's hardly a man left in the battalion what I came out with in '14. Landreecis, Marne, Ypriss, they all took it in turn. An' then there's the general wear and tear, chaps like Sergeant Buck killed in a stray dugout. It all reckons up to a considerable total when you think of it. I've seen fellers come out here, and a month later they were shouting ' Carry on ' in hospital—nice clean Blighty ones, you know, sir. That sort gets home before they've wore out a pair of boots—a-swanking, they are, with gold stripes before they've ever seen an Alleman—others get done in almost before they've seen a sandbag. There's a deal of difference in luck. Some's bad, some's good, and some's middling : that's my class. Twenty-four months I've been on this job, and never a scratch, sir. They offered me a rest a while ago, but I didn't fancy the idea. They puts you into the police somewhere, but that isn't what you'd call a popular job. Some chaps enjoy themselves *watching* estaminays; I don't."

I nodded in sympathy. However, the sergeant's flow of philosophy, entertaining though it was, showed no sign of abatement.

" Well, let's hope the war will be over before very long, sergeant. Keep an eye on that emplacement of yours. I must have a look at the mine shaft, and if you should want me I shall be there."

" Very good, sir," came the inevitable reply.

.   .   .   .   .

Even at midnight, work on the tunnel had not entirely ceased. Far away at the end of its gloomy length gleamed the reflected light of a solitary candle where it burned in its earthy niche. From time to time there came the muffled gurgle of a pump. The narrow shaft sloped downward below No Man's Land for a hundred yards or more, this the result of weeks of labour. Scattered round the entrance of the passage lay sandbags filled by the forward working-party, a sentry beside them, while, trained upon the distant illumination at the end of the shaft, a Lewis gun stood in readiness; for at this point rumours had prompted special precautions. The enemy might be counter-mining. We did not know, but the chance had to be reckoned with. A sudden alarm echoing along the pit props, a few muffled reports—then a stream of grey figures might suddenly round the lighted corner. Who could imagine the echoes of the machine-gun within that confined space, the mounting wall of dead that would choke its further extremity?

Down in the bowels of the earth a deep silence reigned; the corporal in charge had nothing to report. As all was well, there was no need to linger here. From the trench outside, dulled by the walls of the mine entrance, came the sudden sound of an explosion. Evidently the enemy had put over another stray shell.

" What's your ammunition supply, corporal? "

" Thirty magazines, sir."

" How soon could you open fire after the alarm ? "

" Five seconds, sir. 'Number one' stops just there." His gesture indicated a muffled figure that lay asleep in the shadow of the doorway.

A few minutes later, stooping to clear the lintel, one heard the approach of nailed boots and murmured noises in the trench outside.

" I say, you chaps, do you know where the officer is ? "

A dark mass, silhouetted against the bright moon-light, paused at the threshold.

" He's here. What do you want ? "

" Beg pardon, sir, but they've just got Sergeant Gill. He sent me to tell you, and say as 'ow it was only shrapnel in the shoulder."

" Is he bad ? "

" I don't think so, sir. Seemed to me a cushy one."

I couldn't repress a smile.

" If you see him again, tell him from me we shall try to carry on. He'll know what I mean."

.   .   .   .

As the company stood easy after the early morning stand to arms, an air of tranquil repose hung about the lines. A faint mist still obscured the ragged crest of the enemy's parapet and hung like a film about No Man's Land. Within our trench the men were already engaged in sundry occupations : some splintering old S.A.A. boxes with their entrenching-tools, others wiping down their rifles, which had become coated with dew. To any but a soldier there was something incongruous in this care for their equipment, for their own persons were in a worse plight. Though only a few hours in occupation of the line, many were already as unkempt as savages. Their faces, illumined by the early light of day, seemed of a ghastly pallor, and all were smeared with a dry sediment of dust and earth furrowed by trickling sweat. The lines of their skin, emphasised by lodgments of dirt, appeared to be tattooed.

For most company officers the commencement of day routine brings a few hours' respite : now is the time for a little sleep. Through my dugout door, I could detect the cheerful sound of a crackling fire, followed later by the smell of fried rashers of bacon. Footsteps, hurrying in response to a distant call, rang sharply upon a length of duckboards and then died abruptly into silence as the earthen floor of the trench was reached once more. Near to the company headquarters a variety of noises arose denoting the preparation of breakfast. A sudden splutter of fried fat revealed the inevitable fare, eggs and bacon. Next, in response to a murmured word from the cook, someone clattered enamelled plates, then the door of the dugout was darkened by a form bent down to inform you that breakfast was ready.

The bundle of sandbags, so hard a pillow during the night, now feels irresistibly restful. Your body, enveloped in a lined trench-coat, glows with warmth, but your feet seem frozen ; these, owing to the smallness of the shelter, had projected into the trench outside. You try to count how many breakfasts of eggs and bacon you have had in the last few months, and discover that this is probably about the eighty-fifth. How beastly ! But thereupon, you remember that your breakfast, perched upon the fire-step outside, is growing cold. After all, you have a choice. Life is not so bad as it would seem. You decide for hot eggs and bacon, and heave yourself into a sitting position. The next moment finds you lying on your back with eyes swimming from a violent blow on the head. Damn that roof ! A regrettable feature of my abode was the impossibility of sitting upright in it. For this the local building by-laws were presumably responsible.

Eggs and bacon seasoned copiously with much black

grit represented breakfast to us in these days. Following that came ration bread, tinned butter, and tinned jam. The latter was often excellent. In our mess, opinions varied on the question of drinks. While most of the company officers remained staunch supporters of the tea cult, my personal allegiance was pledged to cocoa, for in it the inevitable scum of yellow grease that seems inseparable from trench tea was not so conspicuously evident. What the eye does not see, the heart does not grieve.

By and by, as the cocoa trickles by degrees to my toes, it brings them slowly back to life. The noise of one's stamping feet is secretly resented by the ever-somnolent servants in the adjoining dugout, for presently, wearing a cherubic smile, one of them emerges with a copy of a three-days'-old newspaper, *The Morning Post*. It is already familiar, but that is no reason for not showing gratitude : sometimes, even a London daily contains matter worth a second reading.

Overhead an aeroplane drones fitfully, gliding toward the east. There behind the German lines lies a world of sinister mystery. What will they see ? What will they find ? Below the vanishing speck appears a sudden blotch of white smoke, then another and another. One more day has commenced, charged with the fates of many. So, for hundreds of days past, has this drama rolled on, multiplying and multiplying again its acts of battle, murder, and sudden death.

Wandering idly across the printed sheet before me, my eye dwells a moment upon a casual paragraph:

" The bride looked charming in white satin trimmed with Brussels lace, relieved here and there on the corsage and train with orange blossom. She wore as sole ornament a string of beautifully matched pearls, the present of the bridegroom's father."

. . . . . .

After breakfast, wishing to visit the front line, I

set out down the communication trench. In our present sector, they differed considerably from those to which we had been accustomed in The Salient. Deep and amply wide, these had been well designed with regard to enfilade fire : frequent zigzags and traverses afforded a fair measure of protection. Resulting from this, however, was the fact of our inability to see ahead for any great distance, and it was due to this that, having descended an abrupt hollow which separated our front and second line, I was nearly overthrown by the sudden onrush of a man running at full speed in my direction. A glance at his face was sufficient for one to realise that something had happened.

" Where are you off to, my lad ? "

His reply came in jerks between the panting of his lungs.

" Corporal Wake and another man have just been buried by a shell, sir—Sergeant Thurston sent me down—to fetch the Medical Officer. They're trying to get them out as fast as they can."

" You'll find the Medical Officer at Battalion Headquarters most likely. Give him the message in my name. He will come if he can."

To descend the hill and rush up the farther slope required but a few moments. On my arrival in the front line, a few hasty inquiries were quickly answered by the engineers at the mouth of the mine shaft ; the shell had fallen a short distance away on the left. Soon the grating of spades grew audible, and a moment later a bend in the trench disclosed a scene of great havoc and activity. Six yards of the parapet had been blown in, and all that remained was a tumbled mound of earth and tottering banks.

Crouching low wherever they could find room to ply their tools, a party of some half-dozen men was digging into the wreckage at feverish speed. As soon as one showed signs of slackening his rate a comrade stepped into his place. Soil was scattered feverishly ;

16

bystanders received volleys of it on their legs; but no one heeded. To dig like men possessed was their only thought. Slowly the minutes slipped by; still no signs of the buried men were to be seen. Both were known to be there, but whether dead or dying or alive, none could tell. Sweat coursed from the men in steady drips, from eyebrows, chin, and nose; muscles swelled and vanished; and their breath grew laboured. To maintain such a pace was beyond the powers of human beings. Among their number, I found myself digging as I had never dug before.

" Gawd ! 'Ere's one of 'em ! "

The cry, no sooner uttered, was echoed on every side. Some dropped their spades to dig carefully in the vicinity of the uncovered leg; many tore at the soil with bleeding fingers, digging round the object as terriers after a rat. A corporal, wielding an entrenching-tool with astonishing dexterity, laid bare the head; then, with a mighty heave, the body was raised by a pair of rescuers from its grave. Quickly stooping over it, someone commenced artificial respiration while others tore open its jacket and shirt. Already the face was tinged with the bluish tone produced by suffocation.

The finding of the one inspired the party afresh in its efforts to reach the other. Presently another hail denoted that this too had been found. It was the corporal.

" Seven minutes, sir ! " Throughout, Sergeant Thurston had directed his men with impassive intentness; now for the first time did he permit his feelings an outlet. " Seven minutes," he repeated in a tone of pride, jerking a thumb toward the chaotic heap into which we had burrowed; " not bad going, sir, if I may say so."

" They've done well, sergeant. The first chap is coming round all right."

At this moment the Medical Officer appeared. A

brief examination of the ashen private seemed to suffice.

" Get him down to my place after he has lain quiet for a bit. He'll be all right in half an hour. How's the other chap ? "

Corporal Wake lay like a log, his face pallid, but showing to an inexperienced eye no trace of suffocation. The doctor inquired how long he had been buried. " That's nothing. I've heard of fellows living after forty minutes or more. I'll go on with the artificial respiration."

But he did not. In the act of beginning, his attention was arrested by something, and bending lower, he scrutinised the head more closely.

" Was his helmet still on when you got him out ? "

His face, turned to me over his shoulder, wore a puzzled frown.

" Yes, slipped on to the back of his head."

" And what was his position ? "

" Lying on his back—why ? "

A sudden silence fell upon us. Someone present cleared his throat. The doctor made no reply, but seizing the head between his hands, turned it slowly from side to side. Thereupon, pursing his lips, he gently let it fall.

" His helmet must have jammed on his head—got pressed back by the earth—and broke his neck."

.   .   .   .   .

Evening was approaching. All day an unusual quiet had reigned along our portion of the front, and throughout the long summer hours the sun had beaten unmercifully upon us, hatching forth still further legions of flies. Sheltered in the shady corners of the fire-bays, men sat in the throes of letter-writing, or devoted themselves to picking in their shirts for elusive vermin. Save for the occasional boom of a gun in the distance or the twittering of quarrelsome birds, no sound disturbed the rare silence of the trenches. Poised above the distant horizon were the faint outlines of observation balloons riding motionless at anchor in the hazy atmosphere. If the line did sleep awhile, it was with the deceptive air of a languorous watchdog.

With the advent of night, the enemy stirred from his torpor, and the manner of his wakening was sudden. The warning came but just in time. Though their lines were not more than a hundred and fifty yards away, no one heard the report of the discharge.

"Bomb up! Bomb up!"

Shouted from one sentry to another, the cry sped swiftly down the trench. Those who happened to be exposed fled to safety. A moment later a deafening crash split the evening air. The bomb had fallen over us.

In the direction of its explosion, a white bank of smoke drifted along the hollow that divided the front and second line. The trunks of a neighbouring copse grew dulled, then obscured, as the fog glided slowly across them. It was fortunate that their mortar had not singled us out as a target; we should have been taken almost unawares.

Hardly had the muffled report of their second round reached our expectant ears before the warning cry was heard once more. This time the missile was clearly visible as it shot upward from their line. At the top of its flight it hung for a moment, then, whistling and moaning in a gathering crescendo, it swept down toward our position. It was like a deep-field catch at cricket, and just as deceptive, for, approaching where we stood, it swooped over our heads with a rush. Our crouches for safety were followed by another loud explosion in the hollow behind. Earth pattered around us in a noisy cascade; then all was still.

"Bomb up!"

Once more the enemy trench mortar had given tongue, once more our breathing became unconsciously

suspended while our eyes followed and estimated the
course of the oncoming projectile. Wobbling slightly
in its flight, *this* seemed heading straight for us. This
time we were sure! The conviction had scarcely
been born before we parted right and left in a con-
vulsive dash to escape. The air was filled with a
ghastly wail; the earth quivered beneath and around
us; and a heavy detonation buffeted our ears. Thud-
ding and breaking on impact, large clods of earth pelted
into the trench on all sides. Then came the rain of
dust. Standing up a few moments later, we perceived
some ten yards behind the parados a freshly exposed
rim of earth, above which hovered a pall of dust and
smoke. "Fritz" had missed again.

.   .   .   .   .

The day of our relief had dawned in auspicious
fashion, a common knowledge of our impending rest
calling forth a general light-heartedness. Throughout the morning, the company had busied itself in
scouring the trench and making ready for the
arrival of the incoming unit. Dugouts were swept,
fire-bays cleaned up, and all those sundry duties performed which are commonly expected of a battalion
about to hand over its position. Scavenging parties,
loaded with an accumulation of refuse, clattered to
and from a primitive incinerator. Back in the store,
the company sergeant-major toiled with apparent
ease at the task of checking supply lists, while,
marauding around with ever-watchful eyes, officers
supervised all proceedings.

A company from a battalion of the South Stafford-
shire Regiment was expected to make its appearance
about 2 p.m., so it was arranged that the work of
cleaning up should be completed by the men's dinner
hour. This was done accordingly, and by 12.30 all
was reported correct in the front line.

Scattered in gossiping groups about the fire-bays,

the men abandoned themselves to their own devices, some arguing over a venerable newspaper, others, pipe in mouth, basking lazily in the sunshine. The air hummed to the sound of flies, and, emerging from their myriad nooks, beetles and other insect life paid homage to the summer's day. To and fro, winging their course around the parapet, flitted elusive butterflies, whose satin wings contrasted brilliantly with the background of sky. Blending with the voices of nature, countless chirrups arose from invisible grasshoppers, who, from their forest glades, now raised their hymn to heaven, thereby humbly endeavouring to rival the melody of a lark high overhead. Rising and falling in an endless torrent of sound, this seemed to pour forth the utterance of a fairy world.

No warning heralded their onrush, no rising wail was heard; amidst a confusing concussion and rush of detonations the enemy's bombardment smote our ears. Before our bewildered gaze, sandbags leaped convulsively into space, soil splashed like water, and the gates of hell seemed opened upon us. Dazed and scorched by the sudden blast, one found oneself sitting on the floor of the trench in an avalanche of earth. The Captain, with whom I had been speaking but a moment before, had vanished from view; the freshly scoured surroundings were now a tottering mass of smoking debris; and in my mouth hovered a taste of choking gas. A Whizz Bang had crashed into the parados midway between us: only by a miracle was I alive.

" Are you hurt ? "

His voice arose from around a corner where a passage led into a front fire-bay.

" No! Are you ? "

My fears were allayed a moment later by his appearance. Though covered by dust from head to foot, he seemed quite unharmed. My own condition was no doubt just as dishevelled and scared, because, viewing one another for an instant in surprised incredulity, we burst simultaneously into peals of laughter. And in this fashion were we discovered by a couple of anxious sergeants, who had come up the trench expecting to find a pair of corpses.

The enemy's fire, however, showed no signs of slackening. Into the welter of shell fire there now arose the deafening din of *Minenwerfen*, whose shattering detonations punctuated the storm of 5·9's. Already the copse adjoining our left flank was obscured by a cloud of fumes and smoke, and every moment we expected to witness a terrible calamity; since, heaped in a great pile, there lay yonder an unsalved dump of 60-lb. trench mortar bombs, relics of the days of our unsuccessful attack on July 1st. The Captain had already made off quickly down the communication trench with a view to calling up our artillery retaliation.

Crouching in our dugouts, which trembled to the vibration around us, we could hear above the turmoil outside the splintering upheaval of the neighbouring trees and picture in our minds the ruin of all our improvements. A few moments of such shelling would suffice to sweep away the labour of many nights. Now, over to our right, resounded a gust of heavy explosions, and five minutes later, flying at top speed along the quivering trench, there came a messenger bearing the news that the right flank platoon had been caught by a shower of projectiles.

Before long, acting on his own discretion, Sergeant Davis appeared and reported the partial withdrawal of his men. Through the platoons, now uncomfortably crowded into the centre fire-bays, the order sped to stand to arms. As an attack seemed imminent, breech covers were cast off, magazines inspected, and all preparations made for rushing to the fire-steps. Darting from one emplacement to another, I assured myself that the Lewis gunners were in readiness to man their embrasures, that the bombers lacked no reserve of hand grenades, that the S.O.S. rockets were ready in the event of a sudden crisis.

But these never reared their desperate appeal, there was no need; for crashing abruptly into the thunderous echoes of the bombardment, and thrilling our ears with the tempestuous opening of their titanic music, the voice of the British guns smote earth and heaven. Rolling, echoing, and drumming across the atmosphere, bounding, beating, and pulsating over the intervening ground, they raised their awful hymn to the God of Battles. The air above us, swept by the screams of a thousand demons, now lashed itself into a frenzy.

Something struck my shoulder and bounded to the ground. A half-curious glance showed it to be a fragment of shell-case, evidently newly spent, since otherwise it would have pierced the cloth. But at such a moment as this it was a trifling incident worthy of no further thought. Next came the onrush of a salvo of shrapnel ripping and tearing above our heads. Evidently the enemy had anticipated our concentration in the centre, for they sprayed the neighbouring firebays with their leaden splatter all along our contracted front. By another miracle no man was hit, though more than one steel helmet turned a vicious blow.

The men were ready; the machine-guns were ready; and all that we now desired was the appearance above their parapet of the German storm-troops, for then the plunging gunfire around us would cease. Watching through a periscope for that supreme moment, one beheld a scene of dreadful joy.

Around their parapet there flashed a livid turmoil of fire and flame, in whose vortex whirled many black shapeless objects. The position, resembling already a volcanic eruption, seemed to agonise in an inferno. Convulsion seized it as each salvo struck home, shooting skywards a mingled lava of earth, beams, and mangled things. Lurid pillars of fire gleamed upward left and right, splashing around their streams of orange, red, and yellow; and as they vanished like lightning flashes, they left behind them a rolling sombre pall. Smashing and rending in a ceaseless torrent of blows, the blast of our shells seemed as the frenzied fury of a giant maniac. Before our eyes Bellona had gone mad.

And as the minutes sped by, our spellbound gaze became blind to all other things; the world held but one spectacle. No longer did we heed their fire, indeed, we never felt its faltering onrush, or knew the moment of its final ending; for the scene that fascinated us was a revelation, a promise of things to be. There, in the heart of its fearful conflagration, we saw the dawn of a coming day!

CHAPTER XI

THE SOMME FRONT

OUR forecasts were justified by events: the end of August found the division billeted in the back-area of the Somme front. Our own brigade occupied the village of Méaulte, which lay at no great distance from the district we had visited in the spring.

Here we discovered an unusual amount of scavenging was necessary before the men could occupy their quarters with any hope of comfort, for, owing to the ceaseless flow of troops, the place had become exceedingly dirty. During the first couple of days, the entire brigade applied its energies to the question of sanitation, and a great improvement was soon achieved in spite of some opposition from the inhabitants. These, by wholesale speculation in sundry groceries and stores, were in a fair way of amassing what for them must have seemed small fortunes.

As at this period great blows were being struck all along the line from Thiepval to Leuze Wood, the country-side contained a mass of troops, either awaiting their turn to pass up to the front, or making their way back to army reserve. The great belt of woodland defences had fallen; we were now battling our way forward to the Ridge.

In anticipation of our coming share in the offensive, the battalion started special training in " the attack," and, progressing in this, it soon took part in a series of brigade field-days. To make the best of what time should be left us became our chief concern. Looming nearer and nearer with every new day, our own hours of trial were approaching.

Almost every day fresh news of the Allies' progress came to hand, either an announcement of a further British success or of equally cheering news from the French Army to the south. Thus, on August 24th, the fall of Maurepas became known, followed on the next day by the announcement of our progress southward of Guillemont. Each succeeding day brought with it news of fighting at some point or other, because, as soon as our operations ceased, the enemy delivered a counter-attack. These failed completely, notwithstanding their ferocity and frequency.

The first week in September was marked by a storm of fighting, which, day and night, echoed across the neighbouring country. On the 3rd commenced one of those phases that, like the seventh wave of a tide, seemed to repeat themselves periodically throughout this conflict. It was a day of Allied victory. Guillemont in the centre of the British attack was overrun, also Ginchy ; but from the latter we were ejected by a counter-thrust delivered by the Prussian Guard. Meanwhile the French had been busy with the capture of Clery and the investment of the southern outskirts of Combles. As a result of these operations, two thousand prisoners and a dozen heavy guns fell into their hands.

But, menacing though this advance was to the remainder of the German positions on the high ground, it was soon surpassed by the great attack of the 5th. By the evening of that day, the British had penetrated a mile beyond Guillemont, occupied the whole of Leuze Wood, and had arrived within a thousand yards of Combles on the north-west.

It was while we were watching the spectacle presented by the flaming sky that very evening, that news of this great success reached the battalion. In

addition, we learnt that a new French Army, the
10th, had suddenly opened an offensive along a frontage of twenty-five kilometres between Barleux and
Chaulnes, everywhere over-running the enemy's positions and taking another four thousand prisoners. On
receipt of this news, we were warned to hold ourselves
in readiness to move at short notice. This order
created much speculation and no little excitement.
It was felt that anything might be expected to
happen at almost any hour.

Something of the electrical state of the atmosphere
seemed to have entered our minds since our arrival on
the Somme. The daily series of battles had become
not only an engrossing drama of vast magnitude and
significance to ourselves, but had now come to occupy
the attention of most of the world.

Day and night the entire country-side pulsated with
the fire of the Allied guns, which, even when it rained,
showed no signs of slackening. It was especially by
night that the conflict assumed its most spectacular
form ; then, the heavens blazed with an unearthly
glare. Against a background of flickering fire, one
could see the dark outline of the Ridge, and note the
direction of the heavy guns, whose every discharge
caused a fan of summer lightning to play across the
horizon. At this time, when two great nations were
locked in a death grapple every day and night trembled
at the grandiose scene. The guns knew no rest nor
ceased to hammer earth and sky.

Lying abed at night, we grew accustomed to the
ceaseless rattle of the window casements, and no longer
heeded the noisy vibration of the few remaining panes.
Curtains of split sandbags, screening the open aper-
tures, palpitated backwards and forwards with the
aerial disturbance of the guns. Shaken by the dis-
charges of the howitzers over by Albert, even the walls
quivered convulsively, while the whitewashed ceiling
by the window flickered in response to the storm

outside. So, assailed by the hundred-fold notes of
the British artillery, ears became deadened, and sleep
stole over us at last. Gliding by degrees into a peaceful world, one grew unconscious of the echoes of the
night.

Although darkness rendered the drama more impressive, nevertheless a wonderful sight was to be seen
by day. To accomplish the short walk from Méaulte
to Albert was truly to witness a national pageant.
There, a concentration of fighting energy was displayed
sufficient almost to win the Boer War; all within the
bounds of one man's vision. It was not so much by
the number of troops, though these attained many
thousands, but rather by the latent capacity of the
material burdening the landscape that the spectator
was impressed.

Yonder, where additional railway tracks had been
lately completed, stood long platform-cars of iron
supported on multiple bogie carriages; but it was not
upon these great chassis that the eye dwelled, for all
their imposing bulk, but upon the vast forms
that snuggled on them like beasts in their lairs.
Stretching into the air their long mouthing snouts
arose ponderous forms of 15-in. guns, mammoths
among ordnance. These, grouped at intervals along
the curved railway track, comprised the great bassoons
of Britain's orchestra; here lay the produce of toiling
Woolwich and the lusty men of Armstrong's. Theirs
were the prodigious missiles that, speeding over the
clouds at a height of 15,000 feet, filled our ears with
the shriek of a hundred Valkyries.

Beyond, aligned in ordered rows, battery by battery,
stood a park of pigmy brethren. These were the
18-lb. field-guns—of no great account, one might be
tempted to think—but ask the army of von Arnhim!
These were they whose flaming sleet thrashed down
the massed counter-attacks of Germany; these were
the barrage-makers! At a short distance, rising in

tier above tier of wooden boxes, lay pyramids of munitions : food for the 18-pounders, the 4·5 howitzers,
and the 6-in. field-guns. Long and short, lean and
squat, field-gun, howitzer, naval gun, and giants of
the R.G.A., all might draw their daily rations without
fear of the morrow, for behind these mounds of supplies, flowing ever forward to the front, now rolled the
death-torrents of industrial Britain.

To turn in whatever direction you chose was to
encounter further amazement. There, where the rail-
road skirted a row of silvered poplars, engines of half
a dozen great railway companies at home snorted to
and fro, each thinly disguised beneath a service coat
of paint. Behind them, laden with hundreds of duckboards and miles of barbed-wire coils, trucks were
being shunted amid a continuous clink of couplings.
Down the Albert road, ceaselessly engaged on the up-
keep of the highway, worked a familiar friend of other
days : an English steam-roller, complete even to the
prancing horse that adorned the front of its boiler.
Even these had been mobilised and put into uniform.

But these sights belonged to no particular roadside ;
they covered the landscape, they mingled into the
picture of encampments and bivouacs. This memorable scene was composed of something more than
several divisions of troops, something more than a
scattered mass of artillery and engineers' dumps. Here
lay a tangible proof of England's will, a token of what
the folk at home had undertaken on our behalf.

Gazing at this vast display of industrial power, one
seemed to feel in one's ears the roar of a hundred
thousand lathes and the tumult of a thousand steam
hammers ; see the forests of swinging cranes and the
multitude of humming fly-wheels ; feel on one's cheek
the blast of heated air, as from their boiling oil-baths
arose the molten shafts of a thousand guns ; taste the
acrid smoke of four thousand munition factories ; and
to feel in one's heart the pulse-beats of two million

artisans. Truly each soul of them, man or woman, formed a link in Britannia's coat of mail.

Speeding slowly upon their various errands, long convoys of motor lorries swung past, spraying the unwary pedestrian with a muddy douche, for the recent rains had converted the road surface into pools of water. Behind these came an endless column of waggons. The legs and bellies of the horses streamed with fluid mud, which adhered to them like sugar icing. Everywhere, threading their way through the profusion of stores and equipment, squads of horse and foot meandered on their way. From beyond this sea of humanity and material, over the distant ridge toward Thiepval, where a thin haze rose into the wind-blown rain clouds, came the sullen clang of guns. Blending all into a tempestuous harmony, dominating the impressions afforded by the scene, there rolled an everlasting peal of gunfire. This, more than anything else, represented the spirit of our surroundings. It was the voice of the Somme.

.   .   .   .   .

By ascending the hill that lay eastward of Méaulte, a wide view of the reconquered territory toward the north and east was to be obtained; but, impressive though the panorama undoubtedly was, it fell far short of the audible effect provided by the constant bombardments. The music of a modern battle transcends all other impressions. Over the line of the ridge to the northward jutted the tower of Albert Church. Its diminutive outline resembled a cardboard structure on a stage, and the leaning figure upon its summit appeared at a distance as if in the very act of giving way. It afforded a conspicuous landmark, and for that reason perhaps, it had been made a target for many a German gun. Beyond it, far away in the distance, rippled the flashes of our own artillery as they flickered to and fro across the murky face of the country.

Upon the skyline gushed sombre fountains of black smoke cast up by exploding projectiles. These, rolling aloft in irregular patches, stretched like a wall of fog toward the south. Even as one watched, a cluster of eruptions ascended from the direction of Thiepval. It was indeed a strange sight, for, blended in weird contrast before one, lay mingled the sinister effects of gunfire and the mellow beauty of an autumn evening. Beneath the evening glow the country looked really lovely.

Away on the right stood Mametz Wood, thinned like a great field of bare hop poles, and beyond it again loomed Delville Wood of bloody memory. There, even after an interval of several weeks, lay numbers of decomposing bodies, poisoning the surrounding air for a mile or more ; or so say those who have visited it. These woods appeared as if they had been miraculously transplanted from some dead planet. Seen earlier in the year from almost the identical spot, they then had spread across the land their billowing clusters of verdure ; now not a leaf remained. The blight that had come upon them was more bitter than any known to winter. They were not merely withered : Delville, Trônes, and Bernafay had been exterminated.

To search the foreground for a sight of Mametz was a waste of time. Battered and torn, it had still been easily visible in June : September found it wiped from off the face of the earth.

Turning homewards, one was confronted by a final spectacle. Receding across the undulating land spread the camps and bivouacs of an entire corps : transport lines, cavalry lines, infantry lines ; artillery, motor lorry, and Army Service parks squeezed and jostled each other in an endless mass. Englishmen, Scotsmen, Irishmen, and Welshmen ; Australians, Canadians, and New Zealanders ; almost every British clan was represented yonder. Such an assembly the world had never seen. Seething in a turmoil of dust, spreading to the horizon its uniform tone of khaki, eddying like a plague of ants, the concourse shimmered in the western vales. The scene was unforgettable. There was massed the British Empire on parade!

The setting sun dipped below the distant background, spreading afar its golden beams, and as it sank from view a thunderous peal saluted its departure. Screeching along their aerial paths like a troop of wind-fiends, a salvo of heavy shells passed overhead. To the southward, clamouring sullenly, rose the voice of the French 75's. Their throbbing boom filled British ears with their monotonous refrain: "Verdun, Verdun."

Majestically, the heavy guns of England fling forth their resonant reply, which, rolling across the darkening world, echoes from hill to hill: "Somme, Somme, Somme!"

CHAPTER XII

IN ever-changing hues, the colours of the landscape alternated from gold to grey as rain and sunshine pursued each other over the undulating panorama. Across hill and vale, dark shadows of clouds glided on their headlong course as if engaged in a gigantic steeplechase. As far as eye could see, encampment after encampment of horse and foot lay dotted thickly over the land, their mottled tents looking like corn-stooks in autumn. Such was the view that greeted us as the battalion topped the summit of the ridge beyond Méaulte.

Against our faces we could feel a refreshing breeze, which bore upward from the valley below the muffled sound of drums. Slowly ascending the hillside across the valley, a battalion of our brigade trailed ahead of us. The sun flashed in time to their step as its rays were reflected on the polished drum-case. Following them marched another battalion, nearer to us by several hundred yards; it was the sound of their music that we could hear.

The appearance of these two masses of men, together with our own and that of the other unit behind us, had aroused the attention of the neighbouring encampments, whence a steady flow of men flowed toward our line of march.

For many long weeks, both the Army in the field and the people at home had expected our coming and had wondered at our tardiness, not realising the great quantity of our reserves, or the fact that we had been holding the line in other sectors. But for several days it had been known throughout the district that the Guards were coming up, and here before their eyes the event was taking place.

To sound of drum and fife, battalion after battalion was following in the wake of Rumour, tramping steadily eastward toward the echoing skyline. The entire brigade was visible at a glance : a huge ribbon of men that stretched across the entire landscape. Even to ourselves the sight was fine, for there could not have been less than 4,000 men in view.

Along the highroad hundreds of troops awaited our arrival. As we came up with them, these gazed critically upon our ranks in evident surprise at the presence of our drums, whose pipe-clayed cords and heraldic scrolls bestowed a splash of colour to the scene. Along this crowded roadside, we, the representatives of the past, met for the first time those stalwart hopes of the future, the Anzacs. Eye met eye and smile answered smile as the tribes of Anak came face to face, and many there were among us who drew themselves up an inch or so, or held their heads more erect, for the honour of the Home Country. Thus, amid a peal of fifes and a rattling of drums, the Old defiled before the curious gaze of the New, and the ends of the Empire met for a moment in Imperial fashion.

Halting by and by, the battalion fell out along the side of the road and quickly fraternised with the onlookers, large and powerful men of New Zealand, who seemed surprised that we required the aid of music on the march. Our meagre explanation that to do so had always been our custom in the past seemed to puzzle them still more. Viewing " The Drums " near to, they were interested to hear that the " dago writings " were past battle honours of the regiment. " Oudenarde " and " Salamanca " were devoid of all significance, but " Waterloo " was admitted to be a " proper scrap."

Presently the order came to fall in once more,

and from a crowd of jostling figures the ranks gradually formed themselves anew, company by company, the battalion setting itself in motion like a vast serpent. Down the hill-side the column made its way, now taking up the drumming of the battalion in front, which, as it climbed the farther side, had ceased to play. Swinging forward at the long measured pace of the Foot-guards, companies moved off at regular intervals. In rear of each rolled Lewis-gun carts, drawn with ropes by lusty teams. Far ahead, down the vista of swaying heads and rifles, I could see the figures of the Commanding Officer and his Adjutant; for " Number 2 " was preceded by many platoons of marching men.

Then, in its turn, the head of the battalion rose into view as it began to mount the upward gradient. Above the serried ranks emerged the whirling drum-sticks, and sweeping toward us, unimpeded by the intervening mass, came the sound of pealing drums. But these ceased their play after a while, for the hill was steep and long. Booming faintly in our ears, their echoes seemed to linger on the hill-sides.

Behind us, the rearmost battalion was already debouching over the skyline, their accoutrements saluting the sunshine at a hundred points, and their ordered mass flowing forward down the slope like a sparkling river. For a moment it seemed as if a sudden volcanic agency was causing the hill to erupt from its crest a stream of fighting men.

A quarter of an hour later, topping the rise before us, we beheld the distant battlefields of July and August, which, now swathed in a veil of autumn haze, glinted here and there with the flashes of artillery. Glancing backwards for a last view of the valley we had crossed, one saw the oncoming battalion crossing the hollow. The farther slope was smeared by a scattered trail of sightseers returning on their homeward way. The drums were hushed and silence had returned once more. The Guards had passed.

A RESONANT boom shook the entire dugout and echoed loudly across the valley ; even the candles beside us quivered with surprise.

" This is too much of a good thing ! Why on earth didn't we do as ' Number 3,' and rig up a tent outside ? I'm off to where it's quieter." The speaker threw down his newspaper and rose to his feet, thereby upsetting the 18-pounder box on which he had been seated.

" Good heavens, Raymond ! To hear you talk one would imagine you didn't know there was a war on," cried the Captain.

" Or from the way you block up all the light, you supposed you were transparent," exclaimed another member of the mess.

" Well, it's not my fault there's no window to our 'appy 'ome. The Mess President ought to have thought of that when he fixed on this hole." Hereupon Raymond disappeared up the steps of the doorway.

Silence reigned awhile within the company mess, broken only by the gurgle of an exceedingly foul pipe. Then, once again, the motionless flames of the candles jumped convulsively, while in our ears rang the deep notes of another discharge.

" Plenty of stuff flying around to-day," murmured

The President, peering up from the letter he was engaged on.

"There was more in the night over Ginchy way," replied the company news-purveyor. "They say the Welsh had a very warm time of it."

"Where did you get that from ?" inquired The Captain somewhat dubiously.

"Joey told me when I met him just now. They are supposed to have lost a whole crowd of people in one company. The Huns attacked after shelling them to hell."

"Sergeant-in-waiting to see the Captain !" The voice of one of the servants sounded from the steps outside the entrance.

"Tell him to come in."

Stooping awkwardly, a figure appeared in the doorway and saluted. "From the Adjutant, sir—the battalion is at an hour's notice to move."

.   .   .   .

Lunch-time found us all ready for a speedy departure from Carnoy, with kits prepared and every preparation made for a strenuous period in the line. With the announcement that lunch was ready came the arrival of an unexpected guest, a subaltern from a sister battalion in our vicinity.

"Come in, come in ! We're just dying of boredom. Have you any news ?" The President, acting as host, manœuvred an empty box into position with his foot. John, the new-comer, gazed round portentously; evidently his manner was intended to impress. One by one we feared the worst.

"Well, I don't know whether you folk will call this news, but it's 24-carat fact," he announced. "The hush-hushes are here."

A groan went up from the assembled party.

"My poor fellow," exclaimed The President, "if that's all you can tell us, clear out and report your-

self to your M.O. We are accustomed to lies
these days, but stale ones aren't popular with *our*
battalion."

At this outburst John grinned benignly, since it
denoted the atmosphere he so much desired ; then,
leaning forward across the table, and emphasising his
words with a tattoo from his fork, he delivered his
news.

" I may be first cousin to Ananias and all the rest
of 'em, but what I tell you is sober fact. I've seen
'em."

Five pairs of incredulous eyes contemplated him in
grave silence.

" Where, if I may ask ? " inquired The Captain, in
his suavest tones.

" At their depot, not three miles from this dugout.
Oh, you may smile ! But grinning like a beauty
chorus won't alter facts. I've seen 'em and I've had
a long talk with one of their pilots."

" You aren't rotting, are you ? " The President's
manner showed signs of irresolution.

" Never more serious in my life ! They absolutely
beat the band. There's two sorts, male and female.
The gent carries light quick-firers ; the lady, being
naturally more talkative, spouts machine-gun bullets.
They are said to be proof against anything but
a direct hit from a shell, and do four miles an
hour along a road—caterpillar driving bands, you
know. The crews are priceless ; try to make out they
are sort of land marines, and jaw about ' His Majesty's
Land Ship *Hotstuff*.' They might have been pulling
my leg—probably they were—but the Admiral in
charge told me they could stroll through the walls
of a house or snap a two-foot tree-trunk like a
match."

A long pause greeted this narration, for the news
seemed utterly incredible.

" John ! " exclaimed The President at last,

" either you are the greatest liar in the British Army, or——"

" Or ? "

But The President remained dumb, his imagination still failing to realise the marvellous alternative.

The ensuing pause was ended by the judicial tones of The Captain.

" The yarn would have been quite good enough without your telling us you had seen them."

" But I have, yesterday afternoon. Come and ask our Adjutant ; he was there too."

" You've *seen* them ! "

" As near as I am to you now. You've my word for it."

Something in the speaker's tone compelled belief. Then the amazed silence which had fallen upon the party was shattered by a crash upon the table as Raymond sprang up with a terrific yell.

" My godfathers ! The Bing Boys *are* here ! "

.   .   .   .   .

Outside the Headquarters marquee the heavy howitzers thundered in the dusk of the evening, yet above their echoes the voice of the Commanding Officer rang clear and incisive. Guttering candles flung heavy shadows across the map-strewn table at which he stood, casting into strong relief the features of those crowded around. The conference was a momentous one. Deaf to all that went on outside, we dwelt eagerly upon every word addressed to us, as on our proper understanding of the matter would depend, perhaps, our lives, those of our men, and the honour of the regiment.

" The battalion will therefore be on the left of our 2nd Brigade, and by this arrangement you will see that all battalions of the regiment will be alongside each other. I don't believe that has ever happened before. You have three lines to take; the fourth, if all goes well, will be dealt with by the Irish Guards, who will come up through us. I don't think there is anything more that I have not told you, but if any of you wish to ask questions, now's the time."

"Are we to understand, sir, that the Tanks have nothing to do with us ?" inquired someone, after a pause.

"As far as you are concerned, nothing whatever. They will act according to their own programme."

"And if there are enemy aircraft about when the time comes to show our flares ?" asked one of the front-line company commanders.

"You must do all you can, Charles, to keep your-self unobserved."—Our laughter quickly subsided.—"There's no rule ! You'll have to use your own dis-cretion. If the gunners don't know where you are, the barrage may go wrong. You *must* realise the im-portance of keeping up with the barrage. I don't suppose there will be much interference from the air, but if there is, remember the barrage is your best friend. Any more questions ?"

Apparently there were none.

"Company commanders, stay behind; I won't keep the remainder any further."

And so, with the customary leave-taking, the Colonel's lecture on the impending action came to an end.

It was about an hour later that I, sitting alone in our company mess, was accosted by The Captain.

"Hullo, I've been looking for you," he exclaimed. "I'm sorry, but I've got orders to leave you behind."

"Leave me behind ! "

He nodded, then, divining one's thoughts, he added: "All the seconds-in-command of companies have got to, except in Number 4. Jenkin remains with your party."

I was dumbfounded, but he only smiled ruefully.

" In case of accidents, you know." His comment, uttered in a low tone, did not allude to me.

.   .   .   .

The great day being now at hand, all through the following one the battalion remained at rest. At dawn on the next morning the Guards Division would open its attack.

To cheer our last hours in camp, came the news of the fall of Combles ; the air around seemed infected with the feverish spirit of success. Now that the last hours were running out, we could not help feeling something of the gravity of the occasion. But, however wise the decision as to seconds-in-command, those concerned could not help feeling a sense of being baulked of their share in the doings of the morrow ; worse still were those moments when we thought of the possible fate of our comrades.

To wander round the company lines involved being accosted from time to time by stray N.C.Os whose fate also it was to remain behind, and replying to their entreaties, one realised how insignificant were personal feelings in relation to the great undertaking of the battalion. Before long, stalking me at a short distance, came the company sergeant-major. He, too, was one of the derelicts.

" Beg pardon, sir," he exclaimed at last, catching my eye, " could I have a word with you ? "

" Of course, sergeant-major, what is it ? "

" About to-morrow, sir. I can't stay behind when all the chaps are going in. Isn't there anything you could say, sir, to the Captain so as to let me go ? I'll do anything."

" Sergeant-major, don't imagine I can't share your feelings, but just get this fact into your head : what you'll do is to obey orders, just as I have to. I don't like it, you don't like it ; but for the present that is our job. I can't haggle on your behalf any more than on my own. Try to be reasonable. Our time may come later."

For a moment he gazed sorrowfully into space. There was no doubting the man's disappointment.

"What you say, sir, is quite true," he murmured disappointedly. "But it's cruel hard luck all the same."

"I've been calling it something harder than that," I laughed. "What we've got to do, sergeant-major, is to wish all these boys the best luck mortal man can wish another."

I turned away, as there was no use in prolonging the conversation, but in my ears rang his bitter parting words:

"Twelve years with the Colours, sir! Sergeant at Mons, company sergeant-major since Loos, and now—this!"

But fortune relented somewhat in his case, for in the course of the afternoon, it became known that he and another sergeant-major were to report at Brigade Headquarters in order to supervise the ammunition supply to the line. He, at any rate, would set foot on the battlefield.

.   .   .   .   .

In the gloom, the motionless ranks of " Number 2 " stood present on parade, prepared at every point for the coming ordeal. Though not attached to their fighting strength, I had joined them to bid them good-bye. Beside the shadowy throng of helmeted figures, I felt, wearing a soft service cap, more detached from them than ever. In many cases my farewell of them would prove to be for ever.

The men, generally unimpressed by their surroundings, seemed quieter than usual; some evidently realised the significance of this last parade.

"Number Six Platoon, Shun! Fix—baynits!" Through the obscurity Raymond's tones rang out sharply : the platoons were about to be inspected in the usual fashion. In the distance already arose the clank and clatter of the next company as it moved off toward the battalion starting-point. "Number 2" was to bring up the rear.

Presently amid the darkness loomed The Captain, striding forward in the unfamiliar trappings of webbing equipment and revolver holster.

"Have they commenced the inspection? That's right. I didn't expect you to wait for me."

Five minutes later, the acting company sergeant-major reported all correct and ready to march off. The moment had come.

"Good-bye." Our hands met in a mighty grip.

"Good-bye, and good luck!" More one could not find words for. One after another my mess-mates accosted me before moving to their places on parade.

Then, from the dusky night came the sound one had come to know so well : the three movements of "the slope."

"Move to the right in fours; form—fours! Right!" With a final wave The Captain turned away to the leading flank.

"Quick march!"

The company broke into movement, a rattle of mess-tins came from the shadows, and almost at once the order to march at ease was passed down from the front.

But for once the usual babble of voices was hushed. In the silence, the Battle of the Somme called in thunderous tones. Platoon by platoon, the company vanished into the night. Here, bringing up the rear, came that one which I had once commanded, Sergeant Thurston at their head.

"Good-bye, Sergeant Thurston. God bless you, my lads." The words seemed almost to choke one.

"Good-bye, sir ; thank you, sir," came the answering chorus.

Straining my eyes, I strove to follow their course through the darkness, but rank by rank they were swallowed in the night until at last only the Lewis-gun carts remained recognisable. Then, as they clattered on their way, these in their turn faded from view.

"Number 2" had gone : one's parting pangs remained.

CHAPTER XIV

THE 15TH OF SEPTEMBER

HOUR by hour all through that night I was wakened in the lonely dugout by the detonations of the 60-pounders outside. By some freakish trick of acoustics the noise seemed intensified within the cavernous space, for the dugout drummed to the sound of every discharge.

After a spell of troubled rest, at 5 a.m. I dressed hastily and hurried out on to the hill-side to hear the opening of the battle.

Flooding softly across the eastern sky came the first streaks of dawn, and as they spread, they dimmed the stars with luminous shafts of green. The day of destiny lingered yet awhile, fearful perhaps of passing the threshold of History. Here, at this hour, the echoes of the guns were hushed, and over the mysterious landscape a profound silence seemed to brood. One by one the eastern stars waned and vanished in the glow of sunrise, and on turning about, one could note the retreating hues of darkness where they hovered in the western sky. The air was chilly, for now the nights were growing cold.

Presently, droning faintly upon the ear, the notes of an aeroplane rippled across the silent world, and, swelling louder and yet louder, these soon filled the sleeping valley with their crescendo. Overhead, a gliding silhouette was to be seen speeding swiftly toward the east. In the morning twilight it resembled a monstrous bat. Drifting onward to the coming battle, it cleaved its rapid course above our encampment, and as it passed, it sounded its horn in friendly greeting : *Ave Caesar !* Then, as the notes of the engine melted into the distant dawn, silence crept once more over the land.

Stirred to life by the sounds of the passing aeroplane, a sudden peal arose, trembling in the morning stillness. By ones and twos, flooding heavenward from the surrounding encampments, rose the notes of many bugles calling " revelly." In the solemn silence, their fanfare rang nobly on the ear, echoing the old-time pageantry of war.

Then, transcending all the wonders of the moment, rising over the horizon in response to the clarion call, loomed the crimson majesty of the sun. Hailing its appearance, there crashed forth a dreadful cannon blast, which, swelling upwards in grandiose intensity, struck the opening chords of battle. Thus Mars saluted Saturn.

Already the hands of my watch announced the minute of " Zero." Standing upon the hill-side, one gazed vainly into the mists ahead while a voice within one stammered a broken prayer. At this very moment, yonder amid the Great Unknown, gallant comrades were streaming forward to the attack. . . .

But time was pressing, for the small band of officers which had been left behind had not yet breakfasted, and before long we were due to set out for the first-line transport. This meal proved a sorrowful function, and we were glad when the time came for us to start. A walk, at all events, was better for our state of mind than sitting among the remnants of our late encampment.

The transport lines lay about three-quarters of a mile away, thus it was still at an early hour that we made our appearance there and discovered we were to remain in readiness for further orders. There could be little doubt of what those orders would be ; so we busied ourselves for a while in looking over for the tenth time our equipment and haversacks, and in checking each item of our preparations.

Strolling backwards and forwards along the road near by, we indulged in much speculation on what was happening to the battalion. It was nine o'clock, and so far no news had filtered back.

Beyond a mile or so, no view was yet to be had. Far away to the eastward a dense haze obscured the landscape. From the heart of this lowering veil came the pulsating throb of guns, and here and there the dense atmosphere was rent with their flashes. Though the battle had now reached its height, it still remained practically invisible.

As the mist dissolved, a ridge, veiled hitherto, became dimly defined, and beyond that, another in its turn. Across the face of the slopes, dark lines could be seen crawling upon their way. They were troops and transport.

A sullen roar filled the entire horizon from north to south, rolling like tumultuous breakers across the open heavens. Punctuating the ceaseless noise of the smaller guns, giant howitzers around us thundered on, hurling forth their shrieking missiles into the cloudless sky.

Presently, heard fitfully between the lesser concussions of the battle, an unfamiliar sound stole on our ears. It seemed as if a vast aeroplane might be approaching at a low altitude. Looking about us, we could detect nothing out of the ordinary ; but still the sound continued. Then, a couple of hundred yards or more down the road, we saw several figures running out of view down an embankment. Evidently, as it takes much to arouse such strenuous interest in the average British soldier, something out of the ordinary was afoot. We set off to investigate.

Louder and louder rose the noise from out of the

concealed hollow. "Some kind of engine," we agreed.

Reaching the crest of the hill, we discovered only a short distance away a crowd of men moving at a slow walk beside an incredible apparition. What a monstrosity ! Its identity was evident at the first glance : this vast armour-plated insect could only be a Tank. Its wicked-looking guns protruding forward seemed like antennae, while a huge wheel trailing in its rear suggested a sort of tail. Photographs and newspaper descriptions have made these strange engines of war familiar to all, but at the time in question the Army itself had had no glimpse of them. Our surprise was absolute. A four-horse chariot, with scythes complete, would have caused us no greater astonishment.

But to linger long from our bivouac was out of the question, so, taking a last glimpse of this strange object, we retraced our steps once more, wondering whether during our brief absence news had reached our encampment. There we found everyone in a state of suppressed expectation. Nothing was known as to the fate of the great attack.

How can one forget the racking tension of that day ? Hour after hour throughout its endless course we awaited the order to go up to the battalion, hour after hour we wondered what had happened. Comforting ourselves with the thought that bad news travels fast, we forced ourselves as best we could to bide in patience. From time to time, we would peer through our glasses at the distant cavalry bivouacked on the slope by Montauban, and strove to catch sight of any sign that might indicate an advance ; for cavalry in considerable numbers lay in readiness should a favourable opening present itself. Their lines, however, remained quiet, and our expectations gradually diminished. A long file of horses, hardly distinguishable in the far distance, roused our feverish interest for a while, until it became evident that it was merely a watering party. Thus,

18

alternating between hope and resignation, we passed
the morning.

The first rumours were depressing. On a day such
as this, evil tidings outstrip all others. We had hardly
sat down to an *al fresco* lunch outside the marquee
when Jenkin arrived with the news that Bruce, The
Captain, Pilkington, and several others had been hit.
Here was a bombshell for myself, as " Number 2,"
bereft of the leadership of its Captain, would now
have to be commanded by a subaltern who had
scarcely any experience whatsoever. I made certain in
my own mind that I should be called upon almost any
minute.

The meal had barely ended before further information reached us that Sholto had been desperately
hit; two Ensigns also had been killed, and another
wounded. The battalion had taken its first objective.

But this intelligence was more than " unofficial,"
since, after inquiry, we discovered it had come through
an officer's servant who claimed to have met a wounded
private of the battalion at a dressing station near by.
However, anxiety as to its probable truth urged us to
dispatch one of our party to the place, and once more
we devoted ourselves to a tedious wait of an hour or
more. Returning at last, our companion informed us
of a series of wild rumours which he had succeeded in
collecting from various casualties, rumours that baffled
us by their contradictions. Thus we learnt that the
Guards were being exterminated; the Tanks were
clearing all before them; also that the right flank of
the attack had been held up, but the Guards Division,
pushing home its own advance, had been left " in the
air." So conflicting were the men's impressions as to
casualties and progress, that we could only resolve to
disbelieve all news for the present, whether good or
bad.

Slowly the afternoon wore into evening and the

shadows cast by the waning sunlight grew longer and longer. Still the gunfire showed no signs of slackening. Now with the sun behind us, we could obtain a good view in the direction of the scene of battle, but, except for heavy palls of smoke upon the horizon, nothing of the conflict was visible. High overhead, glistening like quicksilver in the rays of the sinking sun, there floated a squadron of observation balloons, whence come the telephonic directions to the heavy guns on earth. Speeding between these, an occasional aeroplane was to be seen as it glided like a particle of dust through the purpling sky.

The advent of evening brought with it another batch of rumours, many still contradictory, but shedding a little light upon our obscured understanding. A flood of wounded had streamed through the dressing-station all day, but by far the greater number were " walking " cases, as was only to be expected. But out of the confusion of their statements we were able gradually to form an idea of what had taken place that morning, and to accept certain rumours as facts.

Naturally the battalion had suffered, but to a greater degree than any of us had anticipated. After leading the line forward for the second time, Bruce had been hit in two places; Sholto, also, mortally. Besides the Adjutant and two Ensigns, another Captain was unofficially reported " killed." Livingstone, commanding his company in his Captain's absence, had likewise been killed, and very few of the remaining officers were believed to be unwounded. But in spite of these losses, the men had behaved magnificently, and were now reported to be in the third objective. Hundreds of prisoners had been taken, and great execution had been inflicted on the enemy's forward troops, many of whom had been massed in readiness for an attack of their own. Two lines of trenches, it had been discovered, lay between our starting-point and our first objective. Their presence had come as a surprise, but through these the battalions of the regiment had thrust in a great bayonet charge. It had been a terrible and a great day in the annals of all the Guards.

While at dinner within the Headquarters marquee, we indulged in endless speculation as to the reason of our immobility. If, as there was no longer any reason to doubt, the officers of the battalion had suffered heavily, why were we not called up to the front ? We wearied one another with our fruitless arguments and theories. The strain of our long daylight vigil had been wearing to our sorely tried patience.

If possible, outside in the gathering night the sounds seemed to increase. Lifting the entrance flap, we beheld a firmament aflame with lightning, a continuous scintillation of short-lived gun flashes. Leaping forth and backward in the distant darkness, the rugged horizon seemed to be playing a game of hide-and-seek with the elements, now dimly silhouetted against a lurid flicker of fire, now vanishing into the shades of night. From north to south an infernal glare illumined the sky, and, dancing in and out of this upon its entire length, the horizon seemed to writhe in torment. Our ears, assailed throughout the day by the rending clangour of the conflict, suffered now insensitively the beating waves of air that pulsed throughout the atmosphere. They were the heart-throbs of outraged Nature. Tumbling one upon the other in a cataract of sound, waves of thunder raged across hill and dale, shaking the earth and buffeting heaven with the furious concussion of the cannonade.

Within the tent, we were all expecting to be aroused in the night by an order to hasten up to No Man's Land, therefore, rolling ourselves in our trench coats, we lay down in order to obtain some sleep. Prone on the grassy floor of the marquee, we strove vainly for a while against the awful sounds of the night. The beating of one's heart mingled with the throb of the quaking ground, for all the earth seemed to be agonising beneath yonder rain of shell fire. But mighty though the storm around us was, Nature proved mightier still. At last, wearied with anxiety and suspense, I fell asleep.

CHAPTER XV

It was shortly after dawn when I woke on the following morning. Overnight the ground had become chilly, and the cold had penetrated my scanty covering. Outside, while shaving at the solitary mirror by the tent door, we were able to observe the resumption of the artillery fire and to note with satisfaction that the day promised to be fine.

Breakfast, prepared just as if we had been in the trenches, was passed in much discussion of the reason for our prolonged stay with the transport, for almost all of us had turned in on the previous night with the conviction that our time was at hand. It was generally agreed that some effort should be made to obtain more news, so, accompanied by Clive, a fellow subaltern, I set off toward Divisional Headquarters in order to see the casualty lists and the latest telegrams. Twenty minutes brought us to our destination, and entering the office, we found the Prince of Wales seated there with one of the Captains of the Divisional Staff.

Hearing our request to see the casualty list, the latter told us that we should have to wait a little while, whereupon the Prince, who had evidently overheard our words, passed across a document with the remark that he had already seen it. Thus we learnt sorrowful news of many of our friends and fellow comrades in the division.

On returning to our encampment, the first person to meet us was the battalion sergeant-major, who straightway sought leave to go up to the front. This, in face of the definite orders we had received, was absolutely impossible, and so, as the senior officer present, I was compelled to refuse his request.

News of our casualties had now become common property, and the N.C.Os attached to the party became restless in consequence. This state of affairs continued until news, arriving from Brigade Headquarters, informed us all that no officers were needed owing to the small number of men surviving. Two officers, one of whom we learned with profound satisfaction was the Colonel, were now running the battalion; no more help was required. Thus all our chances of participating in the battle were doomed.

Dismay filled us on receipt of this message, not so much on our own account, but by reason of the hint it contained as to the fate of the battalion. We had all anticipated casualties as a matter of course, but never had we expected such losses as this news implied. Our world, composed for many months past of congenial comrades and of loyal followers, had crumbled in a few hours. Never again would the company messes be quite the same; never again would "Number 2" parade as in days gone by.

But after the first numbing sense of bereavement had subsided, we began to conceive the greatest misgivings as to the success of our attack. Had we not trained for it with so much care, and were not the Tanks to have helped us so much ? Though bitter our losses, our growing disappointment was more bitter still.

Gazing longingly in the direction of the cavalry lines across the valley, we searched for some sign that would belie our misgivings, some omen of good fortune; but none was to be seen. Grazing leisurely at their tethers, the horses remained off-saddled in orderly formation, though, it was true, their saddles and bridles lay near at hand.

Roaring sullenly throughout the long autumn morning, the great howitzers in our vicinity maintained their steady fire and shook with their concussions the surrounding neighbourhood. Far in the distance played a ceaseless twinkle and stab of gun flashes, which alone revealed the situation of our countless batteries of field artillery. Once more the noise had swelled until it seemed to fill the entire world from one horizon to another.

As this second afternoon of battle wore on, our doubts of the morning were gradually allayed by the arrival of further telegrams. Now, tales of a great advance were coming through at last. The losses among the Guards had been severe, but their gains had created a new record for the war. This scanty information, coming after so many misgivings, nearly made us shout for joy. The attack had lost direction because, owing to the unexpected check on our right, the division had swerved considerably to its left, leaving its right flank exposed. But though officers had fallen in considerable numbers, the non-commissioned officers had risen grandly to the occasion ; and when these became casualties in their turn, the rank and file had still gone forward. To find a parallel to the men's behaviour it was necessary, according to all accounts, to go back to the day of Inkerman !

As learnt subsequently, the fate of " Number 2 " was characteristic of many a company of Guards throughout this battle. The Captain had been severely wounded before the arrival of " Zero," whereupon a young subaltern had led the attack; but he in his turn was wounded before very long, so the sole remaining officer, an Ensign in action for the first time, succeeded to the command. One by one the platoon sergeants dropped out: Thurston and Davis killed, Ackroyd and Saunders severely wounded. Battling its way forward, the company had delivered a furious charge with bomb and bayonet, and before their onslaught large numbers of Bavarians had melted away. At last, the solitary officer fell a victim to his gallantry, being dangerously hit on this second day. "Number 2," bereft of all officers and sergeants, proceeded to follow the berserk leadership of its Bombing Corporal. This must have been the day of his life, for his leadership and personal example were truly heroic. Five Germans fell before his favourite weapon, a bill-hook, which was already legendary among the men. Thus he fulfilled a solemn vow of many months' standing.

Arising from the leftward swing of the division came the fact that many guardsmen assisted at the storming of Flers. This village had never been included on our programme, but finding it in their path, a rabble of men from almost every battalion of one of the Guards brigades swept into it along with other comrades. Thereupon ensued one of the most striking episodes of the day.

Wallowing ponderously over the scattered heaps of debris which had once been the high street of Flers, firing fitfully from its reeking portholes, there crawled a fearful object. It was one of the Tanks, engaged in making its debut on the stage of war; and it was to a crowded house that it performed. The terror-stricken Germans gaped wildly from amid the tumbled ruins ahead. Toward them the strange apparition made its way, followed by a cheering mob of British soldiers. It was said that men laughed until they cried, for nothing like it had been heard of before. A spluttering German machine-gun was immediately blown to atoms by a point-blank shot from one of the Tank's 6-pounders; an annoying barricade of wire was flattened out of existence; and guns swung threateningly toward any of the enemy whose hands were not already raised. Here, at any rate, the "mailed fist" had met its match.

The garrison of Flers threw down its arms in

the presence of a thundering nightmare, which was escorted down the street by a procession of yelling infantry.

All through the preceding night, hundreds of prisoners had swarmed to and fro across the battlefield, lending valuable assistance to our overwrought stretcher-bearers. By now, the " walking " casualties had long ceased to arrive, their place being taken by more serious cases. Of these, a very large proportion was due to machine-gun fire, for our advancing line had been enfiladed by these weapons from the direction of the Quadrilateral, a large system of redoubts situated beyond our right flank.

Gradually we had gleaned the above items of information from many sources, but toward evening, crowning all, came the intelligence that the battalion would be relieved that night. Part of an encampment lying about a couple of miles from our transport lines was allotted to it, so shortly after dinner I set out in charge of a billeting party in order to make everything ready for its arrival. The business presented no great difficulties except the eternal problem of water supply, since the quarters reserved for our occupation would more than accommodate our slender needs.

It was near dawn on the following morning before our labour was completed and we were at liberty to seek a few hours' repose. By then, the battalion was almost due to make its appearance, but, according to a report, it could not be expected to arrive for another couple of hours; all ranks were exhausted.

After a couple of hours' sleep, I was aroused by my servant and made a hasty toilet. Cyclist orderlies had already preceded toward the route along which the battalion was known to be approaching, and supplementary guides had been posted at all cross-roads to deal with possible stragglers. We had endeavoured to anticipate all their needs, and had, in our humble sphere, spared no time or trouble on our comrades' behalf.

As everything was in readiness for their immediate occupation of this "Citadel" Camp, we strolled out along the track by which the battalion was expected to arrive. The early morning was somewhat squally; scudding clouds swept low overhead, veiling from time to time the struggling sunshine; and the air was fresh with the lingering chill of night. As we walked slowly up a slope in the neighbourhood of our lines, our ears were strained for the first sound of "The Drums," for they had long since proceeded to Carnoy in order to play the survivors in.

Over the skyline presently glided a cyclist, who, on catching sight of us, pedalled swiftly forward. From him we learned a few minutes later that our battalion was now only a mile distant, preceded by its sister battalion in the brigade. After a brief consultation, we agreed to remain where we were, so as to be near the lines, for several tracks converged here from the direction of their march.

Not many minutes had elapsed before the breeze wafted to our ears the intermittent throb of drums; the sound seemed under the circumstances intensely dramatic. Rising and falling on the wind, its mutterings at first grew no louder, and thus, rolling toward us from the invisible country beyond, it seemed almost ghostly. Soon its notes had reached the camp behind us, and men commenced to stream forth along the track in their desire to learn the fate of many a comrade. The breeze murmured to the lilt of fifes; the phantom battalion was nearing the brow. A great expectation seized us all.

Before long, we could recognise the air they were playing, for now it sounded continuously above the noise of the wind in our ears. Standing thus, scanning the hilltop with eager eyes, we waited in suspense.

Now we could hear the melodious tune of a familiar

march—they must be very close at hand. Insensibly one's pulses stirred in response to the rattle of the drums. Over the skyline something flashed and whirled. Our gaze watched in eager fascination. Again the same object appeared, and we knew it for the sergeant-drummer's stick. At last, his head and shoulders rose above the ridge, and behind him surged the emerging forms of the drummers.

"Rataplan—plan—plan—rataplan!" Backed by a swaying row of burnished cases and flourished sticks, he swaggered into full view, and as he strode forward, the full array of " The Drums " followed in his wake. Advancing as with the movement of a machine, they marched toward us in the full pride of their great hour. Next, over the crest loomed the figure of our Colonel marching at the head of the devoted band. Rank after rank these poured over the skyline. Eagerly we counted their strength, wondering every instant how many remained to follow. All too soon a gap appeared, but we, still striving to disbelieve our fears, watched spellbound for the next body of men. But none came : the impossible was true. Before us marched all that remained of the old battalion. . . .

Turning before their approach, we, with many a backward glance, retraced our steps toward the camp. Barely a word was spoken. Here amid our lines we took up our stand and awaited the arrival of the column. Along the side of the road stood many men, gazing in mute contemplation at the band of survivors. Now the drummers were almost upon us. Their music ended with a flourish, silence fell upon all. The moment was almost unbearable. Then, crashing forth with full volume of drum and fife, there rolled the opening notes of the Regimental March !

Dinning our ears with their stirring clamour, " The Drums " wheeled to a flank, whence, facing the road-way, they continued to pour forth their music. All eyes were turned to the lithe figure of our Commanding

Officer, who now led in the glorious remnants. Haggard
and drawn, but erect and admirable as ever, he strode
past us acknowledging our salutes. Next, tramping
forward in a supreme effort, followed the pathetic
muster. They presented an amazing spectacle. At
that sight, the dullest present must have felt that he
was beholding History. A first impression was that
of mud, mud everywhere, from the crown of their
heads to their shapeless feet. Beneath many a helmet
rim, blood-shot eyes stared brilliantly from swollen
and dusty lids ; moustaches seemed like clots of mud ;
complexions were grey, furrowed with dried streaks of
sweat. Though much of their equipment was missing,
here and there we caught sight of German souvenirs,
a bayonet or a round service cap. In many cases
their clothing was torn and stained with blood.
Gazing wonderingly upon their ranks, we noted their
sagging knees and their desperate efforts to pull
themselves together : here a drooping figure propelled
itself forward with the aid of a stick, there, another
stumbled on with fixed and haggard expression. The
music alone buoyed up these overwrought souls. And
as one watched, one's heart went out to them, for
their efforts were positively painful to witness. But
now, at the word of command, every man sloped his
rifle, every man picked up the step. So, lurching
forward at it last gasp, smeared, tattered, but still
tenacious, this vision of undaunted men staggered
past.

CHAPTER XVI

OWING to the ill fortune that had overtaken The Captain, I now found myself in command of " Number 2," so the day following the arrival of the survivors was for me a very busy one indeed. Complete reorganisation of the company was necessary, for out of the N.C.Os there remained but one sergeant and six corporals, and the total strength of the unit did not exceed fifty men. One could only be thankful for that wise foresight which had preserved the company sergeant-major, for now that I was the only officer left his help became invaluable.

Early in the morning of our second day at the Citadel, the battalion received the welcome reinforcement of a draft from the Entrenching Battalion, which was encamped near-by. This, when added to another body of recruits hurried up from the Base, brought our number up to 500 men, and of these new arrivals about fifty came to " Number 2." Among them were several non-commissioned officers of experience, men who had seen active service with the original Expeditionary Force.

By degrees, company commanders were able to evolve some semblance of order out of chaos, and before long the battalion began to regain its former organisation. We were all agreed that to attain our previous standard a period of rest and careful training was necessary, not only for the rank and file, but for

270

officers themselves. We were all novices in our new duties.

But on the following day, we were filled with consternation by the arrival of a rumour that our efforts were not yet ended : the Guards were to deliver another attack !

At first the news seemed incredible. The *cadres* of the units composing the division still existed, but there remained now only a third of those effectives which had travelled southward so joyfully a few weeks before. True, we had just received reinforcements, but these were not either in quality or quantity all that we could have wished for in the circumstances. This news was indeed a severe blow to all our hopes.

Our fate was sealed, however, when toward evening the battalion paraded in the presence of the Brigadier. From him we learnt in the course of a few terse but inspiriting words the fact that a further call was to be made on us shortly. The division was to extend its first advance and try, if possible, to carry by frontal assault the village of Lesbœufs. In this attempt we should receive all the aid that guns and aircraft could give, for our depleted numbers were well known to the Higher Command.

Conversation at dinner that evening consisted of " shop " entirely. This thing evidently had to be, so the best that we could do would be to adjust our minds accordingly. As with so many at a time like this, our fears were held not so much on personal grounds as on behalf of the reputation of the regiment. There lay the crux of all our forebodings. It would be vain to try to assure ourselves that we were equal to our usual standard ; we were not, and no amount of self-delusion could alter that fact. Half of our effectives, newly arrived recruits, had never heard the whine of a bullet ; many of our N.C.Os had only received their stripes within a day or so, and had no experience of leadership whatever, either at home or in the field.

The same applied to some extent to almost all the Captains, while practically none of our junior officers had undergone their baptism of fire. Our own lives might be reckoned as less than pawns on the board, but within our collective assembly there was something at stake that mattered exceedingly : the good name bequeathed us by our predecessors.

With the arrival of dawn on the following morning our last day at the Citadel camp began. Already it had become known that we would move into the line that night.

Hastening on various errands throughout the morning, officers attended to the needs of their various commands : addresses to the men, attendance at a lecture on the forthcoming action, and attention to sundry matters. The whole of the afternoon, however, was devoted to rest and correspondence.

Arriving with the company reinforcements had come St. Helier, an Ensign " out " for the first time. The impending battle was to be his first experience of service in Europe, and no doubt he found in it a memorable contrast with his former activities. One of the newly arrived sergeants, Repton by name, was to act as temporary company sergeant-major in the absence of our old one. His arrival was most opportune, for having done many years' service with the regiment and seen the campaign of Mons and the Marne, he was in every way a tower of strength to the numerous raw recruits now present in our ranks. The Colonel, who had played a prominent part in the battle of the 15th, was not to lead us in our new venture. All ranks heard of this decision with regret. The command of the battalion devolved therefore on the sole remaining Captain of our former days. Though young to occupy such a post, this officer was known to all for his soldierly abilities, and it was with full confidence that we learnt of his temporary assumption of the duties of Commanding Officer.

It was shortly after dinner this day, the 20th, that our very young battalion paraded for the last time and fell into its appointed place in the line of march. Whatever Fate might hold in store for us, she would find us ready ; so, conscious of our lack of experience, and resolved in any case to do our best, we marched away from the Citadel in the gathering dusk.

    .   .   .   .   .

Night had fallen. The surrounding darkness was filled with a multitudinous sound : the indescribable murmur of mud sucking at scores of struggling feet. Here in places nearly up to our knees, there quickening our pace over harder ground, we struggled along the track toward Carnoy. Mingled with the squelching of our footsteps came the occasional tap of a water-bottle as it struck against a rifle-butt, or the rhythmic flap of a mess-tin against a pack. Distinguishable among these noises were many muttered imprecations ; the ground under foot was almost a morass. Against the starry sky loomed the heads of the rearmost forms of the preceding company. But for the guidance of these helmets, the direction of our march would have been unknown to us, for in the stiffened sea of mire no track was to be seen.

As we debouched into the roadway near Carnoy, our march became easier. Here the surface was still hard, though cut up in places by deep ruts and occasional shell holes. As the first hour's march had proved exceedingly heavy, now we were glad of ten minutes' rest. At the end of that time, we took the road once more.

The night was beginning to grow dark and gusty, and banks of clouds drifting across the moon caused us to fear the approach of rain. Ahead of us, the impenetrable darkness was rent asunder by the flare of a howitzer ; then came the blast of its discharge. Our exertions prevented us from feeling the effects

19

of the night air, and it was in a gradually increasing welter of perspiration that we stumbled along the dim road.

Carnoy lay behind us ; one could not help wondering whether one would ever return that way again. Even now, almost at the eleventh hour, the fact that we were marching into battle seemed unreal and hardly credible ; it all appeared like a nightmare, from which we should wake by and by. A few short days—three or four pages of a shilling calendar—would decide the question. For many of us those days would never pass, to others they would just drag on as if each were burdened with a hundred hours. As we all knew, "Zero" was due at dawn on the 23rd.

It was more than strange to feel that the story of my life had become suspended, for that in reality was what I felt. Everything pertaining to the past was finished with absolute finality : never again could one regard it as hitherto—definitely related to the doings of the moment—for it was all over and done with. An impassable barrier seemed to have arisen, which blotted out the past and severed us temporarily from all ties and relationships.

A sullen silence had fallen on the column ; no doubt many a man realised he was face to face with Destiny. A cloud of tobacco smoke, floating in the light of the moon, seemed white as snow. My nostrils were assailed by the pungent scent of a cigarette : evidently a true philosopher strode in the ranks ahead.

Now squeezing into the gutter, now forming "two deep" where the way was narrow, we threaded our course past long lines of limbers and detachments of all kinds, for the turning from Montauban led us now direct to Bernafay Wood, a great and crowded centre that lay on the main track toward the line.

Here the road grew troublesome and appreciably affected our progress. Splashing forward through the ooze, which, shimmering in the moonlight, lay on every side, we plodded along the churned tracks of our comrades in front. In the sombre mass of swaying shadows, the eye would be attracted by the fitful gleam of metal as the moon shone upon a breech-bolt, while undulating in mid-air to the time of our step, a light patch was visible, representing a long French loaf that someone was carrying in the crossed straps of his pack. Then the straggled column, the shadowy roadside, the mysterious tree-trunks, and the slimy expanse of road, were illumined suddenly by an all-embracing flash. Sweaty faces around one glistened with a death-like pallor, and equipment, wheel-ruts, and shattered tree-stems were tipped with silver lights ; then came the ear-splitting crash of a discharge. A moment later, we could hear the receding flight of the shell swooping like a thunderbolt thousands of feet above the newly darkened earth. Down the roadway arose the angry curses of a limber driver who strove to quieten the plunges of a startled horse. Rending the air with their steady cannonade, batteries were firing from their positions behind the wood.

Presently, as we crowded past a long ammunition convoy, we could see the distant glimmer of an illumined dugout door by the roadside, and coming abreast of it a moment or so later, we beheld a signboard proclaiming it to be a dressing-station. Ramped high on either side were massive tiers of sandbags composing its doorway, and through this, receding into the dimly lighted bowels of the earth, a passage was visible wherein lounged a sergeant of the R.A.M.C. There, during the last fortnight or more, must have passed many hours of desperate toil, hours of apparently hopeless endeavour to cope with the influx of stricken men. It was impossible to begrudge him his few moments of relaxation, or his desire to escape from the fetid atmosphere of blood and sweat and drugs in which his present world revolved. He had his job, and we had ours ; each in his own fashion contributed to the efficiency and welfare of the great machine we served.

Forward through the groups of transport we made our way, following blindly the lead of the next company ahead. Soon Bernafay Wood lay behind, and we were heading toward the east. One by one the lighted bivouacs vanished from view, and sounds of human occupation grew rarer. By following the course of a light railway, we had no difficulty in knowing our way, for we were aware that it led direct to the next stage of our march. Ahead of us, the horizon was lit by sudden spasms of flame; overhead, the air was torn by the transit of heavy projectiles, and as these moaned into the distance one searched instinctively for the next sheet of fire that would mark their point of impact. Across the darkened world rolled eddies of gunfire, punctuating the stillness with a measured flow of detonations and sonorous echoes. For many weeks now, the voice of the Somme had known no rest.

Tramping along a rutted road, enveloped in a boundless mantle of obscurity, the battalion forged ahead in pursuit of an ever-retreating darkness. Though the roadway lurched behind at every stride, the outlook remained always as before : an endless desert of ruin and shadow, which seemed to deride our efforts by keeping constant pace with our march. Like creatures in a nightmare, we appeared to advance and recede at every step. To our torpid minds the world had become a gigantic treadmill, and we the slaves of the universe. To slog onward with clodded feet, to ease our aching shoulders, to propel ourselves forward at all costs, these became the tyrannical laws of our existence. Our heads might droop, but there must be no slackening of our pace ; our legs might ache, but still they must fulfil their task. No matter how wearisome our burdens or how stumbling our gait, we must keep our ranks and endure.

As we surged continuously over ruts and holes, keeping always before us the vague forms of our neighbours in the ranks ahead, one recalled to mind a phrase that embodied and gave utterance to our suffering : " Servitude et Grandeur Militaires." In it was expressed all the torment of our plight ; in it was revealed the honour of our great captivity.

Servitude et Grandeur—ah ! de Vigny, at least, had understood. . . .

Now lurching into a hole, now stumbling against a stone, we launched ourselves into the unfathomable shadows. An occasional oath or a shake of a pack alone betrayed our fatigue. Silently and grimly, the column maintained its defiance of the illimitable waste. No view served to distract the mind, no tree or building or even fence to attract remark, only the incessant motion of packs and helmets in front, and on the flanks—the gloom of night and Nature's obliteration.

By ones and twos, figures emerged at last from the night-clad battlefield, voices became audible after an age of silence, and we drew near to human habitations once more. Soon a check arose ; the voice of our Commanding Officer called from the shadows. Looming indistinctly near at hand lay a wall of deeper darkness, a mass of tangled trees and undergrowth. Here, perhaps, we should be granted another rest ?

As if in mockery of our silent prayer, there came the familiar wail of speeding Death. Three blinding sheets of flame dispelled the darkness ; the earth around was lashed by an invisible rain of shrapnel ; and our ears were smitten by jarring concussions. Within the momentary gleam of light, I noted the ducking forms of those beside me, saw the jerk of their cringing heads and the movement of their sheltering packs. Then the curtain fell once more, while our eyes still blinked flutteringly and in our ears sang lingering echoes.

To remain here, even for the brief spell of our hourly

halt, might involve the loss of some of our men, and
they were already far below normal strength. Realising this, we were hardly surprised or disappointed
when the order came down the line to lead on. Passing
along from mouth to mouth, it sped away into the
obscurity behind us, leaving in its track a mass of
shuffling phantoms, who took up again their positions
in the line of march. A few there were who would
have braved the risks and remained where they had
subsided, so overcome were they by weariness.

It was now abundantly clear that not only had the
first hours of our march sapped much of our energies,
but many of the newly joined recruits were unaccustomed to so sustained an effort. In justice to them,
it should be realised that no man, weighing with his kit
approximately seventeen stone, can drag himself for
several miles through half a foot of mud without experiencing considerable strain ; and though the relative
improvement of the ground during the last couple of
hours had somewhat retarded the action of our fatigue,
still the effects of the march had been altogether
unusual by reason of the dreadful condition of the
ground. So surging forward once more, we slowly drew
clear of the threatened area, but not before another
flight of shells had exploded near the trees. We continued to hear their sudden reports long after we had
entered a wood that now enfolded us in its mystery.

Tripping heavily over the logs of the corduroy road,
we were further hampered by the confused shadows
lying across the primitive track. These, mingled with
the medley of our ranks, caused us to step upon a
flickering carpet of darkness, so our progress dwindled
to a crawl. Left and right, there arose a forbidding
chaos, amid which one noticed occasionally the silvery
streak of a flayed trunk or the vivid splinters of a
severed branch. Beyond these scattered details lurked
an impenetrable screen of boles, which blended at a
few yards' distance with the disordered wreckage

of the wood. There brooded an utter silence, which a streaky fog seemed to render only the more sinister. From time to time amid the night, we could smell the horrid odour of corruption, the inevitable scent of a former battlefield.

And what a battlefield was this! These jumbled thickets, masses of gnarled trees, and dangling branches represented all that was left of Trônes Wood! At this late hour, shrouded in its sepulchral setting, it seemed to belie the tales that had gathered round its name, to guard jealously its inscrutable secrets. No leaf survived to rustle gently in the night; no bird inhabited its gaunt remains; only trunks stood like spectres in the gloom, pointing gigantic splinters to the stars. Here a terrible drama had been played, a drama whose details had spread to every mess throughout the Somme. Here was a birthplace of future legends; but for us creeping through the mournful depths knowledge sufficed to reset the abandoned stage.

    ʕ   •   ʔ   •   ʔ

Barely a month before, these martyred acres of woodland had been one of the most frenzied cockpits of the Somme. Backwards and forwards through its dissolving undergrowth the tempest of attack and counter-attack had surged, now favouring the desperate efforts of the defence, now raising the hopes of the stubborn assailants. Day and night the conflict ebbed and flowed, the hours of daylight annihilating the reinforcements of the previous spell of darkness. Fighting furiously in the van, the men of Kent had upheld the honour of British arms; and though the progress of the battle saw the arrival of other units, fragments of that glorious regiment were present at its end.

Again and again the enemy had pressed forward, their ranks heralded by a raging screen of drum-fire and streaming flame-throwers. Filtering through the jungle of fallen trees and yawning shell holes, their massed formations had stormed against the devoted garrisons of the British posts and craters, bearing them backward on the crest of their flood. Then came the British counter-stroke.

Raining into the devastation around the victors, drowning their exultant hurrahs with its bewildering din, into their midst smote the British barrage. A paroxysm of volcanic rage overwhelmed their advance. Crushed and mangled beneath a hail of hissing metal, the leading waves were beaten to earth, and as they reeled from their wounds, other projectiles completed their slaughter. Men were slain fourfold that day, for, like a ceaseless torrent, high explosives, shrapnel, and machine-guns blended into a maelstrom of death. Retribution pelted upon them. Whirling terrifically above their heads, the very trees arose against them and flung their riven stems into the fray. Corpses already dead were crushed and hammered by falling timber, the wounded were brained, the lurking survivors were swept away.

Then once again the smoking glades glimmered with the flash of bayonets, and English shouts resounded through the chaos. Rifles crackled among the tree-trunks and bullets whined across the mangled ground, smacking into the trees.

Thus swaying to and fro, the battle rose and fell in eddies of convulsion. Each German onslaught but added to the havoc of the wood. Companies melted in the furnace, and shattered battalions reeled brokenly to the rear. As the long hours sped by, the brushwood and tortured earth became choked with dead, and everywhere lay an arsenal of equipment and abandoned weapons. Mangling again and again the already amputated trunks and crumbling trenches, the guns of either side had revelled in their work of obliteration : slaughtering the bodies and massacring

the wreckage, their only desire had been to kill and
kill again. Beneath their fire, the wood was churned
and rechurned, everything was pounded into fragments. Earth, bodies, equipment, and all, were blended
in one widespread pulp. . .

And when at last exhaustion put an end to German
efforts to regain Trônes Wood, the place had become
transformed. For long did its depths conceal their
gruesome secrets, but the passer-by, standing a mile
to windward, did not need to guess their nature. The
neighbourhood became shunned by Man. Four thousand dead lay there for several days, and slowly their
dreadful incense rose to heaven.

.   .   i   .   i

Now, on either flank loomed a wall of trunks.
Around us in the roughly formed road, the shadows
of the haunted wood lay thick and forbidding : like
outstretched talons, they seemed to clutch at our
living forms as though minded to devour us in our
turn. Our ranks were pursued by the fetid breath
of a charnel-house.

At last the trees grew thinner, and presently we
emerged into the pure night air. Here in the open
country our vision could roam farther, but everywhere
lay the same desolate expanse. The land had been
shrivelled by a mighty curse.

Plodding onward, the column resumed its endless
struggle against space, but still the track appeared to
march beside it. It was surely an age since we had
left the blessed rest of our encampment ? The long
night march had now become a nightmare. A stupor,
born of fatigue, began to steal over one's senses ; limbs
now performed their functions unconsciously. Our
whole beings were absorbed, not in the effort, but the
need to march.

In this fashion another mile was accomplished ;
time and distance no longer signified anything to our

labouring muscles. We may have been marching for
hours—for how long, none could say—when a group
of tree-stumps appeared near at hand. Here the track
ended and we plunged desperately into a slimy waste,
now lashed by a squall of rain. Weighed down by our
equipment, every step became a struggle to free ourselves from the reeking mud. But we no longer cared ;
our endurance had grown insensitive to everything.

Suddenly the column jolted upon itself and a heavy
recoil bore us back. From the wilderness ahead arose
a murmur of voices and a clatter of equipment, abruptly
interrupted by the sound of a splash and a stream of
blasphemy. Striding heavily through the quagmire
that bordered the way, I groped forward along an
endless line of silent figures, kneading the sticky
soil with leaden feet, glissading from one hole to
another. Then, in the dusk, a man could be seen
hauling a comrade upright, while another kicked
viciously at the air to free his enormous boots of a
few pounds' weight.

"Advance in single file ! " The order approaches
from the front. The motionless silhouettes beside one
surge forward, and you call backward to the company
to lead on.

Wading through an apparent quicksand, we came
by and by to a region of appalling havoc. Here the
earth had been lashed into great furrows and undula-
tions ; craters gaped on every side and even intersected, so thickly were they strewn. Glistening at
the bottom of them like pools of mercury lay stagnant
water reflecting the moonlight. As the column wound
in and out of this misery, we in rear endeavoured to
plant our feet in the tracks of those ahead in order
to ease the strain of disengaging our legs. By now
we were caked with mud up to the thighs, and our
progress dwindled to a painful crawl.

Emerging at last on the ruins of a former road, we
broke through a layer of ooze into a gritty strata that

grated on and checked our iron-shod feet. Sliding one moment in the slough of mud, our legs were next arrested by the resistance of a harder surface. It was with difficulty that we maintained a foothold.

Presently we left the road once more to make way for the passage of a row of limbers. For an instant one beheld a mass of struggling men and horses. Straining forward with all their might, these appeared like an instantaneous snapshot silhouetted against the moon. The rigid forms of the teams hauled desperately against an invisible obstacle, the embedded wheels were buttressed by many a leaning figure, and above the creak of harness and panting of man and beast rose hoarse cries of encouragement from a N.C.O. Slowly, and with infinite effort, the mass lurched on a yard or two ; we could almost hear the creaking of its muscles and the beat of the gunners' hearts. Against the starry background the vision stood like an heroic group of statuary : the apotheosis of physical force.

No word of greeting was heard from either party, as amid such misery all their efforts were bent on forcing their respective ways. Soon, but for the noisy labour of our own progress, all became relatively still once more.

Would the march never end !

With aching shoulders and loosening knees, we abandon ourselves to the ordeal. Checks grow more frequent, for shell holes abound everywhere, and the path is no more than a pounded trail across a spongy wilderness. Overhead, the sky is draped with massive clouds, which drift across the face of the moon like an endless procession of silent avalanches. Even as one watches, their silver edges crumble into ever-changing forms, here fraying into gliding wisps of vapour, there billowing like the edge of a giant dome. Then, as the pale light emerges once again, the immensity of our surroundings looms from its murky banishment like a petrified, tumbled sea.

Here the great attack of the 15th had passed, drawing in its wake a storm that had ploughed and hammered and convulsed the face of all Nature ; here the world was dead, extinct as a planet whose course has run. And as we flounder onward to the receding horizon of darkness, there is wafted from out the night the stench of rotting men.

Now piling itself round some gaping crater, now surging forward through the reeking pestilence of the waste, our column writhes upon its way. Worn out by unending exhaustion, the men have no longer the energy to grumble. In the misery of fatigue they toil on and on, clawing with tortured legs, staggering through the terrible solitude, inhaling at every step the surrounding miasma of death. It is now a *Marche Macabre.*

CHAPTER XVII

THE company was almost at its last gasp when it encountered at last a solitary figure by the roadside. He proved to be the company commander whom we were to relieve. For upwards of two hours he had been awaiting our arrival, and had come to the conclusion that the guide sent to meet us had lost his way. To us standing beside the road the novel situation seemed most unreal; here were no communication trenches, not even to the support line.

In company with this Captain of the Oxford and Bucks, and a sergeant, I set off on a tour of inspection, questioning my fellow officer on the way.

It was soon clear that the position was somewhat isolated. Our predecessors had been barely able to preserve contact with their neighbours on the left, and those on the right were entrenched about two hundred yards in advance of the general alignment. The Ginchy-Lesbœufs road, running in the enemy's direction through a cutting that gradually grew deeper as it receded, marked the boundary of our right flank. The enemy, partially concealed by the fall of the ground in front, were entrenched about three hundred and fifty yards away.

Hearing from my companion that another trench existed just in front of his, I went forward in search of it and came upon it almost immediately. It was newly dug, very narrow and very shallow, but in spite

285

of these disadvantages, other considerations made it preferable to the one behind. It did not take long for " Number 2 " to occupy this position and thus to relieve the former garrison of its duties. No sooner was that done than the Oxford and Bucks filed away into the darkness.

Soon after, a report came from our left platoon to the effect that contact had been made with a company of Guards that was part of a neighbouring battalion ; our trench, though hardly more than a narrow groove, was found to be continuous in that direction. There now remained the question of our right flank. That could only be ascertained by a personal reconnaissance of the ground across the Lesbœufs road, so, accompanied by an orderly, I set out in that direction to find MacIvor's company.

Having the distraction of many pressing matters, I no longer experienced the great fatigue of the march, therefore we hastened across the silent expanse of grass and shell holes, searching as we went along for signs of a track of which we had been told. Amid the solitude of the night, one missed at first the companionship of fellow men ; no harm, however, could befall us, because, though we were as pioneers in the desert, we knew that a friendly trench lay somewhere in the darkness ahead. Through abandoned enemy trenches and clumps of rank weeds we made our way, walking slowly and carefully in order to listen. The time seemed longer, but ten minutes had not elapsed before our ears detected an occasional noise, and, advancing cautiously, we discovered a long line of shadow straggling in front of us. A minute later a few words of English became audible. It was the company which we were seeking.

This trench proved to be both deeper and wider than our own. Here, two men could pass abreast, but in ours that was quite impossible. To judge by a very hasty inspection in the dark, MacIvor's men were in possession of a former German support line; there were even dugouts; but these we could hardly begrudge them, for they stank horribly. In order to discuss the questions of mutual support and communication I set off in quest of MacIvor, passing on my way numerous men of the garrison, who, in spite of their exhaustion, preferred to remain outside the dugouts.

Before very long, my way was blocked by a group of men gossiping in the middle of the trench, so, calling out a warning of " make way," I advanced into their midst. As they fell back on either side, I was confronted by a couple of figures who appeared deaf to the meaning of my words, whereupon, catching sight of a corporal standing by, I told him peremptorily to keep better control over his men.

" They are prisoners, sir," was his reply.

Here was a surprise.

" Were they handed over to you during the relief ? "

" No, sir, they've just come in."

" What, deserted ? " I exclaimed.

" Yessir."

While we were speaking, my eye had not quitted the pair in front; obviously they were endeavouring to follow our conversation. Guessing no doubt from the corporal's manner that I represented a higher authority, they first exchanged a few muttered words and next commenced to fawn on me; for a moment I thought they were going to grovel at my knees. Then, awaiting no order, they tore off their shoulder straps and proffered their pay-books, whining all the while some unintelligible words, among which one caught the expression " *Kamerad*."

Stepping back a pace, I took no pains to hide my disgust. Admittedly, their position as prisoners of war was serious, but there could be no justification for this display of abject cowardice. Not only had they deserted their regiment, but apparently there was no act of voluntary baseness at which they would stop, if by its committal they might purchase their own miserable lives. Smirking and collecting their marks of identification, they next proceeded to doff their round field-caps, from which they wrenched their regimental badge. My gorge rose at the sight.

"Corporal! Take these damned scoundrels away and report their arrival at once to Mr. MacIvor. All badges, numerals, and papers must be collected and given to him."

"Very good, sir."

"You quite understand?"

"Yessir."

And with that I left them.

On my return to "Number 2" there arose the all-important question of communication with Battalion Headquarters. These were situated in a support line lying about five hundred yards behind us. At night, written messages could be sent back by runners along the Ginchy road, but during the hours of daylight the only means by which Headquarters could be kept informed of our affairs was by telephone. The buzzer therefore was our sole resource, and to shelter it as much as possible became imperative.

In rear of the company lay a small shelter used by the Oxford and Bucks as Company Headquarters. This would suit our purpose as well as anything, so it was allotted at once to the signallers. But here the problem did not end: how were we to communicate with the instrument from the new Company Headquarters? These had been installed in a medium-sized shell crater, about fifteen yards behind the company, and equidistant from the trench occupied by the signallers. By day, it was quite impossible to show ourselves above ground, even to cross this intervening space, and to shout messages from this hole to the old trench was impracticable, for thereby grave mistakes might easily arise. The matter resolved itself therefore into a question of ways and means by which written messages might be sent across without attracting the enemy's attention. One obvious method might be tried, but we should have to wait until dawn before testing it. At length, satisfied that all possible precautions had been taken for ensuring the safety of the position, I repaired to the crater in order to obtain a little rest.

Two hours of constant walking and prospecting had followed our arrival in the line, and these, added to the exhaustion of our march, left me broken with fatigue for the time being. Sliding down into our dark pit, I roused St. Helier and conducted him along the company front : refreshed by a couple of hours' sleep, he would be able to keep watch for a while. Then, having explained all the arrangements made, I returned to my primitive lair, and curling myself up in my trench coat, fell straightway asleep amid the mud.

It seemed but a few minutes later when I was aroused by a vigorous shaking. Above me stood a dark mass framed against a circle of pale sky : St. Helier standing over me in the bottom of the shell hole.

" It's ' revelly ' for you ! "

" Good Lord ! but I've only just gone to sleep ! " I groaned.

" You've lain like a corpse for over two hours. You wanted to be called about now."

" What's the time ? "

" Nearly five," he replied ; " it'll be dawn before very long now." Hearing this, I made an effort to sit up, but in doing so was seized by a spasm of cramp and stiffness.

Presently, having risen to my feet, I stretched and bent my rigid legs. On a level with one's eyes the surrounding ground was dimly visible ; everything was as still as a graveyard.

" You turn in now for a couple of hours. I'll see to things until then." So saying, I scrambled pain-

20

fully up the edge of the crater, thereby becoming aware of an attack of rheumatism. Setting off at a brisk pace, I soon overcame these pains, and journeying from point to point, visited all the platoons in turn. The sentries had nothing to report; the brief spell of night had passed without incident of any kind.

At the arrival of the hour of "stand to," word to that effect was passed down the line, and one by one the heads of "Number 2" rose from out of the shallow trench. Here and there the gleam of a bayonet was noticeable; these were soon carefully concealed. Soon, in response to a message, the four platoon sergeants came to receive their orders for the company routine. No man was to show himself above ground during the hours of daylight, nor was any weapon to be raised or object to be thrown out of the trench. Rations and water would come up in the evening. No fire of any kind was to be permitted, and smoking was forbidden. Sentries were to be posted in the usual manner.

In this fashion I strove to impress on the sergeants the need for absolute quiet, for according to our success in concealing our whereabouts would depend our chances of safety. In the meantime, one section was to dig a shallow cutting from the company trench back to my headquarters, deep enough for a man to crawl along unseen. By this means it would be possible for us to speak with N.C.Os should that be necessary. Then, after a final warning as to the need for water economy, the sergeants were dismissed to their duties.

Now came the first rays of dawn. When last the sun had disappeared, we had been at the Citadel; it seemed incredible that all our hours of toil had been crowded into a single night. Gradually, as the sky became tinged with crimson, my thoughts turned to the fateful hours ahead. At sunrise on the day after to-morrow the impending battle would open in all its fury; our front wave would be unleashed into the valley below; and sweeping forward in its foremost ranks, "Number 2" would be charging headlong to its fate. Millions had been confronted by such a problem, but of all their number none had been able to read beforehand the inscrutable writing of Providence. For each human soul the eve of battle had ever retained its mystery—and so it would continue until the end of Time.

Gazing into the mists that screened the unknown ground ahead, we endeavoured to pierce their veil and behold the landscape. But even this was denied us for the present.

Now was the time to test our signalling arrangements. They proved to work admirably, no doubt owing to their simplicity. A few trial messages speedily proved that even from the shelter of the Headquarters crater we might rely confidently on maintaining communication with the buzzer.

Before long the daylight increased, and everyone was ordered to stand easy. In actual fact, this meant that the company was free to sit in the bottom of the trench and to pass its time as best it could. Sentries were able, however, to keep watch on No Man's Land through periscopes, which were rendered as inconspicuous as possible.

Down in our shell hole I now commenced various improvements, and with the aid of an entrenching-tool some degree of comfort was soon obtained. It was impossible to throw up any soil, but as the crater was about seven feet deep, one could afford to let it fall into the bottom. Though this necessitated a partial burial of St. Helier, it was the lesser of two evils, and in any case he slept too soundly to know anything about it. Fortunately the earth was easy to work, so it was not long before I had cut a couple of large recesses in the banks to provide us with arm-chairs. These finished, a rough locker in which to store our

scanty rations was successfully added to our quarters.
The change in our comfort was soon very marked,
for, following these operations, a solid ledge cut along
another side of the place provided a table, and steps
by which to emerge from our hole followed in due
course. By the time I roused St. Helier for breakfast,
the transformation of Headquarters went far to ap-
pease him for the state of his clothes !

Breakfast was a sorry enough meal, but what it
lacked in attraction we made up for in good-humour.
After all, it was only an imitation of a prehistoric
picnic. The only cause for uneasiness was the possibility of our receiving no further supplies ; water
especially was a doubtful item on our list. Yet, as
both of us had survived the march of the previous
night without a drink, each had a full water-bottle
on which to rely for the present.

The day was divided into watches of two hours.
Such an arrangement would afford us as much sleep as
we needed ; but though the opportunity for rest had
now arrived, neither of us felt any desire for it.
Smoking and gossiping, we whiled away the hours up
to midday.   Nothing occurred to interrupt the course
of our boredom. The appearance of a military manual
from St. Helier's haversack came as a veritable
god-send, for at all events it represented some
form of literature ; we could have devoured even the
advertisements of a daily paper with the utmost
relish.

Our next meal differed in no respect from that of
the early morning, save in name. This, like our breakfast, we ate from tins, since plates and other such
luxuries were wanting.   Fortunately, as each had provided himself with a knife and spoon, we were spared
having to use our fingers. Lunch completed, we passed
a while in contemplation of the earthy walls around us,
and having at last exhausted their interest, we turned
our attention to the sky overhead.   Everywhere

reigned a complete silence, stirred only from time to time by the buzz of a wandering fly. They, at least, had nothing to fear by exposing themselves above ground. Beating down from a cloudless expanse, the sun shed its grateful heat upon us, baking our helmets and causing us to open our jackets. To discard our equipment was impossible.·

It was almost with a sigh of relief that we heard presently the wail of an approaching shell. A moment later, the walls and floor of our retreat leaped convulsively as a loud detonation arose.

" Great Scot ! What was that ? " St. Helier's expression of placid boredom had vanished, giving place to a look of astonishment.

" ' That,' if I'm not mistaken, was the call of the 5·9 How. His mate will arrive in due course."

" Damned near, it seemed."

" Not so damned as you suppose," I explained. " It landed about forty yards behind us. Here comes the other."

Tearing overhead, a second projectile exploded in our vicinity. Fifty yards in rear, a black pall of smoke shot upwards into view above the rim of our abode, then a patter of falling dust descended on every side. Arriving at intervals of about half a minute, their shells continued to shake the earth in our neighbourhood until they became a regular rhythm of concussions. Now crouching in the bottom of our refuge beneath a cascade of soil, now peering furtively in the direction of these fountains of earth and fire, we endured the suspense of each brief interval. Several had landed right over us, and the possibility of their range becoming shortened was disturbing to the nerves. Sure enough, one had barely considered the chance before a shriek, louder than any of its forerunners, swooped through the sky. The ground quivered like a startled horse, and a deafening report numbed our ears.

"I'm afraid that must have been very close to the signallers."

"It looked like it," muttered my companion, brushing from his shoulders a coating of dust.

Making a funnel of my hands, I shouted across in their direction and was immediately relieved to hear an answering hail.

"Ten yards over, sir. No 'arm done."

"Have you any idea what their target is ? "

My voice was drowned in the convulsion of another explosion. Then came a brief pause.

"What's that you said, sir ? " came the inquiry.

"Have you any idea what they are shooting at ? "

"No, sir. We can't see much, but they seem to be fallin' round about the other end of this 'ere trench."

Our suspicions were thus confirmed : evidently the old line had been located.

But the bombardment of the empty trench did not last long, for evidently the enemy were satisfied with the results already obtained. By degrees the afternoon lapsed into its former state of quiescence. The world grew still once more.

The hour was now at hand for sending in the company report, so leaving St. Helier to ponder over his first experience of shell fire, I drew up a brief statement of the affairs of " Number 2." When finished, this message was embedded in a handful of clay, and all that one had to do was to attract the attention of the sentry behind us. My hail was promptly returned, so, jumping up to judge the distance, I lobbed the dispatch into the invisible trench close beside him. From the signallers' dugout round the corner the message was flashed back to Battalion Headquarters.

While preparing our dinner some time later, we were annoyed to find our cups and spoons coated with dust. These could only be rendered fit for use by washing, and water was scarce enough without that. However, there was no help for it but to spend a small quantity in this fashion, and accordingly we hoped more than ever that the supply promised us would not fail. At all events, as we might expect a renewal of the enemy's fire at any time, we resolved to wrap up all eating utensils in our trench coats. Eagerly we awaited the coming of nightfall. It seemed a lifetime since we had taken refuge in our dismal quarters. Never had a day appeared so long.

.   .   .   .   .

Strolling backwards and forwards through the long grass in rear of the company, many kept their ears alert for the first notes of a machine-gun, for the hour of gloaming is treacherous. Like spectres in the dusk, scattered forms prowled to and fro, emerging at last from their living tomb. To move, to stretch our cramped limbs, was our universal desire. Occasionally one cast a glance down the slope in front to make sure that we were indeed invisible to watchful eyes. Fading from brown to grey, the mottled expanse of tangled weed and grass grew lighter by degrees ; soon amid the night vapours it would become white and iridescent at countless points beneath the light of the moon. As the shadows thickened across the ground, the grass began to whisper to the sound of gliding feet, the silent earth gave up its hidden men, and the night grew full of subdued murmurs.

The empty portion of the abandoned trench was found to have been badly knocked about. Large craters gaped in and around it, marking the spots where the enemy's shells had fallen in the afternoon, and now striding over the ploughed soil, one could only feel thankful that we had chosen to occupy the trench in front. Though veiled complaints had been made of its discomfort, the choice of it had been the means of averting casualties, and I resolved to continue as before. In a few hours, " Number 2 " would need every man it could muster.

I had barely decided on this and brought my inspection to an end before a message was brought from the Commanding Officer: water and rations would reach us before long, and he himself would visit the company.

This reference to further supplies was welcome news, but what interested us more was the information concerning our right flank. MacIvor's company was to be relieved that night by one from the Essex Regiment. This meant that our battalion would have only one company, "Number 2," in the front line. The Ginchy-Lesbœufs road would mark our boundary as hitherto.

Accordingly, having noted some hours later the retirement of several platoons along the road to Ginchy, I set out to visit the new garrison across the road. They proved to be an unusually energetic lot, for on my arrival, they were already digging another support line which would carry on the alignment of our company. It did not take me long to inform them of our own dispositions, or to learn their intentions—MacIvor had already given them a careful and comprehensive account of the situation—so presently I returned, gratified to know that these new neighbours were men on whom we might rely.

Regaining the Lewis-gun post on the roadway, I there discovered the Commanding Officer, so the affairs of the company were soon thoroughly discussed. As on the previous night, our watches were arranged in alternate spells, and we settled down to what rest was possible under the prevailing conditions. The night revealed no unusual signs; the hours preceding dawn were perfectly peaceful.

Once more the company stood to arms, cramped and chilled by its exposure. A veil of darkness still hung above the hollow ground ahead, and the country lay in partial obscurity. Swinging our arms and blowing on our numbed hands, we paced to and

fro to restore our circulation, and we were thus engaged when a sudden outburst of detonations gave the
alarm.

Along on our left, opposite the front of the adjoining
battalion, there arose a sudden tumult, which, to our
accustomed ears, was easily recognisable as the reports
of many Mills bombs. Like a cluster of rabbits, we
vanished into the earth, every man peering expectantly
into the mist in front. Beyond the stretch of No Man's
Land spurted a sudden jet of flashes, followed a moment
later by the staccato notes of a machine-gun. Next
came a ripple of other stabs, rending the fog at irregular
intervals across the hollow. The air became filled with
the sound of rapid firing.

Many of the recruits made ready to reply in their
turn, but from this they were immediately ordered to
desist, since it was no part of our policy to reveal our
location to the enemy unless there was urgent need.

Suddenly the air above us was torn by the screaming gust of a swinging traverse. Bullets sped overhead like a squall of driven sleet and smothered their
eerie notes in the distance behind. All save the
sentries ducked behind the cover of the soil. But no
answer came from the British line ; even the bombing
party had ceased its noise. Gradually, as no further
events followed, the enemy must have realised his
waste of ammunition, as, not long after, his steady
flow of firing became spasmodic and finally died away.
Though this outburst had done us no harm, it had
notified us of one important fact : "Fritz's" nerves
were none too steady.

However averse we might be to staying all day in
the shell hole, there could be no doubt whether it was
the safest and the most convenient situation for Company Headquarters. After all, our regard for bodily
comfort was a secondary matter, more negligible still
when we considered that this was the last day before
"zero." Bearing in mind this consoling reflection, we

descended before long into the pit and busied ourselves with the preparation of breakfast. Overnight, our supplies had been replenished by the arrival of a sandbag containing sundry rations, but this we had refrained from opening until daylight. Now fired with pleasurable curiosity, we inspected its contents; whereupon our satisfaction was turned to disgust. Plenty of bread was there, it was true, also a tin of sardines and a tin of pork and beans, but water was totally wanting. This deficiency was felt the more keenly by reason of the substitution of a bottle of port and a half-bottle of whisky ; the latter without water was quite useless. When all is said and done, most men's weak spot lies in the region of their belt. To us at any rate the situation was miserable. To pass an entire day on a diet of sardines, chocolate, and ration biscuits, was no great hardship, but to face a second on the same fare seemed horrible. Even the addition of pork and beans to our menu did not compensate us for the lamentable fact that our only drink was port !

Sitting down to a breakfast of sardines and biscuit, we thought sorrowfully of those fabulous meals with which condemned criminals are said to be regaled on the eve of their execution.

In the midst of our meal, we were disturbed by the sound of a hail outside. It was one of the signallers trying to attract our attention. The next moment, in answer to one's shout, a ball of mud landed on the edge of our crater, whence we could easily retrieve it with the crooked handle of a walking-stick. Its contents proved that our morning would be far from dull.

" Any news ? " inquired my companion, noting my grimace.

" Nothing very much ; only a big shoot by our guns, which they want us to observe for them and report on. Lesbœufs is to be knocked about, and their wire cut."

" Oh ! " he cried, realising the significance of my last words, " that sounds pretty cheerful—for us ! "

Breakfast finished, we profited from our late experience by putting away our food and cups into a sandbag, after which, leaving St. Helier to the joys of his manual, I prepared my periscope for the morning's entertainment. It only wanted another half-hour before our guns were due to open fire.

Several months before I had been guilty of imagining that a bombardment by massed batteries commenced simultaneously. I was not surprised, now, to find that at 7·30, the time scheduled beforehand, no great demonstration was noticeable.

A deep moan through the sky was the first intimation of any firing. This ended abruptly in a muffled detonation from the landscape opposite. Then followed sinister sounds as other projectiles cleft the atmosphere overhead and exploded at a distance of nearly a mile within the enemy's positions. Rolling across the countryside, the sullen echoes of each report came distinctly to our ears. In the periscope, sprays of dust were visible as they gushed upward from the trees that enclosed the village, mingling their strange variety of hues. Yonder belched a cloud of lyddite smoke ; there, where a hit had been made on a brick barn, the hanging pall was reddened by the powdered dust of the shattered target. Grouped like gigantic and nodding plumes, the explosions reared themselves along the front of Lesbœufs.

Slowly, merged in the prolonged wail of these medium shells, a new note became distinguishable : the rasping shrieks of high-velocity 18-pounders. These, skimming past at a lower altitude, seemed to rival the noise of their more ponderous brethren up above, and as they ripped by, the air was stirred by their transit. Above the hollow ground at the foot of our slope, they burst in the air like a chaplet of moving pearls. It was a salvo of shrapnel searching the German front line.

Constantly, seen in the small mirror before me, fan-shaped splashes of earth darted heavenward from the distant trees, and amid their folds, gleaming wickedly, there appeared for an instant lurid flashes of fire. Across the face of the smoke-dimmed trunks they seemed like sudden eruptions of a volcano. As recorded by the periscope, the scene resembled a cinematograph; but however lacking in actuality it might appear, its echoes left us in no uncertainty as to its reality.

A sudden squall mingled abruptly with the notes of the cannonade; the air lashed furiously above our heads; a chorus of screams burst from the heart of the tumult; and the pitch of the oratorio leapt to a higher key. The enemy were replying at last!

Happily for us, they sought our batteries rather than our trenches. So long as they did not lower their elevation we should be perfectly safe, though this was hardly credible at first. By degrees, Lesbœufs became obscured by a veil of smoke, and its dark mass of trees grew misty; yet we could still discern its shattered church tower where it protruded like a huge splinter from the mangled tree-tops. Nearer by several hundred yards, a multi-coloured mantle of dust and smoke hung above the enemy's front line like a belt of fog.

Observation of the village became difficult toward midday owing to the clouds of smoke that entirely hid it; but it was obvious that every shot was falling in and around the enemy's support line. In the occasional lulls of the artillery contest we could hear a mighty gurgling far above us denoting the passage of yet larger projectiles. These, wallowing noisily across the heavens, descended into the village amid a terrible eruption of fire and ruin. On our right front, slightly nearer to us, we could see the bombardment of a German redoubt on the farther side of the Ginchy road, but there our fire was not nearly so effective.

Many of our shells failed to explode; a fact speedily telephoned to Battalion Headquarters. Also, their front-line entanglements opposite, so far as we could see, appeared to be but slightly damaged.

So preoccupied were we in "spotting" for the guns, that the arrival of a message from the signallers came as a surprise. Its contents were no less disconcerting: "Zero Day" had been postponed officially until the 25th!

For several minutes it required an effort of mind for us to realise that our day of trial had been deferred. After all, the following dawn would *not* see us swarming forward to the attack. That nightmare thought had pestered us for many an hour past, and now all our resignation and resolution was wasted. This reprieve would add another forty-eight hours to our period of suspense, a period which had already seemed interminably long. To us who had lived the lives of beasts of the field, the prospect of another two days of waiting seemed overwhelming. Nerves which had been strung to meet the direst fate could hardly endure this prolonged affliction.

The possibility of our being relieved, though feasible to oneself, remained far too uncertain for actual discussion, therefore we awaited further news with what calm we could assume.

* * * * *

During the afternoon, the bombardment of Lesbœufs was renewed after a spell of quiet. Bursting out with redoubled intensity, the light batteries now contributed an unparalleled display, for shells no longer screeched overhead independently, but in salvos. Their flight gave forth the note of a rushing wind. Drowned by the torrent of the British fire, the enemy's retaliation seemed insignificant; the sounds of its passage were lost within the din. Powerful though our guns had shown themselves at Serre, their output there seemed now to be totally outclassed.

A clatter of falling clods was our first warning that shells were falling in our vicinity. Turning away from the periscope, I caught sight of a cloud of debris rising like a waterspout about forty yards distant. The cascade interrupted attention to the scene in front. Then came the realisation that the enemy in their turn were bombarding our position. Along a frontage of about a hundred yards, we counted as many as a dozen explosions in a minute, and these, spouting aloft continuously, were filling the air with a dense cloud of dust. As more earth continued to be hurled over us, and driven particles seemed to find a way down our necks in spite of the brims of our helmets, we were presently compelled to turn up the collars of our jackets.

Although the view in the mirror was too enthralling to permit one paying much heed to these detonations, the moment of their arrival was disclosed by the tremor of the picture in the periscope. Every concussion of a large-calibre shell necessitated a readjustment of the angle of the mirrors. It was during such a moment that my attention was diverted by the sound of St. Helier's voice. Turning sharply in his direction, I saw that he was shouting at me.

"There's someone in front trying to attract our notice. He's just crawled into the little trench."

"Just find out from him what it is," I cried, turning once more to watch the enemy's fire.

A few moments later a grip fell on my arm.

"One of our guns is shooting short. Three shells have just missed Number 8 Platoon along on the left."

"How do they know it is one of ours?"

"I don't know, but the message comes from Sergeant Repton."

"No good running risks of that sort; we've been jolly lucky as it is. I'll write a message asking them to check. Try to call up the signallers while I do so."

So a couple of minutes later, our "call" was being transmitted along the solitary wire on which depended our sole hope of salvation. Whatever the truth of the matter, we were not troubled with further complaints from the left-flank platoon.

Just as we were about to commence our evening meal the intelligence for which we had been waiting arrived. "Number 2" was to be withdrawn by and by, another company from the supports taking its place. We were then to proceed to Bernafay Wood, where we should become part of the battalion reserve. There we should remain for a two days' rest.

CHAPTER XVIII

It was nearly 2 o'clock on the following morning when the company arrived at Bernafay Wood. The buoyant spirit with which we had left the line had evaporated long since ; most of us, by the time we had accomplished half our march, would have readily remained in those primitive abodes from which we had set out. Long hours of steady marching had called forth almost our last efforts.

Floundering across acres of wilderness, and groping our way along unknown tracks, we had come near to losing ourselves on more than one occasion, and the resulting feeling of uncertainty had added considerably to our strain.

To make our way back by the former road to Ginchy had been easy, but following that, our troubles had commenced. Continuing along a narrow track, we had filed past many a forlorn spot, whence a terrible odour had risen upon the night. Hour by hour we had toiled onward, our progress resembling rather the timorous gait of blind men than any likeness to a march. Despite the ground having dried to some extent since we had left the Citadel, exhausting conditions had not been wanting. Time and time again, we had been compelled to check our advance on account of the erasure of all signs of a path ahead. To push forward through a maze of shell craters was impossible : the company, extended in single file, would never have been able to keep in touch with itself. Accordingly, scouts had been sent forward to reconnoitre the ground, thus reducing our progress through the darkness to a series of abrupt advances and gradual halts.

After a lapse of several hours, we had emerged at last at some point along the Guillemont road, and thereafter we had been able to move with more assurance. But so exhausted were we by then, that we were only able to crawl along at a snail's pace, and, to complete our misfortunes, a misdirection caused us to make a needless detour of another mile. This, in our condition, represented the best part of an hour's march.

To the recruits freshly arrived from the Base, the toil and fatigue of this night came as another revelation. Their first experience of the line had been a hard one, but now, concluding their ordeal, they had been subjected to this further test. With few exceptions, they had risen to the occasion in a plucky manner, and though hardly possessed of the stoical endurance of the remaining veterans, they had acquitted themselves very creditably. Now, however, we had reached the wood that was to shelter us for the next forty-eight hours ; we could not have proceeded very much farther without a considerable rest.

Scarcely had leave to fall out been given before the entire company subsided by the roadside, crippled with fatigue. Surrendering themselves to their craving for sleep, they lay like logs along the ditch and many immediately fell asleep.

Somewhere in the darkness, the company cooker should be awaiting our arrival. To search for it and guide the company there was my first duty, yet owing to the gloom and the passing traffic, this seemed far from easy. It would probably take some time. I was in no better state than most of the men, so discarding and leaving my equipment with St. Helier, I struggled forward in the direction of Brigade Head-

21

quarters. Near there, someone would probably be able to supply me with the information I so urgently needed.

For the first time that night Fortune proved kind, for I had not proceeded more than a hundred yards or so upon my way before I caught sight of a guardsman standing upon a bank that separated the road from the wood.

In answer to my hail, he informed me that he was not only a Coldstreamer, but belonged to my own battalion.

" What company ? "

" Number 2, sir. The cooker's waiting for you among the trees here." His outstretched arm indicated a sombre mass of trunks.

Ten minutes later, in an open clearing within the wood, the men had grouped themselves round the cooker; as soon as we had warmed ourselves with a tin of tea, we should all be at liberty to turn in for our much-desired rest. Now came visions of a comfortable dugout in which one might lie at full length and ease aching limbs ; a luxurious palace, it would seem, after the burrowed hole in which we had passed the last two days.

By and by, escorted by the company quartermaster-sergeant, I hastened to inspect the quarters assigned to the men.

" What sort of accommodation is there here ? " I asked, following his lead through the shadows.

" Awful, sir ! It's wicked to treat fellows so."

" What ! There must be some kind of shelter for us ? "

" No, sir ; nothing that I'd like to offer to a cow, begging your pardon."

A pause ensued, during which we continued to tramp over the uneven ground that everywhere extended into the trees around us.

" Well, we aren't exactly particular," I remarked

after a while. " The place which we have come from wasn't what you'd call a ' desirable mansion.' "

At this moment the quartermaster-sergeant halted, and indicating the grey obscurity before us, observed drily : " Here we are, sir. This is the company area."

On all sides lay a chaos of upturned earth and splintered trees. Built among the exposed roots of a huge trunk stood a primitive shack ; to judge from the noise arising from its neighbourhood, it swarmed with rats. No dugout, no hovel, was visible ; just a dreary expanse of misty desolation ; no cover, no shelter of any kind.

Staring incredulously before me, I half expected to find myself deceived by my own eyes. Surely it was not for this that we had laboured so miserably on our homeward way ?

Our silence was broken at last by my companion. Never before had I heard so much eloquence expressed by a sniff. The sound brought me back to the grim reality of the situation. I swore heartily—and comprehensively.

.   .   .   .   .

Abruptly I discovered that I had been asleep. My rest had been interrupted by the cold. How short my trench coat seemed, and how chilled my legs ! My movement as I sat up was echoed by a medley of creaks and gratings : the protesting voice of my humble bed. Before me, dividing the darkness in which I had been lying, loomed an irregular patch of opalescent light. Then I remembered where I was.

With stiffened fingers I drew back the cuff of my coat and examined my wrist-watch. It was only four o'clock. Surely I had slept for more than an hour ! Raising it to my ear, I listened intently—no, it was still going.

Recollections of my half-hour's search for a resting-place came distantly to mind. They all seemed so

remote; yet they were barely an hour old. My fruitless quest within the wood; my disappointment at
Brigade Headquarters; my return to the company, and
final resignation; all came flooding back. I remembered
how, in despair and staggering with weariness, I
had discovered this hole in a bank, and my primitive
efforts to arrange a bed. Marauding around the motionless bodies of my men in the hour before dawn,
I had lighted upon some half-dozen of those wicker-
work cases in which German shells are often packed.
With these I had contrived a mattress only a few
degrees more soft than the jumble of refuse that
strewed the floor of my cave, and upon them I had
sunk in a lethargy born of utter exhaustion. It all
seemed so long ago. Those were memories of the night
before; now it was morning.

Stretching my cramped limbs, I crawled forth into
the twilight. Everywhere around lay the silence of
dawn. Yonder among the craters and cavities of the
wood, one could perceive the huddled forms of the
company as it slept. A profound and merciful stupor
still possessed them. How cold it was, and how forlorn!
The aspect of the dreary vistas of tree-trunks chilled
one's very eye.

To restore my circulation, I set off on a ramble
through the trees and emerged by and by into a
road, which ran along the rear edge of the wood.
This proved to be the same by which the battalion
had passed on its march up from the Citadel. Then,
obscured by night, it had seemed to hum with a throng
of traffic, now it receded on either hand along its tree-
lined embankment, an empty expanse. No man or
creature stirred. All was still.

Swinging my arms and stepping out, I set off on my
walk, and as I strode forward I marvelled how even
one hour sufficed to rest a man.

Some hours later, having breakfasted with St. Helier
at the mouth of my cave, I came across MacIvor.
He and his company had been resting here since the
night of their relief. It was but a sorry tale he had
to tell, and my fears were more than confirmed by
his account of his company's experiences. Their fate,
it seemed, had been precisely similar to ours : an
exhausted arrival followed by a rest amid misery.
True they had managed to find a disused German
trench, but even there their plight was hardly preferable
to our own. Tins of stinking meat and other sundry
afflictions could be easily disposed of, but not so the
numerous bodies that choked the surrounding ground.
As for himself, he had managed to annex a tumbled-
down shelter built in the ditch of the road, but owing
to its meagre accommodation and the presence of a
fellow officer, he could not invite me to share it.

My recollection of the abominable discomfort of that
first day at Bernafay Wood is still vivid. Though soon
fatigued after our exertions of the previous night, we
were compelled to keep warm by constant movement;
of hot food there was none to be had. This frequent
strolling to and fro would have been bearable had the
weather kept fine, but it was not long before a steady
rainfall reduced all ranks to the depths of depression.
For all the rest we were getting, we might just as well
have remained in the front line.

But even when assailed by " the blues," the British
soldier remains a man of considerable resource, and
this fact was amply revealed when next time one
visited the company. Ground-sheets and comman-
deered sandbags had been employed with no little
profit ; an hour's labour with an entrenching-tool had
brought improvement to many a hole or crevice ; and
the smoke of several camp-fires served to dispel the
misery of many a sodden wretch.

But however praiseworthy these efforts, they by no
means exhausted the latent possibilities of the place.

While gazing round the desolate bivouac a sudden inspiration seized me; the idea was obvious and easy to carry out. In answer to my call, several N.C.Os came running forward. My order was met with stolid surprise, but presently, as it became known to the men, much curiosity arose on all sides. "The officer" had surely gone off his head?

But ten minutes later the method underlying my madness became apparent to all. With the aid of several former farm-labourers, a very respectable hurdle was fashioned from the abundance of brushwood that lay around. The new occupation, thus demonstrated before their eyes, was instantly taken up by the others, and it was not long before an enthusiastic company had converted itself into a hurdle factory, skilled hands apportioned to each group of workmen.

Later in the afternoon, having occasion to visit my cave, I was surprised, and not a little touched, to find four new hurdles left there by some unknown persons. Then my pleasure subsided. Had my servant "pinched" them? No, in this case I was glad to find he had not.

However, it was not necessary to avail oneself of this offering, for toward evening a great discovery was made by MacIvor, a discovery which was hailed delightedly by all officers of the two companies.

Anyone who has undergone the vicissitudes of active service will readily admit that, without considerably developed predatory instincts, the individual is indeed apt to fare badly. Within limits, it is no exaggeration to say that the hand of every man is lifted against his brother. Now the canny MacIvor was no exception to this rule.

Prospecting in the neighbourhood of Brigade Headquarters, his roving eye had noted the presence of a party of pioneers. "Every picture tells a story," he reminded me in the course of his subsequent narrative. Therefore, pursuing his investigations farther, he had

lighted on a great opportunity. Near-by, a newly
erected hut of corrugated iron and match-boarding
awaited its occupants. Who could possibly do that
more thoroughly than ourselves ?—the miscellaneous
personnel attached to the in-coming Divisional Headquarters ?—surely not! Necessity, acting as a spur,
endowed him with unlimited bluff. No more need be
said.

The rightful owners did not arrive that night, but,
notwithstanding that, there occurred a mighty house-
warming. Four officers regaled themselves with a hot
dinner off a table, laughing and making light of recent
hardships, since they who had lately lived as Gentlemen
of the Road now found themselves amid the magnifi-
cence of kings.

> " Look around and you will find
> Every cloud is silver lined."

Bellowed in uproarious chorus, and defying the possible
approach of would-be dispossessors, the snatch of song
sped from the lighted interior and mingled its notes
with the booming artillery outside. At last, surfeited
with warm food, we laid ourselves down to rest, for
the morrow would be the 24th, and that, as everyone
knew, was the eve of " Zero Day." That night I slept
upon a table-top—three consecutive hours of blessed
sleep—practically the first I had had for four days.

.   .   .   .   .

Bernafay Wood was a weird enough spot even in
daylight. This much I had been able to ascertain
for myself the day before, but having occasion to
wander through it on the morrow, I began to grow
more conscious of its spell.

In a wood that had once been dense, and of many
acres, not one undamaged tree remained. Most seemed
to have been shorn to half their height by the sweep
of a gigantic scythe. Splintered trunks leant at every

angle ; some burst asunder a few feet from the ground, others propped drunkenly in the arms of an upright neighbour, whose branches thus lent it friendly support. Every object revealed the scars of battle. These varied in every imaginable degree. Here the sap-wood fangs of a tortured stem gleamed conspicuously, there another shot-torn pole rivalled their tone, for not only had this apparition suffered total amputation, but its rigid trunk had been subsequently flayed by passing bullets. Small-arm fire had completed the havoc of the guns, scattering on all sides portions of bark and splinters which now lay embedded in the hardening mud.

But strange and terrible though all this wreckage seemed, what struck the spectator most was its unnatural appearance. Leaves and twigs still survived, but, almost without exception, these either dangled brokenly from a tangle of branches or lay in their profusion on the ground. Here was a wood whose foliage grew upside down ! This effect was intensified by the position of the trees themselves, as many now stood upon a foundation of branches and reared their spongy roots upward to the sky. Everywhere the wood appeared to have been immobilised in the midst of a frenzied dance, its wild antics arrested for the benefit of Man's inspection.

Furthermore, the surrounding chaos was not formed by the mangled trees alone, though these would have amply sufficed to create a most awe-inspiring scene ; the ground below contributed also to the spectacle. Here the earth had been whipped by a passing tornado. Huge craters and furrows abounded in every direction, crossing and mingling in a maze of monstrous scars. Soil could hardly have been so churned since those prehistoric days when fabulous beasts had lived on earth : here was a relic of Antiquity, a former battle-ground of mammoths. Not only had it been pitted by shell fire, but its pounded surface had

been kneaded again and again by a relentless convulsion. Here and there among the mass of debris, you
noticed a few yards of crumbled trench, visible at
various intervals, and seeming to shun your gaze.
Battered, bare, and desolate to the eye, these troughs
strove to hide their nakedness by submerging into the
shapeless waves around them.

Over this sea of storm-tossed ground one made
one's way, now descending into a hollow, now scrambling over a hummock. Constant detours were necessary in order to pass a fallen trunk or to avoid a
muddy shell hole. Progress through this stricken spot
bred speculation on the struggle it had witnessed. To
imagine this, no further testimony than what lay
before one was necessary. Several weeks had elapsed
since our troops had seized this wood, but, in spite of
that, a litter of accoutrements still remained. Sodden
and rusted, trampled and embedded in the clogging
mire, an arsenal of discarded kit lay scattered far and
wide. Rifles, jackets, and dented helmets emerged in
all directions, some still recognisable as our own,
others obviously German. Here, as on previous occasions, I was struck by the impression that scores of
men had stripped themselves naked for the contest.
Clothing lay here, there, everywhere.

Beside a crumpled gas-helmet emerged an unex-
ploded shell; close by, a twisted bayonet caked in mud
jutted from a mass of burst sandbags. Yonder, protruding from a matted heap of refuse, a shattered
German rifle caught my eye. The butt was missing,
and a jagged stump alone remained. How could so
stout a weapon have come by such an injury ? Was
it a flying shell splinter, or was it a human obstacle ?
Ammunition may have run out—a clubbed rifle is a
fearful thing.

Farther on amid the trees stood a derelict field-
gun. Its muzzle projected from its crumpled shield,
and from the direction in which it was laid one knew

it must be a German 77. Its wheels had been reduced
to a mass of splintered spokes, and upon its dingy coat
of grey paint, scars displayed themselves like splashes
of silver. Once it had fired at desperate speed, flinging
its thunderous echoes through the wood, but now the
tide of war had swept onward, leaving it like a wreck
stranded on a hostile shore.

A glance in any direction revealed merely a fresh
vista of devastation. Here and there, patches of colour
claimed attention by reason of their rarity. On all
sides undulated a monotonous expanse, in places
relieved only by yellow patches of high explosive.

But it is not by its awful sordidness alone that a
visitor remembers Bernafay. The mind was assailed
to an equal degree by what the wood hid but did not
obliterate. Our burial parties had already done their
work, but it called for no effort of imagination for one
to realise what the tumbled ground contained. Death
encumbered the grisly spot: shrivelled Nature above,
slaughtered Man beneath.

But no Devil's Acre this.

Although hideous and repellent to look upon, the surrounding misery grew glorious to the eye as one recalled
the legends of the wood. Rivalling Trônes—need more
be said ?—here spread a mighty graveyard, a heroic
sepulchre. No altar ever bore a nobler sacrifice.

Stumbling onward, I presently came to a halt.
Near-by, a skinny hand and arm protruding from a
mound of mud seemed outstretched in silent pleading,
as if dumbly beseeching the prayers of the passer-by.

Gazing in meditation on this relic, one beheld an
answer given. There, hovering on the grave, lustrous
in the golden sunlight, flitted a fellow pilgrim to this
shrine of Valour—a snow-white butterfly. But at that
moment its true identity blazed forth : the Spirit of
the Wood. Immortal Bernafay had been transplanted
—borne to the Elysian Fields !

It was on my return to our hut that I found a message ordering both companies to rejoin the battalion in the line that night. "Zero" had been fixed for the following day.

CHAPTER XIX

THE EVE OF BATTLE

THE silence of the wood was broken only by the clatter of our footfalls. Driven to the edge of the track by the darkness cast across it, the company stole over the moonlit ground, glancing occasionally at the silvery glades that seemed to beckon with countless fingers. But to-night, Trônes Wood was robbed of half its grimness ; more forbidding were our thoughts of the morrow. Through the obscurity we stumbled, emerging at last on the farther side shaken and harassed by the irregularity of the way. Here, according to orders, a tool-cart should have been awaiting us, but this proved to be a piece of kindly fiction.

Hereupon, one was confronted almost at the very outset of our march with the unexpected problem of how to equip the company with picks and spades ; for the advance party sent ahead to locate the waggon had failed to discover any trace of it. The affair might have caused us to lose valuable time had I not remembered a detail of our previous march : the tracks ahead of us had been strewn with implements.

Along this portion of our journey our course was easy, since all that we had to do was to follow the light railway toward Guillemont. Along this line we had no difficulty in finding many tools. Within half an hour every man had acquired one.

The march that followed proved just the same ordeal as those which we had already undergone, only it seemed longer and the ground more uneven than ever. We located the sites of Guillemont and Ginchy by means of a few charred stumps ; no surer landmarks were to be found. This country, for all that we could tell, might never have been inhabited by Man. Of course we lost ourselves ; we had never done so before, but on this night of all nights that fate overtook us. For nearly an hour we wandered across the trackless waste east of Ginchy before we chanced upon a battery from which we learnt the direction of our brigade frontage. Steering by compass the course indicated, I managed at last to strike upon a trench. In it, much to the relief of all, we discovered a party of guardsmen that was able to direct us to the support trench of our battalion. At Headquarters, where I presently reported our arrival, I found it was already midnight. We had covered about seven miles in five hours.

The Battalion Headquarters were situated in a deep and spacious dugout, the work of German sappers. There must have been nearly eighteen steps to descend before one entered a musty and gloomy apartment. There the dense shadows were dispelled by the light of a couple of candles, which stood embedded in grease upon a map-strewn table. As I arrived, the Commanding Officer and the acting Adjutant were poring over a series of telephonic messages, and at the sound of my noisy entry, heavily accoutred as I was, and in peril of being precipitated by the abruptness of the descent, they both looked up.

" Ah, there you are ! " the former exclaimed, cutting short my few formal words. " We've been waiting for you this last half-hour. Have you brought those spades ? "

" Yes, sir ; the tool-cart never turned up, so I had to pillage a few R.E. dumps as we came along. As the signposts have disappeared in many places, we missed our way this side of Ginchy."

" Well, that's all over now. Just look at this list and let me know if your men are provided with the things mentioned."

" Yes, we've got everything," I replied a moment later, " except the flares, rifle grenades, and rockets."

" Good ! Then if you'll come along with me, I'll show you where your lot have got to go, and after that, I can take you to the dump where you shall draw the flares, etcetera."

Hereupon, after negotiating the steps, I was conducted by the Commanding Officer along the support line, until, still following his shadowy form, I found myself scrambling up into the darkness in front. Here we heard presently the multitudinous clicks and thuds of a company engaged in digging, and a minute later we could make out their irregular line.

" I hope your people are feeling pretty fresh," my companion observed. "They've got a hard night's digging before them. There's no communication trench up to the front line, as no doubt you remember, and we've got to make one before daylight. Here's your area. Can you find your way back here ? Right ! Come along now, and I'll show you the dump."

To the dump accordingly we made our way, and there we discovered everything in readiness for the company.

It did not take me long to conduct " Number 2 " to the scene of their allotted task, or to dispatch a party to the dump for the purpose of collecting our supplies. Both were quickly done, so, after leaving the men in St. Helier's charge, I hastened to attend a conference at Headquarters. This, among other matters, proved to be a final review of the plan of attack for the morrow : a question of supreme importance to us all.

.   .   .   .   .

The ensuing discussion revealed the following situation. Opposite the battalion front, which I had held a couple of days before, lay the enemy in what was known as the Green Line, distant about 400 yards. Behind that lay the village of Lesbœufs, perhaps 600 yards farther, its near edge abutting against a sunken road that was known to be fortified. This, their support position, was known as the Brown Line. Beyond that again, on the farther side of Lesbœufs, was a third, the Blue Line, which constituted our final objective. The distance to be travelled by our assault was about 1,200 yards.

The right flank of the brigade was to skirt the Ginchy-Lesbœufs road. Running aslant across the line of our proposed advance, and adjoining the diagonal ends of the Green and Brown Lines, lay another sunken road of the same size. In it we suspected the existence of enemy dugouts. This was the Diagonal Road.

These features comprised the principal tactical points of the hostile position, though we were far from forgetting the presence of the redoubt beyond our right flank, from which we anticipated heavy enfilade fire across the exposed downward slope separating the Green and Brown Lines.

In the attack, our battalion would be preceded by one of the Grenadier Guards. This already occupied the front line, toward which we were digging our communication trench. The Grenadiers were to be flanked on their left by a battalion of Irish Guards, and both these units would be supported by the two Coldstream battalions of the brigade. This disposition of the different regiments represented a complete reversal of the order of battle used on the 15th and 16th.

But though our order was changed in the customary manner, no alterations, save those of detail, were contemplated in the method of our advance.

At " Zero " (12.35 p.m.), the leading waves of Grenadiers and Irish were to advance ; a " stationary " barrage would descend on to the Green Line ; and a " creeping " barrage would appear a hundred yards ahead of the foremost wave. This latter, trailing across No Man's Land until it merged into the other, would precede the infantry like a wall of fire. Then, both lifting a hundred yards beyond the trench, the leading battalions would storm the position The movements of "Number 2" during this stage of the action would be limited to occupying the departure trench of the Grenadiers.

In this way, each German line was to be attacked methodically at an hour's interval. Barrages would again be employed as before. Thus, at 1.35 p.m., the leading waves would resume their advance, and "Number 2" would cross to the Green Line in readiness to support the Grenadiers when the time came for their assault on the village. For this duty the company had been specially equipped. Large numbers of Mills and incendiary bombs had been distributed to it, for Lesbœufs was known to contain many elaborate systems of cellars, from which the enemy could only be driven by the use of such weapons. Simultaneously, the remainder of the battalion would move up to the Green Line and consolidate it against any possible counter-attack.

An hour later, the intense double barrage would sweep over the village, drawing in its wake the leading infantry; "Number 2" would deal with all "strong points" in their rear; and the rest of the battalion, leaving one company in reserve in the Green Line, would advance once more and recommence consolidation. This third stage would complete the active operations of the brigade.

. . . . .

The study of these plans did not claim much of our time, since they were already known to us all, and it was only due to a regard for prudence that a last examination of them was considered necessary. After half an hour the officers' conference broke up, leaving us free to rejoin our commands. The moment of our departure was a solemn one. As all understood their respective duties, the flow of questions and replies had ceased. Following the Commanding Officer's last words came an impressive silence, and the pause threatened to become painful, until first one, then another, pushed back his seat and rose to his feet. Unusual gravity had settled on the faces of all. Breaking the stillness, a subdued echo wafted down the narrow staircase, and to our listening ears its sullen note suggested the toll of a muffled bell.

On regaining the company, I found with some surprise that admirable progress had been made in my absence. In spite of the exhaustion of our night march, the men were responding gallantly to the call made on them; a hundred yards of trench had been dug already. Necessity spurred their efforts. This was no time for repining at fatigue. By daylight a trench to the front line had to be cut at all costs; our plans required it, our hopes demanded it. The performance of this night ranks among the most impressive war pictures within my experience. Though only an affair of pick and spade, the episode revealed the great qualities of our recruits. Those who had staggered to their task a couple of hours before now seemed to scorn the trials of their present lot. Weariness and discouragement were vanquished by their sense of duty. Some worked like automatons, others with a smouldering fury. To many troops this eleventh-hour task would have been unachievable, but its infliction came to these men as a challenge to their physique. Racked with exhaustion and the hardships of the last few days, they strove desperately to accomplish what seemed impossible. And they succeeded—succeeded at last— just as the dawn crept upward behind Lesbœufs.

Growing brighter minute by minute, the day of ordeal stole upon us. Watched from the new trench in which we had already sought refuge, it approached

22

with unparalleled dignity. Before its stealthy advance, the green and amber hues of twilight faded imperceptibly, and over the face of the country brooded a deathlike silence, stirred only from time to time by the wakening notes of a lark. Against the rosy glow the village trees turned from black to purple, countless tints of colour tinged the landscape, while over all hung a motionless haze. From one moment to another, the scene unfolded all the colours of Creation. Before our eyes the flush of the eastern sky gave place to an iridescent glow, purple and crimson lit to red and orange. Then, amid the mists, arose a chant of birds : the world was stirring in its sleep. Soon the heavens glowed with reflected light, each fleeting phase surpassing the former in wondrous beauty, and against this background floated a blotch of clouds, diaphanous, and burnished on their lower edges by the first rays of the rising sun. The spectacle seemed to contain an omen.

Now slashing the sky with lurid streaks of fire, the sun proclaims its imminent approach. At the sight, a glorious record of such a dawn steals back to one's memory. Here, lighting the way for History, a soldier's sunrise comes to greet us. Each moment intensifies the impression.

At last the skyline merges into a sheet of fire, the horizon grows dim to dazzled eyes. There! riding upon a flood of glory and mantled in majesty, looms a blazing blood-red orb. It is the Sun of Austerlitz !

.   .   .   .   .

Hour after hour this fateful vigil dragged on and on. The daylight, climbing aloft in the cloudless heavens, must have drawn the thoughts of many in its wake. Already our ears were assailed by a furious cannonade.

Hour after hour the air shrieked in torment. We who watched and waited in the narrow trench found distraction in the wanderings of beetles and other insects that crawled along the walls and floor of our refuge. Against the side most of us had cut a seat, but even that did not serve entirely to relieve us in our cramped confinement. These hours seemed an eternity.

Slowly the hands of my watch crept onward—one could not help wondering whether it would ever be rewound again—in another hour, I reflected, we should have started. . . .

How can one describe the emotions with which we watched the last five minutes go ? For the hundredth time I looked to see—and as I looked, the hour was struck by an uproar of artillery !

CHAPTER XX

" God made them stubble to our swords "

THE moment of "Zero" had arrived, bringing with it a spontaneous tempest of gunfire. Overhead, the sounds swelled to an unparalleled volume, and the earth around commenced to throb and tremble. Merging into the din, a new note grew audible—the note one remembered so well at Festubert—the death-dirge of machine-guns. The Grenadiers had started.

Before very long, the surrounding turmoil developed into a frenzy. Heavy earthquakes shook us from head to foot ; terrible concussions smote the air. Huddling on to our heels and straining our necks upward to watch the grass beside the trench, we realised that the German barrage had opened ; and as it poured on to our line its crashes followed every second, until they blended into a continuous roar. You could only speak to a neighbour by shouting. Gradually, the shocks approaching, and the trench drumming deafeningly to the storm, fear crept into one's heart. Our minds became dazed, dazed like those of the insignificant insects which, shaken down by the vibrations, and alarmed at the inexplicable convulsion that had suddenly engulfed their world, now scurried frantically upon the floor.

Amid this inferno, an order reached us to advance.

The effect of this message was magical, for, bewildered by the storm, one's mind had begun to drift like a ship, driving here and there before a turmoil of impressions; but now, as one crawled forward over the mounds of earth hurled into the trench, the midday nightmare lifted from one's brain.

Soon a check arrested our progress, and an order, coming from goodness knew where, informed us that we were to retire. Again and again the message was howled down the line, but no movement followed; like dazed sheep, the men remained crowded in an immovable mass. Again word was passed along, but with no more result than before. Then, born amid this critical situation, and spreading with incredible swiftness from mouth to mouth, a rumour reached us that the Irish Guards had not started. This panic nonsense found some credence with the men, whose spirits drooped accordingly. A few minutes later, the information reached us from the rear that our support battalion had piled itself upon our reserve company, thus making it impossible for us to retire. This doubtful intelligence was quickly followed once more by an order from the Commanding Officer to advance.

So bewildering and so swift had been our impressions, that it was difficult to estimate the flight of time. Already it was " zero plus one hour." According to the prearranged plan, the company should have commenced its advance, instead of which it had not yet reached its starting-point. Our support might be needed desperately at this very moment.

Vaguely we realised that the concussions had slightly diminished. Turning into our assaulting-trench, we found it crowded by one of the other companies, but not so obstructed as to prevent our passing it. At last, after inexplicable delays, " Number 2 " was reaching its allotted position. All this time, nothing of what had been happening in front had been visible to us in the trench. Along it, the German barrage appeared to have fortunately slackened, so, passing along, I cast about for a suitable exit and, finding one scrambled over the parapet. In the act of doing so I looked back, and could see the last platoon emerging from the communication trench. We were half an hour late.

A heavy explosion shook the ground as the nearest man to me leapt the sandbags: a shell had landed within ten yards of us. Then, in response to a signal, platoon after platoon clawed its way over, and presently, in a long extended line, crouched in the long grass outside the trench. A loud blast on a whistle and a slow gesture galvanised them into motion. A murmur of sound arose as the line surged to its feet. Silent and grim, it faltered an instant. No cheer was heard. A line of swaying flashes rippled along our front as the sun gleamed brightly on a hundred bayonets.

" Forward, the Coalies ! "

Above the clank of accoutrements and the swish of trampled grass, the solitary cry rang like a bugle call. Flitting overhead, the hum of many bullets filled our ears ; others, nearer still, careered past with the crack of a whiplash. Swerving and jumping, we cleared the bodies of numerous Grenadiers huddled in the grass of No Man's Land. Some still moved and even called to us, but we could not stay. Ahead of us, running in a straggling maze of wire and riven sandbags, lay the enemy's front line.

Our feet laboured and pounded with the futility of a nightmare : we seemed glued to one spot. At last, as we drew near the remains of their entanglements, the bodies of our comrades grew thicker, and over them a ghost-like figure drifted toward us. It was a German, who, with uplifted arms and blubbering face, mouthed a terrible appeal. A moment later, in response to an abrupt gesture, he plunged headlong through our ranks, clasping his shaking hands above his head and weeping with uncontrollable relief. Bunched here and there in tangled heaps, the wire lay scattered across a chaos of shell holes, and from it, hanging in splintered frag-

ments, protruded the remains of many stakes. Through
this we stamped our way onward : here on every side
lay numbers of dead Guardsmen. In the trench no sign
of life was visible : the leading wave had already passed
on. Into it I now jumped, a glance sufficing to show how
thorough their work had been, for lying stark and bloody
on either hand were swathes of our enemies on to which
the leaping figures of our line were now descending.

Shouting, swearing, and slipping, they tumbled into
the trench like an avalanche and darted to and fro in
quest of a quarry. But in this we were baulked, because no living soul remained. Running over a human
carpet, one directed the N.C.Os to reorganise their
men. Of the Grenadiers, no traces were visible ; evidently they had already neared the second objective.
They had suffered considerable casualties.

All too soon the time arrived for us to be moving
forward, since, if we were to catch up our time-table,
only a short delay was permissible. Rapidly word
was passed along, and the men commenced to gather
up their rifles and spades, which had been issued to
provide means for entrenching in our final objective.
Bullets were still coming over as we scrambled out of
the captured trench, but in no great volume : a fact
that seemed a good omen. Striding forward through
the long grass, one could observe the admirable appearance of the company as it swept on once more.

" You'd have thought it was an ordinary field-day,
sir ! " Sergeant Repton, accompanied by a couple of
men, came up beside me. He seemed in the seventh
heaven of delight.

Nothing obstructed our advance, no sign of friend
or foe was to be seen, but presently, as we approached
the Diagonal Road, a cluster of grey uniforms arose
from its hollow. Pausing irresolutely at the sight of
our approach, they next ran forward to meet us, hands
in air and whimpering continuously. Their terrified
expressions were eloquent of what they had been

through, and upon more than one, lyddite fumes were smeared like mustard powder. These creatures were obviously half demented by fear and shell shock, therefore we merely jerked our thumbs over our shoulders and passed on. A moment later, the long cavity of the Diagonal Road gaped before us.

Down its steep bank poured the noisy torrent of men, who, with bayonets advanced, peered left and right for sign of a possible foe. Upon the littered surface of the roadway sprawled a considerable number of dead Germans, among whom were scattered a few patches of khaki. Here, as in the trench behind, the Grenadiers had left a trail of slaughter.

As we had anticipated, the near bank proved to contain a number of dugouts, so toward these we hurried. One after another we passed them, until a sudden shout arrested my attention. Looking sharply in the direction of a levelled rifle, I beheld a grey figure stooping in the entrance we had just passed. His hands were unraised. To jerk forward my revolver and fire was an act of instinct. The fellow shook with a sudden spasm, flinched as from a heavy blow, then subsided in a heap across the threshold. Whether he was dead or not, we could not stop to ascertain ; at all events he would trouble us no more.

Satisfying ourselves that no one remained to work us mischief from behind, the company, still preserving its long irregular line, scrambled up the farther bank. There, in full view, the village confronted us. Then for the first time did the men give tongue ! A roar of cheers broke from us all. In front lay our objective, held by a reeling enemy !

Charging down the slope, we felt our blood rise at the thought of the supreme moment that had come. Laughing and shouting, the company gathered speed as it rolled forward, one section chaffing another on account of its laggards. Yard by yard the high-standing grass and looming craters swept behind us as, jumping and

tripping in our stride, we streamed onward. Every
moment now I expected to hear a racket of machine-
gun fire ; but none came. The village remained silent.
Shrill above the hubbub of our onrush rose the sergeants' voices, steadying the eager and calling upon
the stragglers. Soon, before us loomed a disordered
waste, churned by shell-fire and strewn with splinters,
behind which stretched another sunken road. We
had reached the Brown Line.

There, clustered along the farther bank, lay groups
of khaki figures, which, at the sound of our halt, turned
their heads in our direction. By the red " flashes "
on their sleeves one knew them for Grenadiers. A
moment later they became invisible as we, panting
from our exertions, subsided into the surrounding
craters. Here the tempest of gunfire dinned in our
ears once more, for now we were close to our own
barrage. Right and left, grimy faces smiled over the
edges of neighbouring holes.

Since we had left our assault-trench, only a quarter
of an hour had elapsed ! Thus, having nothing more
to do except await the next advance, we turned our
attention to the spectacle ahead.

Into the village not fifty yards distant streamed a
torrent of shells. From the shelter of our temporary
abodes we watched and listened in wonder at their
thunderous roar. Like straws, tall trees were riven
asunder and flung headlong in crackling ruin. Through
the wrack of dust and smoke the remnants of farm
buildings loomed like skeletons, and before our eyes
their tortured husks dissolved in a swirl of flying
timber and rafters. Walls vanished abruptly in a
tornado of brickdust as a direct hit was scored by the
British guns. Now the atmosphere was crossed and
recrossed by a hurricane of screams that engulfed us
in an orchestra of horrible sounds. Around us, the
world appeared to be enclosed by a dome of resonance,
beneath which the echoes of a disrupting universe,

seeking an outlet, swept and pulsated in vain. Stirred
by the shock of this hideous symphony, the earth
seemed to rock upon its axis.

To such a pitch did the storm rage, that our ears
refused to record any further increase, numbed as they
were by the tempestuous notes around. Blasted by
this hail of thunderbolts, Lesbœufs was melting into
ruin. Swaying amid the heart of the flaming eddies,
fantastic impressions flickered before one's mental
gaze. There, phantom Titans splashed the earth with
frenzied stampings; yonder, in a mantle of driven
haze, the Furies swept aloft with thrashing wings.
This transcended everything ; here lay the shrine of
Armageddon. As though attracted by the din of mortal
combat, the fires of Heaven seemed to be unloosed.
Such must have been the day when—

> " Him the Almighty power
> Hurl'd headlong flaming from the ethereal sky,
> With hideous ruin and combustion."

.   .   .   .   .

Over a chaos of tangled hedges and gardens, the
line of mingled Guards flowed ever on. Before
them raged a gliding wall of fire, behind them hung
the heavy pall of battle. Striding forward, eyes
gleaming alertly from beneath helmets, the wave
eddied over and around a mass of obstacles. Many
clutched their rifles " at the high port," for they had
abandoned their spades during their bayonet fight in
the German front line, others held bombs in readiness
for a sudden emergency. Here and there among the
wreckage, a heap of powdered brick and cement marked
the site of a vanished dwelling. Not a soul, not an
insect remained. Across a scene of devastated solitude
rolled the echoes of our barrage. Over jagged beams
and splintered stones we picked our way, peering into
the disembowelled houses on either hand. Progress
was slow ; at every step we encountered an obstruc-
tion, either mound or ditch or prostrate tree-trunk.

Nothing stirred, save our glinting line of bayonets.
Through smouldering ruins, gardens, and orchards we
trampled, a tumult of exultation pulsing in our veins.
It was too great a moment even for a cheer ; our drums
alone could have sounded the note required. So, with
hearts throbbing our *pas de charge,* we burst through
fence and ditch toward our goal.

So overwhelming had been the onslaught of the brigade, that, after a desperate resistance in their front
line, the enemy had abandoned the battle entirely.
Thus by 3 p.m. we were masters of the village. By ones
and twos, the leading wave broke through the line of
trees flanking the eastern side of the enclosures, and
emerged on to a narrow plateau some couple of hundred
yards in width. Scattered in the throng were shreds of
various battalions, but nowhere was an officer visible.

The Blue Line, depicted on our maps as a sunken
road skirting the line of trees, simply did not exist.
Nothing more than a cart track marked the spot.
Before commencing a trench, we should even have to
remove the turf, so, seeing this, and marking
the very prominent target presented by the tall
trees, we decided to avoid them by siting one about
a hundred yards in advance. By doing so, we should
leave our front clear of the barrage for a similar distance.
Moreover, it would afford us another hundred paces
field of fire before the ground merged into a valley
that divided Lesbœufs from the village of Le Transloy.
From it, we should also command an abandoned trench
some four hundred yards away, which ran diagonally
across our front.

Simultaneously with our arrival on the eastern side
of the village, straggling groups of our neighbouring
division appeared on the right flank across the Les-
bœufs-Le Transloy road.   Apparently their attack had
been as successful as our own, for the redoubt situated
on their frontage so as to enfilade our line of advance
had failed to cause us any trouble.

A few moments later the Irish Guards on our left came also into view, preceded by a group of fleeing Germans. As one watched, several of them fell; the remainder escaped by taking cover in the long grass ahead. Beyond these, about four or five hundred yards from where we stood, some scores of panic-stricken figures laboured madly up the slope toward the cemetery of Le Transloy, casting away rifles and equipment in their flight. Promptly one of our Lewis guns prepared for action, the corporal in charge laying it in person.

With a roar of reports the gun opened fire, and an instant later, as I watched through my glasses, its deadly work became apparent. The dust flung up by the flying bullets spurted around their very feet; numbers pitched forward as they ran, and many, hoping vainly thereby to disturb our aim, began to leap from side to side. But in a belching stream the fire of the Lewis took toll again and again. Every moment some frantic figure, sprinting for life, would sprawl headlong in the dust. Deaf to the applause of his comrades, the corporal continued to fire, his face impassive as the Sphinx.

However, time was pressing. Delay with the work of digging in could not be permitted. Working-parties were " told off," and salvage parties dispatched to the rear in order to collect spades, as large numbers had been dropped. In proportion to their arrival did the line of diggers grow, and by incorporating every available shell hole into the new position, cover was provided for a large portion of the men.

All this time since our arrival on the plateau, no barrage from the enemy's guns had been observable, but now, down in the hollow below, a stationary one was established by our own artillery. As good progress was being made with the digging, I turned my attention to the distant landscape to watch for possible signs of a German demonstration. Far away, a couple of their

observation balloons could be seen descending rapidly,
but along the opposite ridge no trace of the enemy
remained visible.

In the midst of this scrutiny I was enveloped by an
earthquake. The ground beneath and the air above
were smitten by a jarring concussion, followed by
another and yet another. Quickly it flashed across
my mind that the enemy's artillery must have seen
us. In wheeling round to shout an order, I beheld at
the same moment a vast eruption of flame, smoke, and
spouting soil, among which the eye noted swirling
forms. A crushing blow hit me on the jaw; a loud
detonation overwhelmed my senses; the world grew
dark and lurched into obscurity.

Staggering a few paces, one wondered if this was
the end. Then my groping outstretched hands encountered a supporting arm, to which I clung for a
moment. Against this invisible friend I leant awhile,
striving to regain command of my faculties. It seemed
a long time before I realised I was untouched!

The first sight to greet one's awakening vision was
that of five of my men lying horribly huddled and
very still. From the nature of their injuries they must
have been killed outright, though a couple still twitched
convulsively. Beside these bodies, two others strove
pitifully to drag themselves from out of the still smoking
crater; and though the sounds were mercifully inaudible
owing to deafness, I could tell from their working
mouths that they were moaning for help.

Heard faintly, a series of explosions arose among
the line of men, and then I realised somehow that
our own heavy guns were causing the mischief.

For a few moments a scene of pandemonium prevailed, and the men, dropping their tools, made as if
they would run off. None the less, their iron discipline
quickly reasserted itself. The line reformed along a
new position slightly in rear. There, if only the
barrage remained stationary, we should be in tolerable

safety from our guns and still avoid the conspicuous landmark represented by the trees.

Heart-rending cries followed our retirement, for apparently the wounded imagined that we were withdrawing altogether, thereby leaving them to their fate. But our first consideration was the establishment of a defensive line. In the event of an enemy counterattack, any ill-timed act of humanity now might lead subsequently to further unnecessary losses. As soon as the new trench had been commenced, stretcherbearers went forward to the casualties and succeeded in bringing in all those who were still alive.

Though thus modifying our position, we did not lose touch with our neighbours on the flanks : the line still presented an unbroken front. In response to a message, the artillery barrage lifted forward into the hollow, whence it presently dislodged several German stragglers. Their appearance from their hiding-places was greeted by an outburst of machine-gun fire, and their forms became added to the many dark dots already covering the opposite slope toward the cemetery.

From now on, our digging made good progress, so much so that, remembering our late experiences and our labour of the previous night, one was amazed at the vigour displayed by these splendid fellows. Soil flew in all directions ; spades rose and fell hour after hour ; and as the work proceeded, their forms vanished from view. Every minute we expected to see indications of a hostile advance. It was a race against time.

Bathed in the sunlight of this autumn day, the prospect before us remained curiously placid after the bewildering tumult of the attack. The world had grown mysteriously silent. Far away in the distance lay patches of crops and luxuriant trees. Yonder country seemed unscorched by the breath of war, seemed in the softening haze like a luring mirage.

About 7.30 p.m., my attention was called by St. Helier to a line of dots advancing far away on our right front.

Seen through field-glasses, it resolved itself into a screen of enemy patrols working in pairs and widely scattered. They were approaching from the direction of Le Transloy. At their present range, rifle fire would be ineffective, therefore the machine-gunners received orders to deal with them by means of concentrated fire. Gradually the Germans came forward, displaying in their advance a caution which, in view of their total defeat earlier in the day, was not unnatural. Covering approximately a frontage of a third of a mile, they proceeded to come on in short rushes, squatting down every fifty yards or so. As the ground ahead of them lay open and fully exposed to observation, we allowed them to make good their advance over an open corn-field before our machine-guns opened fire.

At first no result was discernible, but before long, first one group then another halted and lay down. Some sort of parley must have ensued, for presently a few isolated figures arose and came forward once more. But not for long. Two dropped suddenly, whereupon their comrades, hesitating an instant, turned tail. Then, amid a roar of derisive laughter from our men, the whole line of scouts scattered in the direction whence it had come.

The hours that followed up to midnight were ones of laborious digging. The men's forces had reached their last ebb, and it was only owing to their pluck and the encouragement of the N.C.Os that they maintained their efforts at all. By that time a continuous trench extended across the front of the village.

The company was relieved at 2 a.m. The last couple of hours had seen a considerable improvement to the position by reason of the arrival of a company of R.E., which had constructed not only machine-gun emplacements, but also a system of wire entanglements. At the time of our withdrawal, they were engaged in completing an entirely fresh support-trench. Lesbœufs was fast becoming a British stronghold.

Arriving in the Brown Line, where the company had already proceeded under St. Helier, one cast about for a shelter in which to pass the night. Because nothing better was obtainable, I spent what remained of it with MacIvor in a cavity beneath the roots of a tree still standing beside the sunken road.

．　　．　　．　　．　　．　　．

Early the next morning I awoke on account of the cold, having passed a couple of hours in profound oblivion : my first sleep for forty-eight hours. To warm myself, I set off for a brisk stroll, and by good fortune encountered a servant who was able to promise me a cup of tea on my return. For six days no warm food had come our way. Also, completing my happiness, he informed me that so far no officer had been hit ; our total losses had been few.

Already considerable progress had been made with the work of clearing up the Brown Line, though none the less it remained a weirdly desolate spot. To judge by the general aspect of things, although originally holding it in great force, the enemy had abandoned it completely and hastily before the arrival of the Grenadiers. Uniforms, hand - grenades, boots, and spades were strewn among innumerable other articles in every corner and along every yard of the roadway. Large numbers of rifles still leant against the parapet, placed there before the opening of the attack. These had never been used, for their breech-covers were still fastened on them. The sight of an automatic pistol reminded one that throughout the attack no German officer had been visible, either living or dead.

As on the previous day, a glorious sunrise soon stole upwards through the morning mist. Its appearance was most welcome, for after the night spent in our chilly sunken road we stood in need of a little warmth. Breakfast consisted of a pannikin of tea and a few ration biscuits.

Up to this time, no effort besides that of the reconnoitring party on the preceding evening had been made to molest us, but after breakfast, while most of the troops in support were engaged in cleaning up the position, German shells began to fall into the village. The Ginchy-Lesbœufs road seemed particularly selected. Along it played a continuous barrage for a length of about two hundred yards, and a little later their heavier guns began to search for the Brown Line. The men, no doubt too deeply preoccupied by the illicit joys of souvenir-hunting, did not pay so much attention to it all as otherwise they might have done.

An hour of this salvage work had not elapsed before orders reached us that the company was to move back into battalion reserve and take up its position in the Green Line. By 10 o'clock we had completed our preparations to move, so, after issuing their marching orders to the various platoons, I with the leading party left the village.

Owing to the intense barrage along the Ginchy-Lesbœufs road, we followed the Diagonal. Presently, as we passed along, we noticed that the village itself and many of its surrounding features were becoming obscured by the smoke of bursting shells. Apparently a determined effort was being made to render the place untenable.

As we marched along, gruesome evidences of the battle became conspicuous. Numbers of bodies had fallen along the length of this roadway : nearly all Germans who either had been shot down as they ran or been overcome by their wounds while vainly endeavouring to reach a first-aid post. These latter, propped against the bank where they had sat down to die, surveyed our passage with sightless eyes. Striding on, we kicked against discarded equipment at almost every yard. Higher up the road where it joined that from Ginchy lay a few khaki figures, but these, it was only too evident, had been left there

23

since the battle of the 15th and 16th. Their sunken
features were already blackened by putrefaction, and
upon their dried but gaping wounds swarmed a seething
mass of flies.

Half an hour's march brought us to the Green Line,
where, according to orders, we were to continue
the work of consolidation already begun. Here the
trench was strewn with bodies, upon whose faces one
could not fail to remark every variety of expression.
Some, to all appearances, had met their end instantaneously, and lay now as if asleep; others had obviously died in agony, the result of torturing wounds.
Many one could only think of as splendid-looking men,
dignified in death and often handsome; a few there
were who seemed hardly human, for the rats had
already flocked to their appalling banquet. Here and
there, emerging from the long grass, a hand and arm
were visible, marking the spot where some unfortunate
had striven to attract the attention of his fellow men.
The rigors of death had stiffened the appealing limb,
making of it a forlorn signpost. Yonder where a
dreadful heap of carrion lay shapèless and bloody, a
mass of flies was eating out its eye-sockets. Beelzebub
held revel here.

Passing from one fire-bay to another, we realised the
reason for the numerous casualties suffered by the
Grenadiers. The wire had been only partially cut,
and around the occasional gaps lay swathes of dead.
Clusters of khaki hung from the barbed wire like
marionettes, heads and arms dangling above the rank
grass as if in quest of something they wished to find.
Among them sprawled a splendid type of sergeant
entangled in the barrier. Glancing upon his magnificent physique, one could not but feel indignant at the
death that had overtaken him, for he, the equal of
any two ordinary men, had been shot down by a
fellow probably half his own size.

In many places the trench had been blown in by

our bombardment, and out of the mounds thus formed, legs and portions of German uniforms still protruded. Everywhere lay the scattered jettison of war. The pageants of past battle-painters seemed now a bitter mockery ; on all sides, amid the stench and buzz of flies, our eyes beheld a battlefield in all its grim setting. Here, for a whole day in a hot sun, we had to live and eat, taking our rest in a mortuary, our meals in a slaughter-house.

About midday the bombardment of Lesbœufs swelled to a great intensity, and a heavy barrage of high explosive was put down along our trench with the intention presumably of preventing supports from reaching the village. It appeared as if the long-deferred counter-attack was about to take place. By and by, as on the preceding day, the air shrieked and moaned with a torrent of missiles. Large and small, apparently of every calibre, our guns poured forth a drumming cannonade. Some of us who still remembered early days could scarce believe their ears. Here, above our heads, we could realise from the bellowing atmosphere the extent of the efforts made by the folk at home. Unbounded delight was visible on many a grimy face, and following a paroxysm of sound one heard the cry : " Good old Lloyd George !"

The enemy did their best, but again they were out-classed. Battery after battery of British guns poured forth their reply at maximum speed. Amid this bombardment we ate what little food we still possessed, crouching in the German dugouts, which vibrated heavily from the tremors around.

No infantry attack followed this violent outburst. We heard later that it was supposed to be merely an attempt to shell us out of Lesbœufs, but to judge by the tumult a mile to the south by Morval, it may have been possible that an attack was delivered at that point. However, on the front of the Guards Division none materialised.

Gradually, as the afternoon wore on, their attentions to the Green Line died down. It must have been but little later when a neighbouring incident drew us all as spectators to the fire-step.

Far away toward Gueudecourt we could observe a line of scattered troops moving in extended order across the brown country-side, and behind these, body after body of infantry in fours advancing in support. Gliding like snails over the ground, the varied portions of their artillery formation were clearly discernible as they undulated over the swells and hollows. Several thousand men must have been involved, though only a few hundred were ever visible to us. Gueudecourt, motley to the eye like a patchwork quilt, lay in the distance amid a setting of jagged boles. Portions of recently splintered masonry, catching the sun's rays, stood out in prominent relief, paling however from time to time beside a surrounding twinkle of bursting shells, which danced like scintillating jewels within a hanging pall. It was obvious to anyone that here, on another sector of the line, British troops were carrying all before them, extending the victory of the previous day.

It was not long before our trench burst into a rowdy cheer. Advancing up to the trees of the now captured village, sparkling with glinting steel and tossing heads, appeared a dark line of swiftly moving horsemen. Arriving presently at the outskirts, a portion halted, but by far the greater number continued on its course until it slowly vanished into the haze.

They who have never experienced endless months of waiting cannot form the slightest conception of our thoughts as we beheld this spectacle. Swarming like a crowd of bees on to the fire-step, men clamoured for a moment's use of a pair of field-glasses, and cheered on comrades whom they could hardly see. True, no great body of men rode yonder, but their presence roused our imaginations. Here under our

very eyes was certain proof of that ascendancy for
which England had wrestled so long.

.   .   .   .   .

Night was falling. Grouped along the trench, the
living sought companionship with the living, for in the
darkness within a few yards of us lay a multitude of
dead. From time to time you would hear the clatter
of a mess-tin as someone jerked his equipment into
position, or a low murmur of conversation.

The last hours had been no less eventful than those
which had gone before, since, though wanting in memorable incidents, they had brought tragedy to myself.
Both the Commanding Officer and Clive, the acting Adjutant, had been killed, together with MacIvor. All
three had been good comrades of long standing, and
their sudden deaths left me with a feeling of strange
isolation.

In contrast with these tidings, news had come that
the battalion was to be relieved that night. It was in
readiness for this longed-for event that we were now
waiting, taking our orders from the Colonel of our
sister battalion. The realisation that within an hour
or so we should be marching away from this ghastly
place seemed to bring home to our minds the trials of
the last few days ; now at last we all felt wearied of
and revolted with our surroundings. It seemed incredible that the morning would find us restored once
more to peace and quiet. After what we had undergone, our jaded minds failed to realise fully that such
conditions could exist.

Already! Beyond the scarred traverses arose a
sound of movement punctuated by the tones of
Sergeant Repton. A ripple of anticipation stirred the
waiting men, and a moment later, with a constant
cry of " Make way, make way," the dusky figure of
a messenger appeared.

" Please, sir, the relief's arrived ! Sergeant Repton

wants to know if you'll pass down word when you're
ready to move off."

Presently, after the usual conference between officers,
the men acted on the word and commenced to file
away into the night. So eager were they to draw
clear of the position, that one had to run in order to
overtake the head of the company. Though only set
by request from the rear our pace, in view of our
state of fatigue, was extraordinary. Their only thought
was to quit the battlefield with all possible haste,
for to straining nerves this Place of Skulls now seemed
more evil than ever. Fortunately, in the gloom, much
of the horrors of the Ginchy road was spared us; yet
the rats made their presence only too noticeable. All
the exultation of our advance had become but the
memory of a vainglorious dream. Gone was the
splendour of the previous day; the flavour of victory
now seemed as ashes in our mouths.

"The paths of Glory lead but to the grave."

An hour's march along the road to Carnoy, where
we were to pass the night, brought us to Ginchy, and
there we found the road to Guillemont. Now that we
had put a couple of miles between us and the front
line, the pace slackened, and, the road proving toler-
ably good, the company closed into column of
route.

From somewhere ahead came the sound of horses'
hoofs, and before long a line of mounted men detached
itself from the darkness : an ammunition column engaged in the endless task of replenishing the voracious
batteries in the vicinity.

" Is this the road to Guillemont ? "

" Straight on, sir. You'll reach it in ten minutes."

But as we pursued our way, no signs of the place
appeared. Stretching far and wide on either hand lay
shrouded chaos, amid which our wandering eyes caught

sight of gnarled and riven trees. Quickening the pace
from time to time, we hastened past spots whence
arose a sickening stench of putrid flesh together with
the sound of rustling vermin.

Surely those fellows had been mistaken? It was
farther than they had supposed; mounted troops
naturally misjudged the pace of infantry.

Still, as we trudged upon our way, no sign of human
habitation greeted us, nor even a ruin; everywhere
the night disclosed everlasting abomination and solitude.

Then, glimmering like a haven in the dusk, a streak
of light appeared, issuing from behind a swaying screen
and revealing a dugout beside the road. Halting the
company, I advanced toward it and hailed its occupants. An answering shout was followed a moment
later by the appearance of a telegraphist.

"Can you tell me if this is the way to Guillemont?"

"Which way?"

"Why, here!" I exclaimed, pointing down the road
ahead.

"No, that isn't it, sir; you're going away from it."

"Going away from it, do you say?"

He nodded.

"You've *come through it*, sir—nearly half a mile
back."

* * * * *

Tramp, tramp, tramp, onward through the darkness.

To us, as we toiled painfully upon our way, this
homeward march seemed a penance of the damned.
No more did the ranks behind give forth their guffaws,
or swing forward with eager step; now, voices arose
only to complain, while would-be stragglers only
dragged their leaden feet by reason of a sergeant's
tongue.

"Gawd's trewth! my pore ole back's fair bustin'!"
This and other doleful plaints were frequently wrung

from the stricken men. At last, rather than carry the additional weight of their trophies, they commenced to throw them beside the road : first a German gas-mask—easily spared ; next a saw-edged bayonet—a pity, that ; then, the agony of their muscles mounting to a pang of regret, a curse accompanied the flight of a treasured *pickelhaube*. Thus Nature despoiled the victors in their turn.

Plodding on, we gradually drew near to Montauban. Beyond that lay three more miles. . . .

By now, we had reached the limit of mortal endurance. Our eyes burnt in our heads for want of sleep, our drunken legs would hardly respond to the goading of our wills. Labouring heavily from side to side, many were staggering from unconquerable exhaustion, and the effort of placing one foot before the other rose to a heart-breaking strain. Frequently we had to halt to give time to our tottering laggards, who were now beyond responding to their sergeants' abuse. Then ensued the agony of setting forth once more, for our cramped legs grew stiff in a few moments, and it was only by constant movement that we could sustain our failing bodies.

Midnight had long since passed ; it was now two o'clock in the morning. The last two miles brought to us two hours of awful anguish. Each of us, like Atlas, was burdened with a world of affliction ; each, with bloodshot eyes peering desperately ahead, trailed along his Way of Sorrow.

At last, crawling on to the downward slope that ran above our encampment, a wondrous effort was made. Silent voices arose once more ; a shuffling imitation of a step rippled through the wretched ranks. " We'll be there in ten minutes, boys ! " The words, croaked hoarsely from the rear, acted as a spur. Rank after rank picked up the reviving stride ; once again a rhythm of footfalls beat in our ears : miracle of mira-cles—the boys were *marching* !

At the bottom of the hill, a lantern flashed from the roadside, and from the direction of a mass of forms we heard the tones of our quartermaster-sergeant. Then a cheer went up from many a parched throat, for the sound of that voice seemed like a promise of salvation.

No martial music heralded our return, nor eager crowds, for everyone was asleep. But though "The Drums" were absent, our music should not be denied us. Roaring in unison to the time of our march-step, we, the last eighty survivors of "Number 2" gave tongue to a song we all loved well.

> " Pack up your troubles in your old kit bag
>   And smile, smile, smile ;
>   Pack up your troubles in your old kit bag,
>   Smile, boys, that's the style ;
>   What's the use of worrying,
>   It never was worth while ;
>   So, pack up your troubles in your old kit bag,
>   And smile, smile, smile."

The wordless echoes rang against the slopes, hurling upon the morning stillness the effect of a clamorous *Te Deum.*

PART III

DAY

" Mine eyes have seen the glory of the coming of the Lord ;
  He is trampling out the vintage where the grapes of wrath are
    stored ;
  He hath loosed the fatal lightning of His terrible swift sword :
  His Truth is marching on."

CONCLUSION

AGAIN sickness, that great camp-follower of armies, had laid its hand upon me ; though not for long. Spring had not ended before I returned to France once more.

Bearing in mind my return the year before, I could not help contrasting the present with the past. None could mistake the signs of the times, for they were in evidence on all sides, marking a new epoch in the history of the war. Hindenburg's retreat was not yet a month old.

Though in England we had rejoiced greatly at the news from France, our realisation of its meaning had been vague by comparison with what we were experiencing now as the troop-train bore us onwards. But two short hours before, the draft with which I was travelling had lunched peaceably in Peronne, had read with curiosity the German time-tables on the walls of the railway station, and had strolled like gaping tourists through the streets.

Setting forth once more, by a route that passed through the heart of the Somme country, we had been gradually confronted by a terrible panorama. From the open door of our goods-van, we were able to realise more than ever before the magnitude and fury of the struggle of the previous autumn. In every direction as far as the horizon stretched a desert of brown shell-ploughed slopes and hollows, and scattered upon the face of this landscape, clumps of splintered poles, gaunt and blackened by fire, marked the sites of former woods and copses. Endless belts of wire entanglements, many feet in width, undulated into the distance, tracing rusty red lines across the vast expanse. Craters of every size pitted this land in countless thousands. Along the remains of abandoned trenches and gun emplacements they actually merged into one another, and so granulated by shell-fire was the surface of the country, that it now resembled an extinct planet, its face mottled with innumerable lifeless craters. Down by the river, which now invaded the low-lying ground beside it, zigzags of gleaming water revealed the position of former trenches. Scattered everywhere over the waste, clusters of wooden crosses leant at every angle, telling their tale of past assaults and counter-attacks, and it was still possible for us to trace in broad outline the story of those battles by the rotting accoutrements lying on every side. Here a British shrapnel helmet or a shattered Enfield rifle, there a dented French *casque* or shred of horizon-blue cloth, denoted the two Armies' brotherhood in arms.

Ascending the gradient that wound up the valley ahead, our train pursued its way through this amazing scene. To sit and stare at what lay before us called for no effort on our part, as the country passed before our eyes like a cinematograph display. Thus we continued for an hour or more.

At last the heavy train drew up protestingly beside a few wooden shanties. One or two men of the Army Service Corps, clad in their shirt sleeves, abandoned their lounging attitudes to help unload a consignment of cases. In reply to our inquiry, they informed us that we were at Maurepas. Here, only six months previously, the French had stormed a village after a desperate struggle ; now, no trace of it remained. Maurepas was scattered to the four winds of heaven, mingled with the dust of Sodom and Gomorrah.

And later, when in its turn we arrived at Guillemont, it was the same. Everywhere it was the same : the same drab dreariness, the same sinister desolation. In this land everything had been annihilated.   This was the end.

Such a region as this, exceeding the limit of our vision in every direction, presented a scene surpassing human imagination.   It haunted one like a nightmare.   Neither of my companions accompanying the draft had served in France before, but, like most people, they had read newspaper accounts of the Western Front.   Now, however, they were amazed. Seated beside them in our van, even I was enthralled by the passing spectacle, but it did not prevent me from noting their murmurs of astonishment.   Their feelings were hardly to be wondered at, for, though familiar with the Somme, I, too, had not realised until now the degree and extent of its awful ruin.   Life—human, animal, and vegetable—had been engulfed; not a leaf, hardly a blade of grass, no sound of bird, greeted us ; all was done and finished with.   Here indeed was the end of the world.

Constantly our gaze returned to the harvest of crosses.   Upon one of these, perforated in many places by shrapnel bullets, a French helmet still hung by its chin-strap, and looking at it, one wondered whether all was truly ended.   From all these horrors, something seemed to be struggling to emerge, to cry aloud and make its presence known.

.   .   .   .   .

Since railhead lay only on the western edge of the Somme region, this journey proved but the beginning of our wanderings.   Nightfall found us back at Maurepas ; owing to a mistake in our orders, we had passed through it instead of leaving the train at that point. On arrival there, we discovered that our battalion, which we had been led to expect to find there, had left twenty-four hours before.   It was now encamped near the Canal du Nord, several miles beyond Sailly-Saillisel and Le Transloy.   Accordingly, we spent the night where we were, making the best of our situation. After a hasty breakfast on the following morning we set out in quest of it. To reach its encampment, we should be obliged to pass over the entire width of the former battlefields.

An hour's march brought us to the summit of the hill that overlooks Combles on the east. From here we beheld a wide view of the country-side, now bathed in a flood of sunshine. Peering wonderingly toward the north-west, one could not help contrasting this quiet spring morning with those memorable bloody days of the past autumn—for yonder line of jagged boles arose from Morval and Lesbœufs.

Another mile or so brought us to the position of our recent support-line, where quantities of supplies lay embedded in the hardened mud. Here signboards indicated an old Brigade Headquarters, there, an R.E. dump. Long sections of weather-beaten parapet revealed the sites of our former trenches, these still guarded in front by endless belts of wire and stakes. Now the road was all but obliterated, so we were compelled to step carefully to avoid a fall.

It was a strange thing to be walking thus peacefully through this wilderness, for when last seen, enemy patrols had been advancing across it toward our position in the Blue Line. Then it had represented a wide expanse of No Man's Land, now it was part of France once more.

As we made our way across this waste, parties of men belonging to Labour Battalions paused at their work to watch us go by, while motor lorries, revelling in apparent ownership of the road, choked us with their dust. In the distance, lines of horses out to water threaded their way placidly over the old battle-ground. Everywhere around were to be seen those miscellaneous bodies of men met with on lines of communication, left far behind by the advancing army. No doubt they cursed the country for its discomfort. In their eyes, it represented a region of "rotten jobs" and endless "fatigues," a desert justly spurned by the feet of the forces ahead of them, a world of salvage and of evil smells. Here a motor-transport driver lit a cigarette, turned his nose up at the air, and slipped into top speed.

But to us this place would ever seem the Front! Across it, barrages had trailed their volcanic courses; bayonets had gleamed and footfalls rustled, as, deployed for the attack, we had surged on to victory. Here all the pomp and bitterness of war had displayed their incalculable solemnity. For us, this landscape was hallowed by many a memory. . . .

Viewing this scene, one was stirred by the echo of a recent impression : once again, out of the heroic past the martyred landscape seemed to be calling. Perhaps its cry was more insistent, its appeal more poignant, but now its muffled murmur seemed to swell into utterance. What of the story of it all ? what of the epic deeds accomplished here ? Surely they lived and would live for ever. No ! All was not finished ; something yet remained. As if in the toils of birth, *something* seemed to be struggling into life ; here was the womb of imperishable ideals.

.   .   .   .   .

Toiling forward in the glare of the sun, our draft came at last to the cross-roads near Sailly-Saillisel. Le Transloy lay but two miles to the north. Our way lay through the former village, so we set off along a newly repaired road in the expectation of coming upon its ruins before very long. On either hand lay chaos, where every landmark had vanished. The only thing to do was to direct our course by compass, accordingly, we left the brick-dust road and began to scramble over the maze of craters toward the east.

Everywhere around us a wild confusion seemed to have upheaved the land, leaving behind it an ocean of rubble heaps. French helmets battered to shapeless

24

lumps, and Lebel rifles red with rust, lay in the stiffened mud, scattered among the countless refuse of the
British and German Armies. In many craters lay
great pools of bright-yellow water, whose stagnant
surface disclosed many a rotting corpse. Coils of
wire, like bramble thickets, ran in and out of the sun-
baked hummocks, fluttering bleached tatters from their
barbs. Close at hand, the mangled fragments of a
machine-gun protruded from a reeking mound, and
beside it lay a human skull, picked clean by birds.
Everything was encased by a monotone of mud. Here, as
we turned from side to side, odours assailed us at
every breath, while a profound silence intensified the
dreadful melancholy of the scene.

Presently, in this diabolical spot we came upon a living
man, a corporal of R.E., smoking furiously as he undulated over the wreckage toward us. I fancied he might
be able to inform us of our whereabouts, therefore I
hailed him as soon as he came within earshot. "Sailly-
Saillisel ? " he repeated, "why, sir, this is it." I
remembered the patches of red upon the road we had
just left, and slowly realised that he must be speaking the truth. The powdered brick-dust I had casually noted represented the last traces of the village.
On my map, I had seen the conventional marks that
denote churches and *châteaux*—I had been seeking
their ruins for the last half-hour or more—but even they
had vanished with every brick, beam, railing, or tree,
or sign of human occupation. Here the war had come
to a prodigious end ; this must surely be the final
cataclysm ?

As we laboured across this bleak and dismal waste,
all the incalculable misery since the beginning seemed
heaped upon us as if in a final assault upon human
reason. The endless marches that wear one's very
bones, the exhaustion that breeds oblivion to all earthly
surroundings, the vigils when one fights to keep awake,
all the afflictions of our lot seemed to clamour at us

from the terrible solitude, thrusting derisively before
our gaze the surrounding human offal. The land
gibbered at us madly. In this immensity of churned
matter, wherein sun and rain had corroded all colour
and form, where every object melted into a nameless
mass of putrescence, one could only stare in fearful
wonder.

What did it all mean ? Why had this appalling
Thing come about ? Why were men so monstrously
afflicted ? " The War that shall end War "—the trite
headline of a newspaper came back to me. But would
it ? Every war in history had been a wasted catastrophe, in that the germ had still survived. To think
of the sacrifice around as fruitless was almost unbearable. We, the living, must battle on to prevent that ;
surely this was the message of the dead. Death and
glory this eviscerated land contained, but greater than
these was its summons to the living !

Stumbling from hummock to hummock with such
thoughts in mind, picking my way from one abomination to another, I chanced to lift my eyes from the
shambles at my feet—and in that moment I came to
a standstill. That which confronted me at no great
distance appeared unnatural ; another Age would have
called it a miracle, and who shall say they were wrong ?

The village had gone, and with it all vestige of man-
kind, but, like a Conqueror on the field of battle, the
iron Calvary of its church remained. Here, in spite
of all, the Gates of Hell had not prevailed. Solitary,
amid the accursed and infamous wilderness, the Figure
hung suspended, surveying the scene as if in contemplation and endless waiting.

§   ⸱   ⸱   §   ∗

At last we drew near to the topmost point of the
Sailly ridge, extending here in every direction in
mournful waves. A few more yards would reveal to
us the land that lay beyond. In England, the Press

had been filled with stories of its havoc, and editorials had enlarged upon the topic of German spite. Abandoned by their retreating army, it could only prove a continuation of the misery behind us. Already, having passed the spot where our front line had lain throughout the winter, we had entered the recovered zone.

Looking back at the party in rear, I could see the men crawling through the litter in single file, some smoking, others carrying their caps in hand. Few had any eyes for their surroundings, for a march in full equipment required no false step, and this desert abounded in pitfalls. The region behind us had vanished in the distance; Ginchy, Morval, and Lesbœufs were no longer to be seen.

North and south, the monotony of the ridge merged into an obliterating atmosphere, wherein the devastation, subdued and toned by the sunlit vapour, was not so much in evidence.

But now we had arrived upon the summit. The skyline before us lurched lower at every step; still all that we could see was a wide expanse of blue sky. Then the ground fell away, and the distant landscape confronted us.

For an instant the prospect held one spellbound, so thrilling was its revelation, so placid its majesty. At first I was only conscious of the exclamations of those near-by, for even the attention of the men was centred on what lay ahead. Stretching for miles, bounded by the far horizon north and south, a glorious vision rose to greet us, a riotous pageant of shimmering colour. The low ridges opposite blazed under a mantle of sunlit grass, and scattered upon them, trees, flecked with vivid shoots, spread forth a lacework of slender boughs. Wheeling in a multitudinous swirl in the middle distance, a flock of crows flapped slowly on its way, while at the foot of our slope, a group of mottled roofs was half concealed by branches. Behind all these, displaying a widespread carpet of unblemished pasture land, glowing in the full radiance of the sun, the country undulated into the distance, luxuriant with verdure, scattered spinneys, and a patchwork of fields, and revealing at every point the freshest tints of an awakening world. Greedily we feasted our unbelieving eyes, scanning the far perspective of the land until baffled by the distant haze. So suddenly had it appeared that it seemed at first only a mocking mirage. But no—still it lay there inviting contemplation. There lay Spring in all her vastness and all her splendour, pæaning the resurrection of the Earth !

All this was France once more. Here lay the legacy of countless men, bequeathed to a posterity for which they had been martyred.

Standing here at this supreme moment, one recalled to mind those distant days two years before when we had all hoped to see the day of England's advance. Gone were those days of unequal odds. Now the uphill trail was ended, now after months of bitter striving we had topped the summit. Here was the fulfilment of all our hopes : before us lay the Great Redemption. By comparison with this, our memories of what lay behind seemed like a fading dream. The Somme battlefields, bearing with them their records of the past, of glory, of death, and of dire appeal, were receding into their sombre place in history ; here, smiling its welcome, lay the Future !

Accomplished once, our hopes might be fulfilled again, and someday from the east might spring a dazzling dawn, proclaiming to all—

" The day of Glory has arrived."

For its coming, not the French alone, but millions of Allied soldiers waited. In such a host the hope had blossomed to a creed. Was it for nothing that our armies battled toward the sunrise, for nothing that this wonder followed our sight of the lonely Sentinel ? Surely our beliefs were sanctioned ? With this background behind it, His effigy now seemed the advance-guard of the Future.

A sound, unheard for many hours, caused me to turn my head. Inhaling deep draughts of untainted air, the men had unloosed a running fire of comment, and now glad laughter arose on every side. They, too, realised the call of the land ahead.

As we stood with our backs to the desert we had passed, the enthralling view lay spread before us like the Promised Land, luring us onward with its radiant charm, whispering words of transcendent hope. Then, hardly did we wanderers curb the triumph in our hearts as again we strode forward—down the hill.

Lightning Source UK Ltd.
Milton Keynes UK
UKHW02f1120210118
316558UK00004B/37/P